AVANT-POST

edited by
LOUIS ARMAND

þ

Litteraria Pragensia
Prague 2006

Published 2006 by Litteraria Pragensia
Faculty of Philosophy, Charles University
Náměstí Jana Palacha 2, 116 38 Prague 1
Czech Republic
www.litterariapragensia.com

The publication of this book has been supported by research grant MSM0021620824 "Foundations of the Modern World as Reflected in Literature and Philosophy" awarded to the Faculty of Philosophy, Charles University, Prague, by the Czech Ministry of Education.

Cataloguing in Publication Data

Avant-Post: The Avant-Garde Under "Post-" Conditions, edited by Louis Armand.—1st ed.
    p. cm.
      ISBN 80-7308-123-7 (pb)
      1. Poetics. 2. Literary Theory. 3. Cultural Studies. 4. Aesthetics.
      I. Armand, Louis. II. Title

Printed in the Czech Republic by PB Tisk
Typesetting & design by lazarus

Contents

Introduction

The Organ-Grinder's Monkey

The day will come when one original carrot will be enough to start a revolution. —Cézanne

Is an avant-garde viable under the conditions of post-modernism? This question immediately gives rise to others, concerning the status of avant-gardes historical or conjectural, and concerning the various cognates of post-modernism and the numerous other post-s and isms that have populated critical discourse in literature and the arts during the latter half of the last century. Consequently our initial question may come to appear purely definitional, while any endeavour to respond to it programmatically will nevertheless remain ambiguous, eclectic, even contradictory. The reason for this has not to do simply with the diversity of possible positions vis-à-vis avant-gardism and post-modernity, nor with the ambivalences of historicity or interpretation, but with what has been called (in deference to the poetic legacy of the Russian poet Velimir Chlebnikov) "the discoveries of forgotten but never completely lost archaic resources of construing, which lead to unexpected significations of the language structure."[1]

It has been argued that all art worthy of the name is in some sense experimental, and that experimentation is inevitably bound to innovation by the same thread that binds the purportedly new to the idea of a tradition. Such a formulation

---

[1] Jan van der Eng, "Introduction," *Avant Garde* 5.6 (1991) 3.

1

reveals an inherent "referential indeterminacy," wherein words like experimental, avant-garde and tradition come to approximate "heterologous signs," without indicating whether they should be read literally or metaphorically, while demanding that we nevertheless interrogate their meaning within an increasingly conventionalised *discipline*. This "metacritical" dimension to the question at hand has in various quarters been perceived at bringing about something of a renewal of the trope of the "avant-garde," lending it a critical force which extends beyond the domain of aesthetics into the entire field of thought, sign systems and technology.

While today it might be possible to speak of avant-gardism with respect to cognitive science, for example, and quantum computing, this in itself may simply reflect that the history of avant-gardism has always in some way be bound up with the question of consciousness, its transformation and re-invention. Its proper domain, we might say, has increasingly tended to encompass the encyclopaedic "lifeworld of man" and the prospect of what humanity might yet become by grasping its own-most possibility in what "it is" and what "it has been." This curious temporal conjunction of the "avant" and the "post," mediated by the trope of experiment (or of *experience*), has a long historical genealogy that only in relatively recent times acquired the self-consciously aestheticised character that, in the twentieth century, became institutionalised as "the" avant-garde, and which is often said to have terminated in the discourse of post-modernism. At the beginning of the twenty-first century, this account of the "end of the avant-garde" is once again under contention, as the viability of a continuation, renewal or reinvention of avant-gardism—in tandem with the end, exhaustion, death of postmodernism—is raised by artists, critics, thinkers generally, unsatisfied with the pre-millennial wisdom that everything is permitted, hence nothing is any longer possible.

The promise of liberation is always a precarious one, and if the advent of the global economy, equal opportunity, the new media and communications technologies, and the end of the Cold War suggest—as the end of the twentieth century—a future world utopia, then this half-decade of the twenty-first century has violently dispelled that illusion. Beneath the guise of cultural pluralism and permissiveness, the hard edge of socio-economic ideology continues to give purchase to a critical engagement that previously (under post-modernism) was said to no longer be viable. And with it, the critical necessity of something "like" an avant-garde, not simply as a reaction or counter-action to a present state of affairs, but as an active intervention in futurity, in the very possibility of a future.

For these reasons, the title of this volume—Avant-Post—should not be taken as signalling a merely historical project, or one of cultural pessimism, but rather something like a call to order and a call to address the situation, today, of those outposts (*avant-postes*) that ensure a future for *critical* culture.

1

In his study of the New York school of poets—John Ashbery, Kenneth Koch, James Schuyler, and Frank O'Hara—improbably entitled *The Last Avant-Garde* (1999), American critic David Lehman (echoing Zygmunt Bauman, Jürgen Habermas, and others)[2] contends that: "the argument against the viability of the avant-garde today rests on the assumption that there is no real resistance to the new, no stable norm from which the defiant artist may depart." The contradictions of the "new," as a term largely inherited from Ezra Pound's injunction to "Make it New!" cedes here to the characteristic complaint that postmodernism in the 1970s and thereafter stole the carpet out

2 David Lehman, *The Last Avant-Garde: The Making of the New York School of Poets* (New York: Anchor, 1999); Zygmunt Bauman, "Postmodern Art, or the Impossibility of the Avant-Garde," *Postmodernity and Its Discontents* (London: Polity, 1997) 95-104; Jürgen Habermas, "Modernity—An Incomplete Project," *The Anti-Aesthetic: Essays in Post-Modern Culture*, ed. Hal Foster (New York: The New Press, 1983) 3-15.

from under critical experimentation. Moreover, having stolen the carpet, postmodernism then went about stealing the rest of the avant-gardist décor as well, which henceforth was reduced to a mere retro "style" or historical fetish. Thus Lehman writes, in the first person plural: "If we are all postmodernists, we are none of us avant-garde, for postmodernism is the institutionalisation of the avant-garde."[3]

Following the major ideological, technological and economic upheavals in the post-WWII American cultural landscape— mediated, in those eminent domains of literature and the fine arts, by the "scandalous" figure of Pound and by the predominance of what Clement Greenberg in 1955 felicitously termed "American-Type"[4] painting—the concept of the "present as a moment of revelation" (a time, according to Habermas, "in which splinters of a messianic presence are enmeshed"[5]) was sacrificed in the cause of a new historicism, from which avant-gardism succeeds modernity in the form of mass-media culture, "kitsch," neo-liberalism, and compulsory global democratisation. This sacrifice of "the tradition of modernity"—to what Harold Rosenberg termed the "Tradition of the New"—was repaid in the *currency* of historical tradition traded in a merely present time. Setting aside the problem of tradition and the present, or of a tradition of the present, Habermas's remarks, coupled with those of Lehman, draw attention to the particular politics of the institutions of literary and art history emerging from the 1970s, according to which the future of cultural production would forever more assume the form of a repetition of the "end of culture" represented by the end of Flower-Power utopianism, the debacle of the Vietnam War, and the Watergate affair.

---

[3] Lehman, *The Last Avant Garde*, 11.
[4] Clement Greenberg, *Art and Culture: Critical Essays* (Boston: Beacon, 1961) 208-229.
[5] Jürgen Habermas, *The Philosophical Discourse of Modernity*, trans. Frederick Lawrence (Cambridge, Mass.: MIT Press, 1990) 6.

That this view of history could be described as specifically generational and local—for example, in terms of the post-Greenberg generation of art critics like Rosalind Krauss and Hal Foster, or in terms of American post-Cold War cultural arbitration (as apart from a mere commentary on postmodernist globalisation)—has not been sufficiently commented upon. The widely reported death of the avant-garde, on the contrary, has come to be attributed (within cultural studies, fine arts, and the literary critical media) a degree of universal social significance that, in life, it ("the avant-garde") could hardly have aspired to. Indeed, the death of one culture's avant-garde has acquired the status of a veritable end of history, characterised by a universal—so we are told—disillusionment of (primarily leftist) ideologies, a radical pluralism of style, the eschewal of any mainstream, and an overwhelming tendency to retrospection. It seems to matter little that this laissez-faire view of cultural history fails to account for the fact that large sections of the so-called avant-garde were dominated by conservatism or radical right-wing ideology, or that pluralism is an idea bound from the start to the myth of bourgeois liberalism "opposed" by successive avant-gardes; that its often revolutionary posture was orientated towards the establishment of a mainstream in its own image, and that even the least socially-engaged of avant-gardes were preoccupied with their own internal politico-aesthetic programmes.

In this sense, both Lehman and the generation of "1968" appear to succeed primarily in elevating their particular discursive paradigms, of modernity and postmodernism, to the unique status of a last call before historical closure, ideological futility, eternal repetition, self-parody, and the messianic promise of "no future." Thus we encounter the chiliastic echoes of Baudelaire's "Painter of Modern Life" (1863) and Nietzsche's critique of Cartesian modernity in *Human, All too Human* (1878), under conditions in which the death of the avant-garde is made to strangely resemble the conditions of its historical birth.

Something like paternity of the historical avant-garde (as viewed through western eyes) could arguably be said to belong to the otherwise unlikely figure of the Compte de Nieuwerkerke, Director-General of the Imperial Museums in Paris—whose interventions in the jury procedures for the 1863 Salon was the immediate cause of Napoleon III's inauguration of the *Salon des Refusées*, at which Édouard Manet's notorious *Déjeuner sur l'herbe* was first exhibited, thus indirectly ushering in Impressionism and the history of European "avant-gardism."[6]

Born of the institutions of Imperial French culture, the avant-garde has ever since maintained a type of parasitic relationship with the dominant apparatuses of official taste and of moral and intellectual permission—even if this relationship fashions itself as an "adversary relation," by which (as Roger Shattuck has argued) the avant-garde "gains its special status" through its critique of "the main body of the culture to which it is reacting."[7] Pound's self-promotion from the London drawing room circuit—as private lecturer on Provençal poetry—to harbinger of "the New," is indicative of the very character of the avant-garde's origins. Pound's career finds an immediate antecedent somewhere between that of Fillipo Marinetti—bourgeois media savant and sole inaugurator of Futurism—and that of Manet—covetous of success at the official Salons, yet driven by circumstance to assume the leadership of the "first coherent, organic, and consciously avant-garde movement in the history of modern art."[8] The curiosity is that it was the mechanisms of official culture itself that caused a significant

---

[6] Ian Dunlop, *The Shock of the New: Seven Historical Exhibitions of Modern Art* (London: Weidenfeld and Nicolson, 1972) 10-53.

[7] Roger Shattuck, *The Innocent Eye: On Modern Literature and the Arts* (New York: Farrar, Strauss, and Giroux, 1984) 74.

[8] Renato Poggioli, *The Theory of the Avant-Garde*, trans. Gerald Fitzgerald (New York: Harper & Row, 1971) 132.

number of such otherwise highly individualistic artists, writers, and thinkers (like Pound), to purvey ideas of *collectivised action* and to gather around themselves "consciously avant-garde movements." For Pound and Marinetti, such action arguably remained bound to personal prestige and, like Théophile Gautier before them, to claims of cultural arbitration, education, and social transformation.

More curious, then, that the failure of collective action has, particularly since 1968, became the primary criterion in judging the success or failure of the so-called avant-garde project. Aleš Debeljak, for example, has written that the failure of "the avant-garde effort to transcend the institution of autonomous art" and to "integrate art into everyday life in the name of utopian social change," can be attributed to the fact that the avant-garde project "ended in a collapse of the aesthetic and practical dimensions without liberating effect."[9] This view remains incomplete in many respects, not least because its failure is accounted one of *modalities*. This is similarly the case with Habermas's rejection of postmodernism on the grounds of an "incomplete project of modernity," linked to a critique of Enlightenment rationalism. As Lautréamont famously said: "Plagiarism is necessary; progress implies it." And if the work of the avant-garde—whatever, or whoever that is supposed to be—has been historically directed at the revelation of this seeming contradiction in the logic of progress, then the "collapse of the aesthetic and practical dimensions" is not an *end* of avant-garde history, but rather its *condition* as a "critical counterpart" of the very bourgeois system of values to which it is said to be opposed (and whose illusion it has nonetheless always functioned to sustain, as the very raison d'être of avant-gardism). In this way, progress retains a satirical dimension: a détournement of the very priniciple of origination and invention which has always been advertised as its sumum bonum.

9 Aleš Debeljak, *Reluctant Modernity: The Institution of Art and Its Historical Forms* New York: Roweman and Littlefield, 1998) 128.

It seems to be no accident that the series of political, social and epistemological ruptures and recursions that had led up to the installation of Napoleon III should have found themselves mirrored in the revolutionary discourses of avant-gardism, in which the "new" has always, in some sense, affected itself by way of a détournement of the received tradition—but above all of the revolutionary tradition itself, born alongside eighteenth century Romanticism and the open-ended progressivism of the Enlightenment project. Likewise the ambivalent relationship of successive avant-gardes to industrialisation and the status of the machine in modern life. Successively an object of satire and utopianist praise, "the machine"—from Jonathan Swift and Jeremy Bentham, to Marinetti and Marcel Duchamp—has emblematised the inherent paradox of the avant-garde hypothesis. Moreover, in terms of a "programme," whose success or failure is necessarily measured in progressivist and socially redemptive terms, avant-gardism appears itself to be nothing more than a particular détournement of the very social ideologies that gave rise to it.

3

It is for this reason that the birth and presumed death of the avant-garde mirror one another in contemporary critical lamentations in such an uncanny way. After a century-and-a-half, the avant-garde's principle legacy, it seems, is its own disappearance: a vanishing act corresponding to a type of rectified perturbation in the system of western historical consciousness. Hence, Debeljak writes: "While liberal bourgeois individualism implied the provinces of privacy, self-development, dignity, and autonomy, the emerging form of the individual self in advanced capitalism is instead articulated in terms of fragmented and narcissistic consciousness."[10] And all of this not because the avant-garde was driven from the streets,

---

[10] Debeljak, *Reluctant Modernity*, 128.

like the once ubiquitous organ-grinder, but because it had long ago learned to convert its radical currency into a mix of public sinecure and private fund, and in the process turned from antitype of social conformity into one of conformity's very safeguard.

Moreover, given the uneasy association of revolutionary "aesthetic practice" with politico-economic idealism over the course of the second half of the nineteenth century and the first half of the twentieth, it is hardly surprising that debate over the status of avant-gardism and of the various modernisms should come to mirror those about the necessary phases of Western industrial, liberal-democratic, industrial "evolution." According to such analogies, the history of avant-gardism commences with the "second phase" of the Industrial Revolution in France and ends with the media revolution following WWII and the advent of "globalisation" (previously anticipated by Marx), signalled in Guy Debord's *Society of the Spectacle* and elsewhere as a descent into pure simulationism—culminating "today" (in the shadow of "11 September 2001") in a mode of politico-economic *avant*-ism whose instrument is the affective contretemps of a globalised network of ethical inequivalence masked by a pseudo cultural uniformity and enforced by way of what Antonio Tarbucchi has termed "that which arrives before Time and against Time," exemplified at the turn of the 21st century by the transformation and regulation of conflict as a social fact by the spectre of pre-emptive war, "des guerres faites *avant*."[11]

In many respects the prospect of the spectacle of a perpetually reiterating state of affairs must always have held perverse appeal to the sort of solipsistic/nihilistic temperament that views all of history as tending inexorably towards itself, as though "it" were its natural apotheosis and end-point— whether this be the revolution of Marx of the New World Order of the American neo-conservatives, viewed through the prism

[11] Antonio Tarbucchi, *Au pas de l'oie: Chroniques de nos temps obscurs*, trans. Judith Rosa (Paris: Seuil, 2006).

of a western cultural apparatus and media that has increasingly come to be characterised by a functional ambiguity: an ambiguity which anticipates and incorporates "in advance" its own critique and thereby affects a type of discursive *law*.

4

Antonin Artaud's excursus on *Heliogabalus, or the Anarchist Crowned* (1934) provides a paradigm case in the unmasking of precisely this type of aesthetico-moralistic ambiguity, one which always accompanied both judicial messianism and the counter-hegemonic claims of political anarchism, as well as their aestheticisation by way of "avant-gardist" theory and praxis. For Artaud, it is precisely in the body of the Law itself that the rule of order is overthrown, given over to the serial, almost mechanistic, iteration of its otherness in "deviance" and "perversion," and to the equating of these terms with the real politics of, for example, social justice.[12]

Like the anal-aggressive phase of infancy delineated by Freud, the historical avant-garde has acquired for itself something of the caché of the diminutive tyrant emblematised in Charles Fourier's "little hordes"—those anarchistic street urchins cum trash collectors in whom the work of social hygiene is transformed into endless play. It was Fourier's basic contention that it was not man but civilisation that needed reforming. And like Jarry's Ubu, Fourier's social monstrum posed a challenge to the moral dictatorship of utopianists and utilitarians like Robert Owen and Jeremy Bentham (just as it does to the present day ideologues of "democratisation"), exposing the fundamentalism of—and fundamentally normative distinction between—the role of social engineer and that of social "revolutionary."

Fourier's legacy has more recently been taken up by Guy Debord, in whom the "no-work" ethic functions as an uncanny

---

12 Antonin Artaud, *Selected Writings*, ed. Susan Sontag (Berkeley: University of California Press, 1998) 317-36.

counterpart to the social fictions of consumer culture; and by Peter Bürger, whose *Theory of the Avant-Garde* (1974) yokes together the systemic disorder of Dada with the disordered system of revolutionary praxis called Surrealism. In both cases, the logic of the "new," and the counter-logic of its resistance, are merely available stereotypes in the round of laissez-faire deregulation and re-appropriation. As Theodor Adorno says: "Even where art insists on the greatest degree of dissonance and disharmony, its elements are those of unity."[13] The dream of aesthetic social praxis has in this sense always served a homoeostatic function, in which the ruptures and discontinuities of avant-gardism have served more as a deflection from the fact that the idea of linear progressivist history was itself never more than a political expedience. The enervations of what is called postmodernity were thus forecast from the very outset of the modernist project.

"It is possible," Karl Mannheim wrote in *Ideology and Utopia* (1936), "that in the future, in a world in which there is never anything new, in which all is finished and each moment is a repetition of the past, there can exist a condition in which thought will be utterly devoid of all ideological and utopian elements."[14] Confronted with the redundancy of both traditional social taboos and the "novelty" of transgression, permissibility itself recedes from awareness as the sole universal actor in a social theatre devoid of a stage. The absence of ideology is perhaps, then, merely the latest manifestation of a hegemonic structure whose regulatory power seems to be everywhere visible, but nowhere verifiable. If such is the condition of the postmodern, then the decried lack of a point of critical "resistance"—of a critical object as such—is simply one

---

[13] Theodor W. Adorno, *Ästhetische Theorie* (Frankfurt: Suhrkramp, 1970) 235: cited in Peter Bürger, *Theory of the Avant-Garde*, trans. Michael Shaw (Minneapolis: University of Minnesota Press, 1984) 56.

[14] Karl Mannheim, *Ideology and Utopia: An Introduction to the Sociology of Knowledge*, trans. Louis Wirth and Edward Shils (New York: Harcourt, Brace & World, 1968 [1936]).

more ruse in the aestheticisation, and consequent anestheticisation, of shock-value.

In any case, the necessary belatedness of postmodernism as a discourse carries with it the sort of historical stink that always accompanies the resurrection of old corpses to adjudicate on matters of social or cultural permissiveness. The trick has been for it to present itself as lacking any historical dimension at all—as though it were, in essence, a timeless mechanism arrived at through the technologising of all critical orientations towards a possible futurity. A purely disembodied stink. Hence, for Jean François Lyotard: "*Post modern* would have to be understood according to the paradox of the future (*post*) anterior (*modo*)."[15] Its status, as future-anterior, links it to a perpetual recursion in which everything is made to look and smell more or less "the same"—since what is being looked at or smelled is no *thing* but rather a kind of trope: the commodity relation according to which Coca Cola, the Mona Lisa and a sexagenarian Mick Jagger achieve a discursive, timeless equivalence.

5

The question that has consistently been raised over the last thirty years is: if the condition of criticism is continuous with that of modernity, is postmodernism thus predicated on a post-critical condition? Or, contrary to received wisdom, is the perceived ambivalence of criticality today due not to a lack of a "point of resistance," but rather to an oversubscription of antecedents; or else to the fact that criticism itself has become "mimeticised," as it were? That the criticality of the historical avant-garde, founded upon a supposed relation to the otherwise unpresentable, has ceded to representation *as* criticism, thus constituting itself as a post-effect? And if such is the case, is it inevitable that "criticism" be left with no other

---

[15] Jean-François Lyotard, *The Postmodern Condition: A Report on Knowledge*, trans. Geoff Bennington and Brian Massumi (Manchester: Manchester University Press, 1991) 81.

option than to adopt a strategy of "acceleration," in an effort to regain at least a nominal vantage point in this ever-shifting, virtualised terrain? This has been one of the conclusions put forward by contemporary media theorists like Vilém Flusser, Friedrich Kittler, Jean Baudrillard, Paul Virilio, Donna Haraway and Katherine Hayles, re-echoing the prescriptions of McLuhan thirty years earlier and Walter Benjamin thirty years before that—suggesting that the technical, mass reproduction and circulation of images does not serve to conceal a social reality, rather it reveals *the inherently technological dimension of that reality.*

If Habermas, to the contrary, identifies the radical phase of modernity with the Enlightenment and Industrial Revolution, this is because he perceives in its social orientation a criticality without direct antecedence, without a *model.* Modernity's attempt to come to terms with the unpresentable, as Lyotard likewise contends, is thus tied to a certain condition of crisis in the accession to an experience of discourse removed from one of epistemological foundations. Hence, a condition of crisis vis-à-vis the representable is taken as the *condition of modernity* as such. Nevertheless, as Bürger and numerous other commentators have pointed out, "when Duchamp puts his signature on mass-produced, randomly chosen objects and send them to art exhibits, this provocation of art presupposes a concept of what art is,"[16] just as Tristan Tzara's cut-ups presuppose an idea of what literature is. And indeed, just as Bruce Nauman's "Fountain" and John Ashbery's "Europe" presuppose an idea of *avant-garde* art and *avant-garde* literature. To paraphrase Marx, the conventions and clichés of all the dead avant-gardes weigh like a nightmare on the brain of the living.

In these terms, the application of electronic computing in contemporary poetics, with its explorations of hypertext, hypermedia and other aleatory mechanisms of inscription, has made only modest advances upon earlier forms of "avant-

---

16 Bürger, *Theory of the Avant-Garde,* 56.

garde" writing—such as the algorithmic constraint-based poetics of Raymond Queneau and the Oulipo—other than in incorporating aleatory *mechanisms* directly into the "work itself," wherein the aesthetics of probability and chance operations become part of the textual edifice while their actual mechanics remain invisible. This is perhaps a condition of all forms of technical supersession, yet the ubiquity of techno-aesthetics accompanied by a too-discrete dependency upon a sublimated technics (exemplified by such things as operating code, as Kittler has long observed),[17] stands at odds with a certain "criticality" vested in the appropriations of an historical avant-gardism that today finds itself more properly expressed, we might say, by way of hacker subcultures than by the burgeoning institution of digital art.[18]

Consider, for example, the textual interventions, détournements and chance operations in now canonical work like John Cage's *Roaratorio* (1979), wherein the "operating code" is itself *performed* alongside the works so-called content, and is endowed thereby with certain "metatextual" properties that assume for themselves the function of a conductor/composer, insofar as the rest of the performance (of which they assumes the role of metonymic counterpart) takes its cues from them: i.e. they produce instructions or recompose indexes of subsidiary operations performed by other instruments and so on. Which is to say that such performances comprise a *diagrammatic field*, indeed a schematisable sign system. Much of the new media, meanwhile, has been employed in the arts in a primarily imitative manner—either to automatise the type of work pioneered by Cage and others, by way of computer programmes, or to redploy such things as analogue video art within the digital field, or else to surmount the perceived limitations of print media's fixed typo/graphic distribution by

---

[17] Friedrich Kittler, "Protected Mode," *Literature, Media, Information Systems*, ed. John Johnston (Amsterdam: OPA, 1997) 156ff.
[18] Cf. Thomas Foster, "The Rhetoric of Cyberspace: Ideology or Utopia?" *Contemporary Literature* XL.1 (1999): 144-160.

way of the mutli*linear* schematics and visual kinaesthetics of "electronic writing."

This, perhaps, remains today the proper "task" for an avant-garde, in overcoming the traps of analogical thought in the conception and supersession of the formerly "new" by way of a simple transition form one platform to another—regardless of which critical domain we choose to speak of. Gene Youngblood, author of *Expanded Cinema* (1970), has made similar remarks concerning the status of "new media" within the discipline of the arts, arguing that video art, for example, "can only have a formalist reference—the graphic properties of the image." For Youngblood, "the new avant-garde is about creating autonomous social worlds that people can live in. Art is central to that, but the art is not what's avant-garde. What's avant-garde is metadesign, the creation of context."[19] The notion of context as content is born of the very idea of communications technologies, from McLuhan to cyberculture, in the re-appropriation of corporate media space, through public access cable TV, satellite, internet, GPS and WiFi.[20] A critical, ecological mode of thought—networked, transverse, topological—here assumes the practical function of "avant-gardism" in effecting the structure of how things come to mean, and how meaning is lived.

CODA

We know that the history of experimentation did not commence with the "avant-garde." Nor has social transformation always accompanied a *project* of aesthetic transformation, even if the term "culture," for example, implies

19 Gene Youngblood, "Life in Counterculture," *Umělec* 2 (2006): 13.
20 Cf. *Prefiguring Cyberspace: An Intellectual History,* eds. Darren Tofts, Annemarie Jonson, and Alessio Cavallaro (Cambridge, Mass.: MIT Press, 2002); also *Virtual Realities and their Discontents,* ed. Robert Markley (Baltimore: Johns Hopkins University Press, 1996); and *Cyberspace/Cyberbodies/Cyberpunk: Cultures of Technological Embodiment,* eds. Mike Featherstone and Roger Burrows (London: SAGE, 1995).

it. The experimental viewpoint—from John Dewey, Gregory Bateson, Buckminster Fuller, Louis Pouzin and Ted Nelson to the contemporary "technopoetics," "codework" and "meta-design" of the likes of Metz, Stelarc, Kenneth Goldsmith, Kit Galloway and Sherrie Rabinowitz—necessarily holds that avant-gardism is first and foremost an attitude towards life if it is to be anything at all. This raises the question of whether the long-standing debate over "the avant-garde" and its various manifestations is simply a contest over terminologies or whether it is tied-in to a broader aestheticisation of ideology and of ideological purchase upon critical "praxis" and upon the "real."

Louis Armand
Prague, May, 2006

Rachel Blau DuPlessis

Post-Avant / Avant Post: An Imaginary Conversation inside Real Practice*

A. Is the avant-garde viable under prevailing "post" conditions?

P. "The A-effect consists in turning the object of which one is to be made aware, to which one's attention is to be drawn, from something ordinary, familiar, immediately accessible, into something peculiar, striking and unexpected. What is obvious is in a certain sense made incomprehensible, but this is only in order that it may then be made all the easier to comprehend. Before familiarity can be turned into awareness the familiar must be stripped of its inconspicuousness; we must give up assuming that the object in question needs no explanation."[1] Even to choose the words "the object" is not enough—too bounded. I have always wanted to write a work called "Provenance" in which the intricate origins of every made thing can get traced to its social, ethical, political, material sources, a work constructed in order that we feel the networks of impingement and intricacy. I'm sure it's been done ...

*   Parts of this text appeared in an essay published in *PORES* on-line (2002). Joan Retallack's words "continue the conversation" inspired the form.
[1] Bertolt Brecht, *Brecht on Theatre; The Development of an Aesthetic*, ed. and trans. John Willett (New York: Hill and Wang, 1964) 143-4.

A. Is the "A-effect" the Avant-effect? It's true that what you just cited about the Alienation Effect also sounds like a definition of the goals of the avant-garde. This is not an unusual insight, but it's a curious one. Does that make the Post-Avant create the A-effect by using the avant-garde as "ordinary, familiar, immediately accessible"? Would that work? The "alienation effect" of Post-Avant is a distancing and questioning of avant-garde ideas? Or does that point just reaffirm the endless cycle of replacement fantasies and not change any assumptions whatsoever? This is the fake Hegelianism of avant, post, post-post and so forth. Stagy position taking and sabre rattling. The new and newer and newest new. No transformative sublation. Anyway, what happens if we talk about "alienation effect" and not "avant-anything" for a minute?

P. I like to return to that Brecht citation because it talks about an art experience that does not resolve the contradictions (contradictory emotions and allegiances, cross-hatched identifications and investments), but insists that the viewer take the contradictions beyond the experience of the artwork into the pinch-me-it's-real, historical world. Those contradictions are both intellectually and viscerally imbedded in the body-mind, they unsettle, arouse, disturb and displace; thus they may lead to action and then to social solutions. Real gardens provoked by the imaginary toads in them? Anyway, in order for that to occur, all parties in the exchange need to resist normative, affirmative art (begging the question of just what this might be and how these words can always be deployed as terms of accusation and contempt). The artist/maker thus must refuse the conventional desire and norm-laden aesthetic demand to provide conclusion (simply) or catharsis (more complicatedly), thus making restlessness permanent. By producing restless artworks that do not settle, the artist somehow induces the viewer to become alert with the Eros of political arousal and enraged with the stubbornness of political rage. And the viewer must agree to enjoy or accept or endure being unsettled, indeed, to live within the non-escapist ethos, to enjoy the feeling of the contesting contradictions and emotional conflicts now layered inside her.

A. "Somehow induces"—what is the content of that "somehow"? And what if an unsettled viewer just walks out, walks away, untouched?

P. It's unproven whether walking out means you are untouched; it could mean you are shaken to the core. And "boredom" could be defensive. It's true, however, that "walking out" is an undesirable situation for this theory: the conventions of audience behaviour in theatre (and in other performance) are indeed pressure against walking out as they are also against throwing potato salad at the performers or joining the orchestra on stage with your violin or kazoo. (Funny, then, that this a-normative theatre depends on certain social manners. Indeed, in David Antin's performances, one hears him welcoming people—and this is an allegorical invitation—to walk in!) But one does graze and walk freely (touched or untouched) in a museum or gallery. And as for reading? No one prevents you from closing the book, from skipping or skimming. How to prevent the viewer from failing to be gripped? This suggests that the *aesthetic* negotiation of "alienation-effect" or unresolved contradictions—pace of presentation, manner of frustration, the degree of pleasure or pain at this, sense of address to the whole situation—is actually central to continuing to engage the attention of readers/ viewers. So this still involves aesthetic judgment and precision as well as, let's say, socio-political acuity and precision. We are, here as always, tumbled back into the fundamental questions about making art as well as thoughts about making a political intervention through art. Sometimes we think (rigidly) of these as "different" realms, different claims. This rigidity is so curious, anyway, given that we live, are formed by, are tempered in the material and political particulars that make the "self" or its "life." I want to see those particulars; I want to register them; I therefore want to resist theorising that separates the aesthetic and the material/socio-political. But I don't want to oversimplify, either.

A. I think Brecht's theory is brave, and maybe the best we can do, but I think it also underestimates the degree of multi-tasking and self-repression any person "does," how we swallow hard transitions down and just live with the comic, ironic, or ridiculous figure we cut moving from—let's say the stunning awe at the threat of a volcanic explosion to the fact that it's time for lunch. I am thinking of the first section of Wallace Stevens's "Esthétique du Mal":

> He tried to remember the phrases: pain
> Audible at noon, pain torturing itself,
> Pain killing pain on the very point of pain.
> The volcano trembled in another ether,
> As the body trembles at the end of life.
>
> It was almost time for lunch.[2]

Really, the terms we want are more like Joan Retallack's "poethical wager": "that we do our utmost to understand our contemporary position and then act on the chance that our work may be at least as effective as any other initial condition in the intertwining trajectories of pattern and chance."[3] Act in life, act in art, act engaged is how I translate that, though Retallack is here defending the unpredictable impact of a complex artwork set on its merry way into a real life zone. But of course radical form does not mean anything about actual political agency; those processes may intersect but they are not synonymous.

---

[2] Wallace Stevens, *Wallace Stevens: Collected Poetry and Prose*, eds. Frank Kermode and Joan Richardson (New York: The Library of America, 1997) 277.

[3] Joan Retallack, *The Poethical Wager* (Berkeley: University of California Press, 2003) 46.

P. Radical form does not make anyone a radical. But it is such a temptation to play hopefully along the edge of those two concepts that use the same word.

A. Or maybe Roland Barthes on pleasure and bliss would be a happier theory, a theory of extravagance, acknowledging the painfulness of desire for the unknowable, the edge beyond. He argues that bliss emerges in the sense of the unsettled, the unresolvable, the non-thetic, in negativity. Pleasure is affirmative, closural, but bliss is something beyond. One is aroused to a sublime awe at the intricate worlds whose rationales and meanings we can barely intuit.[4] Like finding a whole ecology of life-forms thriving in the hot vents in the Pacific.

Or something to return to from Barrett Watten: "The constructivist moment is an elusive transition in the unfolding work of culture in which social negativity—the experience of rupture, and act of refusal—invokes a fantasmatic future—a horizon of possibility, an imagination of participation."[5]

P. The terms of this conversation are already overwhelming; we have barely begun, and I'm getting hungry; it might be time for lunch. But, no matter that noble avant-garde goal of rupturing the affirmative, still I look at the avant-garde sort of cock-eyed. Most avant-gardes I know about in the modern period have not self-consciously critiqued their own gender and racialised assumptions, although they are rife with these materials and often run on them, are fuelled by them. Avant-gardes have worked "overwhelmingly" from "male subject position(s)" as Susan Rubin Suleiman says about Surrealism.[6] Yet they rarely

---

4   Roland Barthes, *The Pleasure of the Text*, trans. Richard Miller (New York: Hill and Wang, 1975) 3-24.
5   Barrett Watten, *The Constructivist Moment: From Material Text to Cultural Poetics* (Middletown, CT: Wesleyan University Press, 2003) xxi; 191.
6   Susan Rubin Suleiman, *Subversive Intent: Gender, Politics, and The Avant-Garde* (Cambridge, Mass.: Harvard University Press, 1990) 26.

examine or question the issues and materials of masculinity and manhood, whiteness and privilege, anti-effeminacy, or the scintillating dark-exoticisms created, but rather affirm them as part of the palette, unquestioned assumptions as usable as pigment squeezed straight from the tube. Indeed, when many avant-gardes have proposed gender and racial issues as part of their arsenal of representations, a good deal of evidence shows that these considerations of social location and power replicate to perfection, or even exaggerate melodramatically, the gender and racial relations of the bourgeois society that the avant-garde is, in its other presumptive claims, contesting. Same old, same old. There has been at least a feminist epistemic shift in the past years, as well as other parallel shifts. So why should I get excited about "the avant-garde"? Perhaps it is simply the past and a term from the past.

A. Yes—thinking as a feminist always confronts one with the ethical choice: do I overlook this specific problem in favour of greater solidarities? Or do I critique and go out on a limb, never to be seen again? I heard a piece by Sofia Gubaidulina, the "Feast During a Plague" (2005), performed by the Philadelphia Orchestra and Simon Rattle in February 2006. The piece is a stunning, noble, monumental and risk-taking orchestral work that ended in a non-dialogue between the classical materials and a heavy rock set of stuff played over loud-speakers. That was certainly an apparent contradiction between two art forms, but it was not a true contradiction; I felt the "answer" had already been set, made in the Adorno-esque mode of resisting the brazen sound of pop culture, or barely beginning to have a dialogue with it. So surely if there is to be contradiction, it must be real, not faked, and not, like Socratic "dialogue," skewed to favour one side. This is harder to do than it seems, and hard to do without seeming wishy-washy, non-committed, soft, just fooling around, "playing".... But what I really liked was the take-no-prisoners sublime of Gubaidulina's work; it made me awe-struck, ennobled, uplifted. These are humanistic, confrontational-evocative qualities. And just look at those terms! Maybe what women artists have to do is begin culture all over from the beginning!

P. Well—do what you need to do. But don't just light up a zillion watts with illusions! I'll say one thing about this "post" moment, whatever it is, and whatever we want to call it—it is raising every single question we ever had about art, its terms, its functions, its mechanisms, its purposes, its histories; this moment compels us to propose and relive all the debates about aesthetics and politics and social location again, and at a serious, necessary pitch.

A. Post-avant. So is this the same term as "avant-garde" or a different term? What does it mean? I've seen "post-avant" used by Ron Silliman on his blog and elsewhere (including www.bostoncomment.com/debate.html), and I accept it, sort of vaguely, as a helpful generalised rubric. It's an umbrella / catch-all category for all of what has been thought of as oppositional poetics over the past fifty-plus years—Black Mountain, New York School, Language writing, and ethnopoetics, and, and, and. If it has a particularity, it might mean writing coming after the Vietnam Era experimental Language Poetries (and sometimes, indeed, it's writing made by the people who actually participated in that formation), writing that does, more and more, seem to collect itself in, into, and toward political comment—from Tenney Nathanson, from CA Conrad, Deborah Richards, Frank Sherlock, from Laura Elrick, Rodrigo Toscano, from Juliana Spahr, Redell Olsen, Erin Moure, Ed Roberson, Rob Fitterman, Erica Hunt—there really are a lot of people doing this work—many more than that list of folks, which is mean to be suggestive only. However—and this is quite interesting to me—in part because of the penetrating self-consciousness about group formation visible at least in the New York School(s), the Language groups, and in the freemasonry of ethnopoiesis, anyone coming up now (generationally) has seen the sociology of art groups up close, actively, eagerly digesting materials, has seen the debates that build and exclude in public forums (like blogs). Thus I think some post-avant thinking is self-consciously trying actively to build a "generation." Although I am not sure one builds a generational sense only from one's own acts and agency—I think it also happens, activates, congeals, from historical pressures external to the small-ish formations of poetic groups. I can see why the term "world spirit" seems so useful an explanation!

P. So what you mean is post-avant exists as a term—now we have to give it a content. That list of people you just gave is not exactly "generational" but cross-generational.

A. Well, it's some people who are simply temporally *after* the avant-garde formations, doing experimental work. And it's people drawing upon modernism, but resisting the universalising, triumphalist ethos of modernism. Plus it's people who are self-consciously using experimental tactics directly to confront politics and ideology and issues in their representation and critique. These are somewhat different emphases (like the difference between Kenny Goldsmith and Bruce Andrews—Andrews has more social bite in his combinatory urgencies, although Goldsmith represents the streaming of sensation and stimuli in our world with hyper-realist goals), but they get simply all bundled together under the rubric post-avant. For reasons of such flexibility alone, it is a useful-enough term that will probably stick. And it, like many such terms, will continue to have its definitions constructed in process as various artists continue functionally to participate in this formation. To me, post-avant means artworks from the mid-eighties on. (In the US, thus with the neo-conservative blockage of social democracy and then the 2000 coup taking over government functions.) This is art made under political and social conditions that cause one to reopen all the questions about the meaning and function of art, given our sense of, and our objectively palpable political crisis. Which might be as simple as a lack of ideological political parties and proportional voting (rather than what we have—dysfunctional Big Tent parties and the Electoral College). That is, the US is a democracy in name only. Which might be a crisis of our agency, powerlessness, and our sense of out-of-control exploitation and despoiling happening very close, indeed, sometimes happening "in our names." But to generalise, to get off culture-bound United-Statesness I'd say that fundamentalism, wherever found, is what post-avant must stake itself against.

P. But "post-avant" has a built-in rhetorical problem in its verbal closeness to "avant-garde." The avant-garde, the vanguard party, the ones who claimed to be ahead in a necessary, teleologically crucial historical direction also implicitly or explicitly claimed leadership roles in the advance. This is a structural part of the ideology of the avant-garde. This position has severe ethical problems, casting others as followers only, instrumentalising them, while the claimants become Seers or Visionaries seeing the direction of history, and thus, while possibly acting in exploitive ways in their personal, sexual, economic and ethical life, being excused because of that visionary élan. This vangardist ethos, no matter where it appeared and for good reason or bad, has been a disaster. The separatist claim of the lesbian vanguard, for instance, was a cul-de-sac for the women's movement, which does not mean—don't misunderstand—that sexual preference and those particular aspects for social justice are not central issues, because they are. In any event Post-Avant may be "after" that conceptualisation of the forerunners, the military scouts, but does it not still claim that same vanguardism of terminology and positionality? It did not get intellectually "beyond" that kind of vanguardism. Is it not, in its terms, a new-new, or the latest thing, or the thing beyond the thing out front? Thus—in terminology, and taken at its face value, the term "post-avant" participates in the vanguard ethos it is presumably resisting.

A. Yes, There is plenty of semantic, not to say deconstructive, irony in the term post-avant. *Post* indicates "after in time, later, and subsequent to" and thus indicates a new firstness, in front of the former firstness. And in that, the term may simply be descriptive: we do come after, chronologically. Another definition of *post* is "after in position, behind, posterior to." Saying post-avant, or avant-post we still line up behind the avant-garde, those historical, noble, excited, beneficial, experimental, shocking, disgraceful groups and movements. This is getting funny: so are we before or are we after? Are we behind or are we in front? *Post*, in another definition is something placed as a benchmark. We are a post placed near the historical avant-garde, which is still a bigger post. The lines we string depend on them. Or—it's "post" — a system for delivering mail, begun in the series of relays along a fixed route, for couriers. So avant-post is just delivering the "letters" of the avant-garde to another generation. We travel quickly, post-haste. So we are "post-age"; the age of after, the stamp and ticket. And the price of first-class mail has risen again: 39 cents. So we can "post"—on the internet. Anyway, I'd rather not be "post," meaning hasty and quick; "shoot first; aim later" is amusing (except if you take the shot), but if you do the "shoot first" too much, you'll regret it. And then suppose I don't want to line up, as you don't, for gender reasons, with or as anything like the historical, twentieth-century avant-garde. I need a quieter term: Experimental. Innovative.

P. These terms are agreeable and accurate, but they have no particular historical edginess. Part of that edginess of "post-avant" is precisely the flirtation with an avant-garde history that is also being critiqued. And partly "experimental" and "innovative" can be over-generalised terms everyone is happy to have a friendly little piece of, turning strategies into rhetoric only. Maybe post-avant is this: it is the ethics of resisting the sheerly avant-garde. So it's beyond the avant-garde while participating in some of its terms. Well—it's a good cluster—

experimental, innovative, avant/post-avant. So long as edginess and critique are central.

A. I say I want to "torque" things. The challenge, it seems to me, is to write precisely inside one's social historicity, not ahead of it. And so for whatever reasons, I am beginning to think that I'm pre-avant, although I am certainly living in certain "post" conditions. I am not "after" anything; rather I'm before, waiting still for modernism to happen, waiting for real modernity to happen—the sense of justice and social democracy promised in the radical movements of the later 19th and early part of the 20th century. Utopian desire, ethical hope, sickened astonishment, and intermittent despair are my present. Pre-avant is the Gramscian optimism of the will, pessimism of the intellect.

P. Poetry as a form of words can sometimes lead to political arousal and transformation. Songs can seem to sum up a generation's urgencies. A poet/writer who has experienced having her/his words accomplish this (like Adrienne Rich, Ntozake Shange, Allen Ginsberg, or Eliot Weinberger with "What I Heard about Iraq"), a poet for whom this is a decisive desire (such as Anne Waldman, Ezra Pound, or Sonia Sanchez) can probably never let go of the tremendous feeling of having achieved words that change people's minds, hearts, consciousness. But do these words cause something to happen in the political sphere? Only as part of the political conditions, as one contribution among many. There is not a direct correlation between writing and action. This is to the good. I would imagine there is a split among these artists—between those who seek and accept the cultural responsibility of being a conduit for something that they feel needs to be said and those who discuss and examine what they see is vital, whereupon, by a series of interesting accidents, their words accidentally become talismanic. Ginsberg did not write "Howl" in order to achieve the response he did; the response was an unintended consequence, one, however, that created a feedback loop that induced him to continue to speak for his generation.

The bard, the spokesperson, the arouser, the one on whom our investments pour, the one who seems to be speaking for us, the one whose rhetorics appear to have invented us—this is a generative cultural position, but it is not either an exclusive function for poetry nor is it the top of an imagined hierarchy of poetry's function. Poets might think of their words as bridges, reaching between, living in betweenness.

A. Do you realise we haven't really said what "post" conditions we are talking about—? I mean, with all this invoking of historicity. I'd say post-Vietnam (a big power loses to a guerrilla army), post-9/11 in the USA—the shock of an attack that should have been declared a "crime against humanity" but instead solidified a minority government and its calculated "pre-emptive war" policies both inside and outside its borders; post-Fall of Berlin Wall in Europe; and post-national on the economic level (rabid companies and ministries of economics, global integration, exporting exploitation, despoilers— otherwise called investors—in collusion with national governments against peoples). This is one mix, and its dates range from 1975 to 2006—thirty years! But mainly it is about small powerlessness, the lack of agency of the small as against the machineries of power: states, armies, global companies. So what I want to say in considering the post-avant is: We have not mourned the failure of modernity enough.

P. Tell me more.

A. What went wrong? Torah in Hell. Atlas of Slavery. We have not mourned and comprehended (taken the knowledge inside us) because its failures are pocked, pebbled, irregular (unevenly developed). In our world sector or cadre, we have the more developed gains of modernity, although unequally distributed even inside our sector. (*We*, is defined here, in a friendly way, as made up of people who have enough education, equipment, and access to participate in this discussion) Class, race, ethnicity, region, gender, religious culture are some of the filters that bar or inflect the dissemination of the benefits of modernity. But we have not mourned because we are often dazzled by the baubles modernity has given to us. We were thinking that this unrolling crisis is not about us: globalisation, not about us. Possibility of nuclear war, not about us. Our standard of living, not about us. Ecological disaster, not about us (well, maybe about us). The militant claims to impose fundamentalist religious laws, not about us. Hence our consciousness has been pallid and apolitical; this has been going on for years now; it seems our consciousness is paralyzed and half-poisoned. Will we wake up? We are still living in some amnesia and obliviousness. We are not enraged enough about injustice, about the lacks and losses of others, because we don't see these are part of us. Living in the long "twentieth" century (in modernity, whenever that began—let's say with African enslavement, accomplished by a toxic coalition of the willing—this is not white vs. black by any means!), we have also lived with unacceptable brutality and political malfeasance: genocide, rapine. We have gotten used to the tragedies we inflict on each other while invoking peculiar names: science, religion, nation, development. We have to become desperate for our values. These values involve sustainable development, liberal tolerance, and social justice.

P. Post-Gardes from the Volcano? The ajvar of Dada, a jar of it, all red, is open on the table. Sometimes people passing by will take a spoonful and throw it in whatever they are doing. I shrug. Or, a student paper on a poem. "It has a revolution at the end." We should be so lucky. She meant, probably, either "resolution" or "revelation." These are notes in "Shorthad." Right now, we've been "short had." The power of hands on the levers of power which are shameless, unchecked, and willing to lie and never swerve is one of the more shocking—and fast-moving developments on the past (approximate) decade—six years of a callow, shameless, criminal clerical-authoritarian president of the United States feels like forever.

A. When Celan changed his name, making a poet's name from Antschel, his family name, I think what he did was cast out particular tainted letters: the H for Hitler and the ST for Stalin.

P. Post-avant feels like the knowledge of networks. We are not one single thing. This may be because of the internet, information access and information saturation, instant communication. It may be because of the plagues and illnesses that travel round the globe. It may be that we intuit or are shocked by ways various far-flung economies interconnect; or we feel the "butterfly wing" of politics whose links and odd causations shake us to the core. The breeze (often one we have created, financed, underhandedly encouraged even when it violates our laws or human rights norms) sets up a tidal wave of shattering.

A. "No Proof Children Were Told To Kill." Headline, 30 November 1993. This headline is typical of our times. You can hear its weaselling, lying tone even across the years.

P. I'm still unclear about whether we are participating in the post-avant or critiquing the concept. But whichever, ideologies—that is consciousness, assumptions, values, and modes really have played a strong role both in the real world, as religious ideologies, mainly fundamentalist ones in the current world crisis. You can see why Mina Loy thought, in 1918, that artists should work together to use a combination of fashion, snob appeal, and high culture to absolutely change the symbolic order.[7] The symbolic order (which exists in literature

---

[7] Mina Loy, "International Psycho-Democracy" (1918), *The Last Lunar Baedeker*, ed. Roger L. Conover (Highlands, N.C.; The Jargon Society, 1982) 276-282.

and religion, in national ideology and so on) is precisely part of what we, as artists, engage.

A. That's why there is a desperate necessity to act against fundamentalist thought wherever it is found. It is one enemy of art. And that is just one reason! Right now it is found in four of the major world religions. Hindu fundamentalism in a kind of purgative violence. Israeli fundamentalism that wants to capture Judaism for Israel, as if these were synonymous. They are emphatically not. Christian fundamentalist denizens have "captured" the government of the United States. This has been achieved through a series of astonishing acts around the severe tainting of the electoral process, acts with consequences of serious import. We are its hostages. Christian fundamentalism has not gone un-resisted, but it is still powerful, and its moralist millenarian thinking is grotesque and dangerous in a secular society. Militant, military Islamic fundamentalism, already active in national settings, has made startling claims for attention in this toxic situation, creating a four-cornered danger. Islamic fundamentalism has captured some of the ideological institutions of Islam, such as small schools and mosques. I would take seriously its desire to impose a retrograde moralism and anti-modern social norms on the secular institutions of the world. As I would take the fulminations of the Christian Right in the United States, particularly, though not exclusively, their continuing social war on the female gender, but also on sexual minorities and by their concerted justifications of suppurating social inequality.

P. It is probably not enough simply to say what we stand for. Ethical nuance, linguistic richness, forms that sustain interest, and a resistance to affirmation especially affirmation led-by-the-nose. Compassion, empathy, justice. The creation of, simultaneously, space for one's work and respect for the achievements of others. Heritage, transmission, transposition, regeneration. Resistance, articulation, hope. Poiēsis and curiosity.

A. Go back to the beginning: "Is the avant-garde viable under prevailing 'post' conditions?" What is "viable"? Does this mean "who's listening"? or does it mean "having a real-world impact"? Does viable mean capable of being actualised, or surviving, developing, practicable? To me, viable is a strange word. Really, anything can be done; can be made. The issue is— what is worth doing. If I want to wrap islands in pink cloth, is this worth doing? Should I not think about the birds, the shellfish, the tides? Is mastery, heroism, and imperial vantage the only model of ambition? This art—a project of Christo—is hardly avant-garde; it parallels the ecological despoliation model of Big Corporations, and prettifies that mind-set by draping coloured fabric around big territory. Further, the model of sheer rupture is tiresome. It disallows the poise of an artwork, or says to the reader/listener/consumer that the sense of achievement, peace, poise, pleasure, awe, sense of location, satisfaction at the end of an artwork is null, or is a coarse satisfaction, not prone to change the world.

P. You know—David Antin opens his "what it means to be avant-garde" with this anti-Christo riff. And he also says "practically every role classically attributed to the avant-garde has been pre-empted by something else" –like advertising.[8]

A. Take my little riff as a footnote to his

P. I hate the Poetic.

A. Forget Poetic. Try idiosyncretismatic.

---

[8] David Antin, *What it Means to be Avant-Garde* (New York: New Directions, 1993) 44.

P. Stop making up ways, or words, to make me feel better. I want art that is the work of thought. Not the work of certainty or dull craft running on empty. I want art to get at the joy of the pain of being here. The pain of the joy in such an intractable world.

A. Some art is improved by leaving it behind.

P. I dreamed of seeing workmen and well-dressed men throwing women. Just picking them up and throwing them, throwing and breaking them. This dream was in 2002.

A. Antin's "What it means to be avant-garde" is an extended parable that hardly "discusses" the proposition of the title in any conventional fashion. However, there is an extended meditation on the temporality of the avant-garde, as it lives in the present and responds to the present humanely and with a situated ethics. Meaning "if you have to invent something new to do the work at hand you will," and this "without worrying about making it new or shocking."[9] Articulating the present to itself is a task, a work, a responsibility. This is why Antin spends some energy "leafing through the [local San Diego] newspaper looking for the present,"[10] a corny, cunning positivism at which Antin is quite adept, as his tactic is hardly aleatory, but allegorical and holographic He also draws an intricate picture of a network of family history, of aging relatives and family loss. The sense of loss, gap, processes of losing it, indignities of age, pain, the bravery of facing what is with dignity and compassion central to this work. Antin's final excursus in the piece is his three-week search for Uncle Irving, playing cross-country telephone tag, and then his suddenly being informed, by the stunned widow, of Uncle Irving's death a few hours after Antin had last talked to him. Whereupon the piece ends: "and it seems to me that if you cant respond to that

9   Antin, *What it Means to be Avant-Garde*, 46.
10 Antin, *What it Means to be Avant-Garde*, 55.

youre not in the avant-garde."[11] Thus the avant-garde is about humane, ethical, frank response to the human condition. It is, in a sense, humanism, but inflected with ec-centric critiques, present alertness, an attitude of investigation and discernment, a temporally moving social dynamic, an articulation and exploration of "the present." It's also a claim about scale—no more world historical scope. The local; the particular; the ethical as acting in the present as one faces that present. I suppose I could go for something of that as the "post-avant."

P. You know that famous title? It's not *Minima Moralia: Reflections from a Damaged Life*. People often quote that title wrong. Or they say *Reflections of a Damaged Life*. As if it were all personal, all Adorno's "problem," his life, his problem. Here's the real title. It's *Minima Moralia: Reflections from Damaged Life*. There's no "a" about it.

A. We are all damaged; our collective life, damaged, and deliberately with complicity and deliberation, especially by people who wanted to destroy social fabric in the name of profit and power in order to make more profit and power. "Je est un autre" now has ethical and geopolitical meaning. Consciousness IS network.

11 Antin, *What it Means to be Avant-Garde*, 61.

R.M. Berry

The Avant-Garde and the Question of Literature

> If we take eternity to mean not infinite temporal duration but timelessness, then eternal life belongs to those who live in the present. —Wittgenstein, *Tractatus* (6.4311)

It seems increasingly apparent to me that formally experimental writing is running counter to the main current of history. Whether we consider the global expanse of capitalism, the unrivalled position of the United States in international affairs, the rise of the Republican party nationally, or the worldwide audience for Hollywood film and American popular music, the general direction of the last three decades has been toward increasing consolidation of the dominant. My aim in acknowledging this bleak fact is not to minimise the real fissures and counter currents of recent history. It is to motivate a question: Why does formally experimental writing persist, at least for some of us, in the face of what appears to be its growing marginalisation? In what follows I will not be providing a historical explanation for this persistence, nor will I be seeking a political or ethical justification, although it's essential to the force of my remarks that, on occasion, they compete with such accounts. My background idea is that the continuation into the new millennium of literary experimentation, despite its widespread neglect, is forceful evidence that modernism was not a response to historically circumscribed conflicts and crises but, on the contrary, arose from necessities internal to literature itself. I'll try here to give concreteness to this idea, to indicate how these necessities arise, what they look like, why they're not generally recognised, while attempting some rapprochement with the history I'm bracketing. After all, what I've situated internal to literature, counter to history, is simply the necessity for change, that is, for history. Said another way, it's unclear whether I'm looking for the necessity of formal experimentation or perhaps for freedom from necessity altogether. These could be the same thing.

For those of us who are committed to radical change in literature, there are good reasons why we might want to avoid using the term "avant-garde." The philosopher Stanley Cavell, whose writings on modernism have been influential for me, has noted three confusions endemic to the concept.[1] First is its tendency to overemphasise art's future at the expense of its past, leaving present work ungrounded. The result of this lopsidedness is an impression that contemporary art bears no relation, or only an arbitrary one, to those historic achievements that have given rise both to art's significance and to its problems. We could speak of this first confusion as the avant-garde's misrepresenting possibility as indeterminacy, its misinterpretation of art's unforeclosable future as a hedge against its historical specificity, its present fix. A second confusion has to do with the avant-garde's uncritical enthusiasm for any and everything that calls itself innovative, regardless of an "innovation's" sterility, irrelevance, or just plain stupidity. Cavell speaks of this tendency as the avant-garde's "promiscuous attention" to newness, a phrase intended to suggest both indiscriminate coupling and infidelity. The idea is that the avant-garde habitually conflates novelty with change, imagining that artistic advance results from mere unconventionality, from difference as such. Call this the

[1] Stanley Cavell, *The World Viewed: Reflections on the Ontology of Film*, enlarged edition (Cambridge, Mass.: Harvard University Press, 1979) 216-7.

"farther out than thou" syndrome. And the third confusion is a tendency, already implicit in the avant-garde's military metaphor, to represent artistic advances as historical or political advances, as though significant changes in the forms of art could be validated by their political efficacy. Although Cavell wants to keep open the question of art's relation to politics, not to imply that there is no relation, he means here to criticise the habit, so characteristic of 20th century avant-gardes, of underestimating the real differences between artistic practice and serious political action. How to characterise this last confusion is difficult, since we're still in it, but it has something to do with art's paradoxical autonomy, with the political significance of art's irreducibility to political significance. Taken together these confusions emphasise the avant-garde's tendency to turn on itself, to represent the historical conditions of art as mere obstacles, and thus to undermine those problematic continuities on which, not just mainstream art, but even revolutionary art, depends.

In her 1926 lecture, "Composition as Explanation" Gertrude Stein offers an account of historical change that, while insisting on the necessity for advances in art, seems to avoid Cavell's critique. Her originality stems from two ideas, both involving what she calls "time-sense."[2] First is her idea that the goal of any advance is not the future but the present. That is, every generation lives instinctively and un-self-consciously several generations behind itself, in a kind of anachronistic hybridity, preoccupied with earlier emotions, reflexes, styles, and concepts, and discovering its own time only afterwards, in narrating it. Her paradigm of this belatedness is World War I, which she says the generals imagined as "a nineteenth century war ... to be fought with twentieth century weapons,"[3] a time lag that suppressed modern warfare until too late, after the carnage had forced contemporaneity on it. Part of what Stein

2 Gertrude Stein, "Composition as Explanation," *Selected Writings of Gertrude Stein*, ed. Carl Van Vechten (New York: Vintage, 1990) 514.
3 Stein, "Composition as Explanation," 513.

wants from this example is the contrast between the academic and the modern, a contrast she'll develop later as something "prepared" versus something "that decides how it is to be when it is to be done." But more immediately she wants to deepen the problem of time itself.

For Stein, the present is never what the present naturally wants. On the contrary, wherever the present achieves expression, those living in it will find it confusing, irritating, unnatural, ugly. Consequently, art cannot be made present by accommodating it to popular styles or dominant ideas, and art's motivation to become present has nothing to do with striving after novelty. Instead, changes in art occur because in some befuddling but life-determining way, they already have occurred, are already present, inescapably so, even when repudiated. Stein's idea is that what changes from one generation to the next is a form, not a content, what she calls "composition," and although each generation's composition controls its consciousness absolutely, i.e., "makes what those who describe it make of it,"[4] it does not itself readily submit to consciousness, to description. It's as though everyone can feel how out of synch things are, can recognise the obsolescence of what our leaders, parents, peers have to say, but as soon as anyone tries to *say* what's out of synch, he or she becomes obsolete too. Art's problem then is to acknowledge something as inescapable as an entrenched enemy but that resists our direct advance as forcefully as a machine gun. As Stein says, "No one is ahead of his time,"[5] one of several remarks meant to dislodge our confidence that we already know what she's talking about. The avant-garde—in *Stein's* sense—is merely art's struggle *for* its time, for embodiment of those formative but unrepresentable conditions on which art's continued presence, and possibly everything else's too, depends.

But Stein's second idea seems to complicate, if not undo, this first one. Her word "composition" is meant to set up an

4 Stein, "Composition as Explanation," 513.
5 Stein, "Composition as Explanation," 514.

analogy between the action of history and the activity of painters, writers, and musicians, the point being that the modern work is one that incorporates this new "time-sense," the consciousness of the present, into itself. However, when Stein tries to explain what this change means concretely, she comes out with a stupefying series of redundancies: "a thing made by being made" "what is seen when it seems to be being seen," "the thing seen by every one living in the living they are doing," and most dizzyingly, "the composing of the composition that at the time they are living is the composition of the time in which they are living."[6] Despite their circularity, these formulations seem to me uncommonly precise. What they all share is a suggestion of something already in existence that is the means by which it is itself brought into existence. The idea seems to be that what has always existed unrecognised in art—i.e., the creative power of presentness—is in the modern work, not just what is recognised, but what actually does the work of art, what makes art "art" specifically *by* being recognised. This is what her phrase, "a thing made by being made," tries to bring out. But now everything has gotten turned around, since presentness no longer seems limited to the present. It's as if modern art weren't just the latest change in art, say, the form of Stein's own generation, but were instead a change of a wholly different order, one that has revealed something about *all* art. That this is, in fact, Stein's idea is indicated by her lecture's first sentence, which insists on a historical changelessness underlying changes in composition, as well as by her later, more paradoxical insistence that what results from incorporating the new time-sense is not a historical document but something timeless, a classic. It is as though what Stein's generation needed to do to make art was to find out for the first time what art was. In other words, the whole point of acknowledging the present for Stein is to disclose what, once laid bare, seems always to have existed. When this happens, art

6 Stein, "Composition as Explanation," 514-6.

happens. Understood in this sense, the avant-garde isn't just the struggle *for* its time. It's the struggle *in* its time for something suppressed by time itself. Stein's term, both for this struggle and for its object, is "a continuous present."[7]

Despite the difficulty of making these ideas clear, I think Stein's account of artistic advance is basically right. If literature is to exist in the present, then it must be *discovered* there. This is, I believe, what the idea of an avant-garde meant for Stein's generation and what I believe it still means, even if ignored. To write after modernism, not as though before, is to acknowledge modernism's discovery of this necessity of discovery as such. Initially, this implies that nothing known about forms of writing can count as a guide for producing novels and poems now. That is, we are to imagine an inadequacy of our current knowledge that is not overcome by newer or better knowledge, an inadequacy intrinsic to knowing itself. Stein's idea seems to be that what needs discovering—our time—has the character of obviousness, as though the new composition were too proximate, *too* present, for knowing. Understood in this way, the problem isn't so much that current knowledge is obsolete, as that it's neurotic. What can be taught in writing workshops and literature courses—i.e., the version of poetry and fiction we are presently prepared to recognise—has the same status as the version of his or her present life that the analysand enters psychoanalysis prepared to recount. One can say about such versions that they repress what needs discovering or that they incessantly reveal it, but either way, an unacknowledged presence controls all that's said. It is this paradox that Stein brings out by saying, not that nations are behind the times, but that they are "behind themselves,"[8] as though our anachrony comprised an essential dividedness. The implication is simply that discovering will not take the form of narrating. That is, the present cannot be revealed as a new or further episode in any story we are prepared to recount, and being present does not

[7] Stein, "Composition as Explanation," 517.
[8] Stein, "Composition as Explanation," 515.

mean recounting it. Nothing obvious to us about machine guns was unknown to WWI generals. This failure, even impertinence, of current knowledge is what remains right about modernism's insistence on newness, innovation, experiment.

At the same time, the impertinence of knowledge does not mean literature must be, or even can be, created directly from present experience. Nothing seems further from Stein's idea than that changes in art are identical with changes in taste, sensibility, cultural style, or fashion, which is what we're likely to have in mind if we say every generation's experience is unique. Quite the contrary, Stein's idea is that present experience will be as anachronistic, as much a hybrid of past experience, as poetry and fiction, and for the same reasons. To insist that literature must be discovered means that, far from creating poems and fiction *ex nihilo*, from literature's absence, literature can only be created—as contradictory as this sounds—from literature, that is, from something always already in existence, controlling in misunderstood and largely unrecognised ways every writing. This is what Stein's "continuous present" tries to name. I take it to be a version of what Heidegger had in mind when, in apparent defiance of logic, he insisted that art was its own origin.[9] That is, what the present discovers is not just a new composition or form. It discovers literature, as though for the first time. Stein's originality was in seeing that, where the present is at issue in this way, acknowledgment proves more radical than even the farthest-fetched invention. In her account, the avant-garde writer undergoes, succumbs utterly to, what in other writing exists as frustrated, ignored, incomplete. In other words, the notorious irritation and ugliness of avant-garde art can be said to measure, not the present's distance from the past, but the present's distance from itself. It is a dividedness of the same kind, and with similar consequences, as the analysand's dividedness from his or her own body. Between linguistic

---

[9] Martin Heidegger, "The Origin of the Work of Art," *Poetry, Language, Thought*, trans. Albert Hofstadter (New York: Harper & Row, 1971) 17-8.

materiality and literature's presence there persists this gap. Or stated in a sentence, after modernism, literature ceases to exist as history and materialises as a question.

Probably the best way to give tangibility to these remarks would be to examine Stein's own writings, since her lectures were always meditations on her own literary practice, but because my interest is less in what the avant-garde was than what it is, I want to conclude with some reflections on Carole Maso's novel *AVA*. Although the order of my paper suggests that I am using Maso's novel to illustrate a theory developed independently and beforehand, I think the opposite chronology is more nearly the case. At any rate, if I had not come to understand what literature is by discovering from specific works of fiction that I didn't already know, then none of what I have said so far would have been for me of more than academic interest. Which is another way of saying I wouldn't have written this.

AVA is my candidate for a present representative of the avant-garde in fiction, that is, for a novel that continues modernism's advance into the present. Ultimately, my commitment to *AVA* does not result from its mere difference from other novels but, as I'll try to show, from its revelation of what novels are, what they have always been. However, I'm highlighting it initially because its form seems a version of nothing that, before *AVA*, I was prepared to recognise as a narrative. Its originating predicament is that Ava Klein, professor of comparative literature and ardent lover of life, is dying at age 39, and Maso's text purports to be a record of the phrases, images, writings, and recollections that pass before Ava's consciousness on the morning, afternoon, and night of 15 August, 1990, the day Iraq invades Kuwait and Ava dies. The problem Ava faces on this day is how her life can be whole, complete, even while coming to such a premature end. She recalls a remark by Eva Hesse, "Life doesn't last, art doesn't last,"[10] one of countless passages that imply something closer than an analogy, more like an identity, between the problem *in* the novel and the problem *of* the novel. What Ava the character seeks, what *AVA* the novel seeks, is something that, as long as there was God, meaning provided, call it lasting significance or a higher end, but something that atoned for the shortcomings of flesh and matter. However, without recourse to the everlasting, Ava's death cannot be redeemed through any spiritual allegory. Her salvation has to be literal: "Here is my arm," she tells the chemo nurse. "I want to live" (49). Nothing not complete in itself, nothing that stands for something else, can matter to Ava now. All that will atone for life is life. The problem then, for both novel and character, is time.

AVA's pages seem a material realisation of Stein's anachronistic hybridity, their lines comprising a congeries of times and places, texts and experiences, each with its distinctive mood, inflection, rhythm still intact. Some lines express regret, as though the past had presented itself too late ("How could I— why did I hesitate, given all that we knew, even then?" [173]), while others acknowledge present longings that still look toward future consummation ("Because decidedly, I do not want to miss the grand opening scheduled for early winter, still some months away, of the new Caribbean restaurant down the block that will serve goat" [11]). Several lines allude to events that were never more than partly present, even on their original occurrence: Schubert's unfinished symphony, a deferred marriage proposal, a fragment of orchestral music heard on a car radio, a miscarried pregnancy, Moses dying within sight of the promised land. Taken together, these lines epitomise a frustration that seems more than just accidental, an anachrony built into Ava's very existence, as though to be mortal were simply to be balked. She recalls George Steiner's remark, "Moses fails to enter Canaan not because his life is too short, but because it is a human life" (100). That is, deprived of

10 Carole Maso, *AVA* (Normal, Ill.: Dalkey Archive, 1995) 185. Subsequent page references are cited in-text.

paradise, human finitude seems itself a broken promise. It's as if Ava's capacity to imagine a future without herself, or possibly just her ability to say the words, "If we could live forever" (102), projects a limitlessness by contrast with which every present, regardless how extraordinary, seems truncated. "So many plans," she thinks, then adds, "time permitting" (162). Some lines attribute this frustration to language. Ava repeatedly recalls Hélène Cixous's wish "to create a language that heals as much as it separates" (52), a wish frequently juxtaposed with Ava's hope for cure, as though the two forms of brokeness, Ava's body and Ava's dying words, were each forms of a single disruption. More than once Ava flirts with the idea of a lost, primordial wholeness, as if articulation were not her natural condition, juxtaposing the remark, "Let me describe what my life once was here," with the fragment, "Home before it was divided" (22), and wishing repeatedly for the fluency of music. A recalled quote from Monique Wittig (37) attributes this linguistic disruption to maleness.

Interpreting Maso's myth of lost origins is tricky, since it can express either a wholly satisfactory solution to Ava's problem or a temptation to repeat it. It's to this temptation, for example, that Ava and her first husband yield, seeking ever younger lovers in an effort to make their love present again by replicating its inaugural moment: "You were looking for the way I was once," Ava tells him, "the age I was when we first met" (167). That is, interpreted as the projection of fullness into a retreating past, Maso's myth reinstitutes the temporal confinement Ava's literally dying to escape. Although Maso means for her myth to recall us to a forgotten promise, she doesn't mean that Canaan could only be entered by going backwards. On the contrary, if Ava's life is to be whole, its wholeness must come, not through a return *to* the past but *of* it, as of the repressed, a return identical with Ava's absorption in the present. In other words, the incompleteness of Ava's life is not its discontinuousness, or not if by that we mean life's comings and goings, its punctuation by silence and questions, its parsing into discrete experiences, what Ava calls "moments." If language is implicated in Ava's problem, then that's not because it is articulate—i.e., not because it is language. If anything, as Ava draws closer to *AVA*'s end, she seems increasingly affirming of all that separates words, thoughts, feelings, people. "Learn to love the questions themselves," she tells herself. "The spaces between words. Between thoughts. The interval" (171). No, the complicity of language in her life's incompleteness must involve something with which the discontinuousness of words, their articulations, can be readily confused, some capacity of a word to dislocate from its origin, from those moments in which its occurrence brings fulfilment or relief, and recur where its presence can create division. If we have difficulty seeing what this is, that is probably because, in reading *AVA*, we are doing it too.

What makes time problematic in *AVA* is narrative. Or perhaps it would be more precise to say that Ava's predicament, like the reader's, is not that she lives in time but that, being mortal, she must tell it, recount every moment. The source of life's incompleteness, then, is not its division into words but its division into beginning, middle, and end. It is this schism that Stein's continuous present means to repair. When Ava's consciousness, when Maso's page, is split into what Stein calls "the time of the composition and the time in the composition" (516), even the fullest moments resemble forestalled actions ("And what in the world were we waiting for?" [24]), unfinished developments ("I might have gone to China" [241]), dashed hopes ("We lost the baby, Anatole" [81]), or epiphanies that came too late ("Everything in me is suddenly beginning to emerge clearly. Why not earlier? Why at such cost? I have so many thousands of things, some new, some from an earlier time, which I would like to tell you" [241]). It is this representation of her life as *never wholly present* that periodically rises up in Ava as an insatiable demand for more time: "Find a cure … Find a cure … Find a cure" (221). Either the past returns as reminder of her life's fullness—"You were all I ever wanted"

(61), "You gave me the world" (178), "It was paradise" (43) — or it retreats eternally, trapping her in finitude: "But I am only thirty-nine, Dr Oppenheim" (55). Everything can be narrated except what must be present for anything to be narrated. In other words, the solution to the problem of Ava Klein's life — and therefore to the problem of representing it — is not discovered by postponing death a few more years, for the problem is not life's shortness. And the solution remains hopeless only so long as representing it substitutes for undergoing it, which is roughly what Wittgenstein meant in the *Tractatus* when he called aesthetics "transcendental."[11] Ava's solution remains where Ava has always discovered it, in the living out of every moment in its completeness, fully, up to the moment of life's close in death. That is, whatever enables words to come and go, anything to be a preparation for anything else, each moment to be a conclusion, a complication, a denouement, a beginning, or time in its continuum to be punctuated by now, now, now — whatever permeates every present, making it count, that is what makes *AVA*, both novel and character, whole.

I realise this way of speaking can seem frustrating, almost as frustrating as calling the deathbed question of Ava's lover — "But what, after all, is wrong with now?" (87) — an answer. Either nothing needs explaining here or nearly everything. I feel like saying: You simply have to hear the words! But the problem is, if you did hear the words, then saying you have to verges on an insult, and if you didn't hear the words, saying you have to *is* an insult. We're banging our heads against a limit. What can't be said can't be said. However, if I were to try to give concrete expression to this present I find so absorbing, I'd turn my attention to the most immediately striking but readily overlooked feature of Maso's novel: the deluge of white space on every page. This white space represents something no novel has ever existed without but whose precise significance

[11] Ludwig Wittgenstein, *Tractatus Logico-Philosophicus*, trans. D.F. Pears and B.F. McGuinness (London: Routledge, 1978) 6.421.

for novels went largely uninvestigated until the latter half of the twentieth century. It is in terms of Maso's further discovery of this significance that I want to speak both of *AVA*'s continuous presentness and, in retrospect, of its historical advance.

To explain what I mean, it will help to contrast the relation of white space and text in *AVA* with that of two other earlier novels with which it seems to have some affinity: Raymond Federman's *Take It or Leave It*, and David Markson's *Wittgenstein's Mistress*. White space in *Take It or Leave It* is used, for the most part, as it was by modernist poetry from, say, W.C. Williams through Charles Olson, primarily, as the spatial equivalent of a break in speech, a breath stop or syntactic division, and secondarily, as a way of foregrounding linguistic materiality, the print as a visual object. The opening lines of Federman's "Pretext," despite their initial appearance of disorder, seem on closer examination arranged in near perfect accord with speech rhythms, syntax, and grammar:

in the beginning
words scattered
by chance
and in all directions!

Similar vertical series of syntactically or grammatically parallel units can be seen elsewhere on the novel's opening pages:

a shy silhouette
a profile
a shiny saxophone

or in the lower right corner of the second page;

treees
roads
cars
people
rooms
… puppets

... people.

However, the jumbled text on the right margin of the first page,

u c n r l e e e g e
n o t o l d n r i s!

operates by another principle, providing something like a
visual mimesis of its own sense or meaning. While arranging
the text according to rhythm and syntax works to emphasise
the spokenness of the narration, its saturation with voice, the
visual mimesis seems to disrupt or compete with this voice,
asserting the autonomous existence of page and print. But in
both instances Federman's relation to the white space is that of
using it, that is, manipulating it for expressive ends or to
actualise his narrator's character. Despite the expanded
signifying repertoire of *Take It or Leave It*, its white space
remains—in some sense still to be articulated—passive and
inert, incidental to the action in the same way as commas and
periods. Federman's artistic advance is to reveal his pages as
white, not blank, not just lacking printing, but even if
considered a disclosure of materiality, the ultimate effect of his
use of white space is to foreground, not the page, but the
voluble Franco-American whose self-representation provides
both the novel's matter and manner, its speech and its writing.

We could call *Take It or Leave It* a graphic performance or the
graphic representation of a performance, but either way,
Federman's novel represents an investigation of narrating as a
kind of action, one happening on the page. The kind of action in
which its white space is involved is that of interrupting, of
breaking up what is continuous: i.e., lines, sentences, phrases,
meanings, letters. We could say that, for Federman, white space
becomes a new form of punctuation. However, for this use to
count as presentness, as a discovery of fiction in the terms I've
laid out, it would need to reveal something about novels
generally, about the function of all white space, and here one
can feel unsure whether Federman's deepest discoveries are

really of the page. That is, unlike the edge of earlier paintings, which modernism revealed to be only apparently accidental, line breaks in earlier fiction *are* accidental. Their location remains irrelevant to the significance of the line. What makes them essential to *Take It or Leave It* is the action of the narrator, who, no longer contained within the dematerialised space of representation, has penetrated the fourth wall of materiality, breaking into Federman's book. White space for Federman is expressive. In this sense, we could say that Federman discovers the page as a space of action, dispelling its blankness, but leaves unexplored the action of that space itself.

Wittgenstein's Mistress continues Federman's investigation of the page as a white space, but Markson's novel does not make the action of this space the narrator's doing. That is, although the white space in Markson's novel does something *to* the narrative, or tries, it does not do anything *in* the narrative. It does not punctuate. Here I want to record a peculiar fact about my experience of Markson's work. I first thought to compare it with *AVA* because I remembered, or thought I remembered, that the pages in the two books looked alike, that in *Wittgenstein's Mistress* a white expanse separated each of the narrator's statements. Therefore I was quite surprised when I returned to his book and discovered, on first glance, that the pages appeared wholly traditional. That is, the white space appeared to be merely a passive background on which the text was printed. What had created my false impression was the similarity between Maso's and Markson's narrators, specifically, that both seem to express themselves in short, disconnected utterances, utterances that resist closure, that seem unable, at least without disappointment or frustration, to stop. It was as though I had wanted space to intervene, felt the rightness of or need for Federman's punctuation. When I didn't find it, I felt a little panicky.

This misremembering is, for me, the first clue to Markson's discovery. In *Wittgenstein's Mistress* the impression created by the narration is that of breathlessness, as though the absence of any naturally occurring divisions in speech or thought, of pauses, resting places, were the condition of an augmenting claustrophobia. We could speak of it as narrative gone mad, as though the present were wholly absent and all that remained were the continuous, unsatisfying transformation of past into future, future into past, a hellish parody of timelessness—call it never-ending static. The contrast I want here is between Federman's voluble narrator, whose interminable digressiveness expresses his irrepressible life, and Markson's tormented solipsist, whose run-on utterance is pure compulsion. Within the context of this compulsion, white space becomes active. Its action is, in one sense, perfectly familiar, merely its action in all novels. That action is to enclose. That is, Markson's advance, if calling it an advance makes sense yet, is not in its *use* of white space but in its disclosure of what might be considered every novel's use of white space, its revelation of what white space has always been doing. What white space does in *Wittgenstein's Mistress* is fill every void, every opening the narration offers, as though the ceaselessness of narrating were a continuous effort to keep it out, to keep at bay whatever would be there but for the narrator's run-on voice. I do not know if I am speaking metaphorically or literally here. This is the significance of what, on a second glance, one can see is the new look of Markson's page, i.e., that the margins appear unjustified. Or almost. The left is a ragged column of indentations; the right is broken repeatedly by long incursions of white. It's as though silence were struggling to break in, to contest speech. That is, Markson's page does not look like a surface on which text has been laid. It looks like an active presence, a natural force. In short, *Wittgenstein's Mistress* reveals white space to be a surrounding.

It should be apparent now that what makes the function of white space in these books both newly revealing and newly significant, is the novel as a whole. That is, when we're speaking of white space, we're not talking about a primarily visual phenomenon, that is, an appearance of essentially the same kind as a picture. Despite the enhanced importance of visual experience in both Federman's and Markson's works, the significance of the visual remains a function of the narrator's voice, of various qualities of the discourse that give to the novel's appearance its interest. It is this interaction of inflected text and white space, that makes the page, not merely a background but an integral part of the work. Likewise, the significance of white space in these novels is not the same as in modernist poetry. Even in Federman's usage, its significance is not a function of the line so much as of the event, of the nature or kinds of discursive continuity staked by the teller's predicament. That is, it is the encounter of fiction, i.e., both narrator and situation, with reality, i.e., the physical book, that transforms the accidental into the essential, the page into the meaning, matter into spirit. What makes white space new in these novels is seeing this.

These remarks are intended to show that white space in *AVA* is distinctive in just the ways *AVA* is distinctive. Like *Take It or Leave It*, Maso's page is a positive fact, not a blank, not just an absence of print. That is, the appearance of her page is not of a text laid onto what would otherwise be an emptiness. There is just too much page, too much bare paper to call Maso's book the material support for her narrative. (One feels like saying, "*What* narrative?") The appearance of *AVA* is more nearly that of a field or plane, something composed essentially of space and merely interrupted at sporadic intervals by incursions of text. That is, what punctuates in *AVA* is not white space but print. Which is the most obvious way in which Maso's novel diverges from Federman's. In *AVA*, as in *Wittgenstein's Mistress*, the significance of white space does not seem to be the narrator's doing, resulting instead from something already present, conditions more fundamental than anything represented. In *AVA* white space seems prior. However, whether we'll want to describe its presence as active seems uncertain. That is, the presence of white space in *AVA*, at least in my experience of it, feels nothing like an event. One could risk gibberish here and refer to the whiteness of Maso's page as a *continuous* event, a *ceaseless* action, but my point is that Maso's text, unlike both Federman's and Markson's, isn't narrated. I want to say it's breathed. I realise that this way of characterising Maso's discourse may be just too metaphorical, too impressionistic, but I know of no other words that could describe so precisely what I have in mind: specifically, that the fragments of text do not represent anything Ava Klein *tries* to say—they aren't her efforts to explain what happened or comment on her life, are rather what escapes from her, slips out, like a sigh—and that they are weightless, light as thought. That is, regardless of the gravity of Ava's predicament, her lines remain free-floating, detached, suspending all action and leaving events up in the air.

In other words, while Maso's discovery is of the page itself, not only or primarily of its availability for use (as in *Take It or Leave It*), her discovery is of something more fundamental than, prior to, a surrounding or enclosure (as in *Wittgenstein's Mistress*). I want to call it a ground. That is, the oddest fact about Maso's novel is that its parts are separate. Unlike compositions in which the basic units (e.g., sentences, lines, phrases) are grouped on the page into larger units (e.g., stanzas, paragraphs, verses, chapters), every fragment in *AVA* is separated by a uniform distance from every other. With the exception of the three long sections "Morning," "Afternoon," and "Night"—marked off by two expanses of white on pages 123-4 and 213-4—only the fragments' occurrence in the same book, on the continuous field or plane projected by the space of its pages, implies that they have a connection, are all parts of something. What this something is cannot be a voice, since the speakers are changeable, and the occasions (e.g., "Brazil, 1988; Venice, 1976; Quebec, 1980" [6]) seem as discontinuous as the fragments themselves. If we say the fragments are connected by or in Ava's consciousness, we will be interpreting what connects them, not describing it, and saying that they aren't connected, that the reader must connect them, only confuses the issue: first, by suggesting that the reader could just do this, as if we knew some way of connecting the fragments of *AVA* that didn't raise the same problems as *AVA* itself, and, second, by suggesting that the reader could just *not* do it, that we knew some way of reading *AVA* *without* connecting its fragments. No, the problem of reading *AVA* is simply the problem of Ava's remarkable life, that it occurs in time. That is, if in order to be complete reading must presuppose a finality impossible of rearrangement, then the reader's plight is as hopeless as Ava's. No single life will exhaust life, no text will comprehend the meaningful. Reading cannot be the origin of what it seeks.

The question to ask is: What does Maso's ground ground? That is, if the white space in *AVA* reveals properties independent of the novelist's use and if these properties prove more fundamental than the enclosure of narration, then what white space grounds is our ability to make of Maso's words, or of any novelist's words, a novel. To read *AVA* we must acknowledge what goes without saying in every other novel we've ever read. I want to say that this more radical discovery—call it the discovery of literature—makes *AVA*'s relation to its predecessors historical. That is, *AVA* is both an advance over Federman's and Markson's innovations and a transformation of them, as though the history of the page that Maso's novel, in my experience of it, culminates, had not been tellable, in no way connected Federman's novel to Markson's, was simply no history, before *AVA*. *AVA* dates Federman and Markson by revealing their white spaces to be discoveries for the first time. The way that it does this is by achieving presentness. That is, what fixes *AVA* in time, what situates it at a specific historical moment (e.g., after publication of *Wittgenstein's Mistress* in 1988), is precisely its revelation of what for the duration of that moment—a period without fixed limits—remains timeless: the space of telling. A page is not a surface onto which a pre-existing entity, e.g., a novel, has been laid, nor is it an agglomeration of particles. A page is the presence of a novel before my presence to it, after its presence to me. This very autonomy, this material subsistence, threatens to make every page immaterial, as negligible as earth underfoot. Maso makes hers matter again, uncovers her page's presence, by making its space our means, almost our only means, of telling Ava's life from an agglomeration To see white underlying the dividedness of Maso's words is to see, for the duration of a moment—August 15, 1990—Ava's life wholly there.

In this way white space solves the problem *of* Maso's novel *in* her novel, i.e., how a life can be complete while coming to an untimely end. What seems crucial here is to acknowledge that the white space in *AVA* is no more complete than Ava's life, or not if "complete" means it could not extend beyond what we have now. It certainly seems possible to imagine more of it. In fact, saying that the last line, "You are ravishing," *completes* the white space seems as groundless as saying that it *completes* Ava, assuming that this means something partial from beginning to end required just this one sentence to be entire. When Maso quotes Cixous, *.".*..[E]ach page I write could be the first page of the book" (58), she suggests that the space of her telling is as protean, as utterly without predetermined limits, as human being itself. And yet it is just the strange thing about a page, at least when it ceases to be seen as blank and begins to be seen—"seen"?—as white, that it appears complete in a way no writing could surpass. We could say that its dazzling surface composes a picture of total expression. It is against this background of austere purity that every word must come to matter. I have at times regretted that, in my 1995 Dalkey Archive paperback version of *AVA*, Maso's notes and the publisher's advertisements follow page 265. That is, it has sometimes struck me that we should conclude with white pages, as though confronting the thing itself—*AVA*. The wish is fanciful, of course, but it poses a serious question: where does Maso's novel end? If what I have said is correct, then its last sentence is no more conclusive than any other, or only accidentally so. Or said differently, if the space of telling has become necessary to telling *AVA* from an agglomeration, then the materiality of Maso's book has ceased to be accidental and become essential. Something artificially truncated but potentially boundless—the white space upholding *AVA*'s / Ava's words—has imparted wholeness to what exists in time, in history, as fragmentary. The seeming incompleteness of Ava's life is not a function of its ending. Everything needed is present—continuously. All that's lacking is me.

The problem of history, that is, of the representation of life in time, is not our limitedness, not our inability to see and do and say all. It is more nearly our *awareness* of our limitedness, specifically, that this awareness continually threatens to displace what we do see, denies the significance of what is constantly before our eyes. When Wittgenstein remarks in the *Tractatus*, "The solution of the problem of life is seen in the vanishing of the problem," [12] he doesn't mean that there just aren't any problems. Ava's dying, for God's sake! What could be more of a problem? He means that the desire for life constantly projects us beyond life, making human life incomplete *metaphysically*. "Death is not an event in life,"[13] a remark meant to recall us to here and now. Or in the terms I've set forth, narrative is the present working out of a problem, an attempt to acknowledge what's past, and where narrative isn't, then narrative *is* the present problem. Can a book be as full as life, as complete for the moment of reading as what exists without bounds? I find myself divided between saying that white space in *AVA* is allegorical, that it stands for what underlies all narration, what continuously presents itself throughout history, and that it's literal, that it *is* what underlies all narration, continuously presents itself in history. Either way, it seems a version of what Wordsworth called nature, what Heidegger called being, what Beckett called silence, and what Stein called the continuous present. That is, it is an *absence* of human saying and doing that represents no *lack* of anything

12   Wittgenstein, *Tractatus Logico-Philosophicus*, 6.521.
13   Wittgenstein, *Tractatus Logico-Philosophicus*, 6.4311.

said or done, an absence of lack itself. If we wish to represent the present more concretely, the problem will not be that the representation proves lacking. The problem will be that the present proves lacking. Wholeness isn't history's other. Or as Ava herself remarks, "It was everything while it lasted."

Robert Archambeau

The Death of the Critic:
the Critic-Pasticheur as Postmodern
Avant-Gardist

Can there be an avant-garde under postmodern conditions? The question is large, indeed too large to be properly answered here. I do wish to contend, though, that certain projects of the avant-garde can still be accomplished. In fact, I believe the radical project of the avant-garde has been carried out by at least two contemporary writers—David Kellogg and Benjamin Friedlander—working in a kind of prose that is best described as critical pastiche. Since pastiche is an idiom generally recognised as postmodern, one could say that their avant-gardism succeeds not despite postmodernism, but because of it.

The most imposing obstacle facing anyone foolhardy enough to ask whether an avant-gardism is possible under postmodern conditions, I imagine, is the much-contested nature of the terms themselves. The terms "avant-garde" and "postmodern" are, after all, among the most contested and over-determined in the critical lexicon. Since my claim here will be that a postmodern avant-gardism is not only possible but manifest in that most conservative of arts, the art of criticism, I hope I may be forgiven for deferring a demonstration of that claim until I've established just what I mean by "avant-garde" and "postmodern" in this particular context.

The Linguistic Scepticism of the Avant-Garde

Renato Poggioli gives a classic definition of avant-gardism in his 1968 study *The Theory of the Avant-Garde*. Poggioli's idea of the avant-garde, which is essential but not sufficient for my purposes, proposes that avant-gardism proceeds from the assumption that languages and systems of expression are, by their nature, entropic. Avant-garde artistic and literary praxis are, in this view, inevitable reactions to "the flat, opaque, and prosaic nature of our public speech, where the practical end of quantitative communication spoils the quality of the expressive means." For Poggioli, the "conventional habits" of expression in a bourgeois, capitalist society are subject to a "degeneration," and the role of the avant-garde must be the renewal of whatever language (literary, visual, etc.) the artist chooses as a field of operations.[1]

This idea, of course, does not originate with Poggioli, but derives from a long tradition of thinking about experimental art, much of it from the era of the historical avant-garde itself. Much of what Poggioli has to say, for example, was already present in Victor Shklovsky's seminal article of 1917, "Art as Technique." Here, Shklovsky presents the problem of linguistic entropy as a problem of ever-decreasing experiential returns: "If we start to examine the general laws of perception," he writes,

> we see that as perception becomes habitual, it becomes automatic. Thus, for example, all of our habits retreat into the area of the unconsciously automatic; if one remembers the sensations of holding a pen or speaking in a foreign language for the first time and compares that with his feeling at performing the action for the ten thousandth time, he will agree with us.[2]

---

[1] Renato Poggioli, *The Theory of the Avant-Garde*, trans. Gerald Fitzgerald (Cambridge, Mass." MIT, 1968) 37.

[2] Victor Shklovsky, "Art as Technique," *Critical Theory Since Plato*, ed. Hazard Adams (New York: Harcourt Brace Jvanovich, 1992) 753.

Only the artist devoted to new forms of representation can overcome this automatism. If, as Shklovsky claims, "the purpose of art is to impart the sensation of things as they are perceived and not as they are known," then the technique of art must be "to make objects unfamiliar, to make forms difficult, to increase the difficulty and length of perception..." (758).

This view of the avant-gardist's role as the eternally vigilant regenerator of languages, symbolic systems, and modes of experience appears in countless manifesti of the historical avant-garde, and is handed down to us through thinkers like Poggioli and Clement Greenberg (whose "Avant-Garde and Kitsch" made the idea central to American academic thinking). The idea of the artist as the revitaliser of language is a vital element of art's role in our time. But while this view of the avant-garde is correct as far as it goes, it is limited by its formalism and aestheticism, by its deep-seated tendency to see art as independent of its institutions and social situation.

The Institutional Scepticism of the Avant-Garde
One irony of Shklovsky's status as a kind of patron saint of the avant-garde is that the examples he chooses to illustrate his idea of art as defamiliarisation are not drawn from the powerful currents of avant-garde practice that flowed through Russia in 1917. Suprematism and Zaum are absent, Mayakovsky does not appear, and there is only the briefest mention of Khlebnikov to indicate that Shklovsky even knew Futurism existed. Instead, Shklovsky derives his most extended and convincing examples from classic nineteenth-century Russian writers such Tolstoy and Gogol.

The very fact that Shklovsky can illustrate his argument with these writers indicates the insufficiency of defamiliarisation as a defining characteristic of the avant-garde. If older texts enact defamiliarisation, defamiliarisation cannot be the defining characteristic of the avant-garde. The avant-garde may well be sceptical about language's ability to remain fresh, but such scepticism certainly predates the historical avant-garde. As Jochen Schulte-Sasse points out, scepticism about language's ability to remain fresh and retain meaning was already present in the late eighteenth century,[3] the period in which Schiller and Goethe wrote:

> All dilettantes are plagiarisers. They sap the life out of and destroy all that is original and beautiful in language and in thought by repeating it, imitating it, and filling up their own void with it. Thus, more and more, language becomes filled up with pillaged phrases and forms that no longer say anything ...[4]

If the avant-garde is to be understood as something distinct from the artistic and literary traditions that preceded it, it must possess some quality or propose some project other than linguistic regeneration. Schulte-Sasse follows Peter Bürger's *Theory of the Avant-Garde* when he maintains that this additional project is the avant-garde's questioning of the institutions of art. Schulte-Sasse begins with the premise that the late-nineteenth century Aesthetic movement was predicated on Kantian notions of aesthetic disinterest and autonomy. While the Aesthetic movement was critique of the bourgeois, utilitarian world, it was also a dead-end in that it removed art from the world of power and praxis. Art became otherworldly, incapable of intervening in civil society, and its critique of capitalist values became a matter of an impotent refusal rather than a force of active intervention. As Schulte-Sasse puts it,

> Aestheticism's intensification of artistic autonomy and its effect on the foundation of a special realm of aesthetic experience permitted the avant-garde to clearly recognise the social inconsequentiality of autonomous art and, as the logical consequence of this recognition, to attempt to lead art back into

---

[3] Jochen Schulte-Sasse, "Theory of Modernism versus Theory of the Avant-Garde," foreword to Peter Bürger, *Theory of the Avant-Garde*, trans. Michael Shaw (Minneapolis: University of Minnesota Press, 1984) ix.

[4] Johann Wolfgang von Goethe, *Werke*, vol. 47, ed. Paul Raabe (Weimar: Weimarer Ausgabe, 1990) 313.

social praxis. For Bürger, then, the development of the avant-garde … is not a continuation of tendencies already present in Aestheticism. Rather, for him the turning point from Aestheticism to the avant-garde is determined by the extent to which art comprehended the mode in which it functioned in bourgeois society, its comprehension of its own social status. The historical avant-garde of the twenties was the first movement in art history that turned against the institution "art" and the mode in which autonomy functions. In this it differed from all previous art movements …[5]

The avant-garde, in this view, turned against the existing institutions of art (literary journals, art galleries, museums, good taste and connoisseurship, etc.) and the theory of art that underwrote those institutions.

Postmodern Pastiche and the Project of the Avant-Garde

At least one project of the avant-garde—its regeneration of entropic language through defamiliarisation—has been dismissed as impossible in postmodern conditions. Frederic Jameson, for example, argues that attempts at defamiliarisation have become "meaningless," and their emphasis "on the vocation of art to re-stimulate perception, to re-conquer a freshness of experience back from the habituate and reified numbness of everyday life in a fallen world" cannot function in our cultural climate.[6]

Central to Jameson's concept of the postmodern is the idea that we have moved into an era in which the idea of the modern self has been largely undermined, and with it the notion of individual literary or artistic style. "The old individual or individualist subject," he writes, "is dead" Indeed, from a postmodern and poststructural point of view, the bourgeois individual subject is "not only a thing of the past: it is also a myth" that "never really existed in the first place; there have

---

5 Schulte-Sasse, "Theory of Modernism versus Theory of the Avant-Garde," xiv.
6 Frederic Jameson, The Political Unconscious: Narrative as a Socially Symbolic Act (Ithaca, New York: 1982) 121.

never been autonomous subjects of that type."[7] The defamiliarisation of experience through a heroic feat of individual style is impossible in the face of this realisation. Such heroic feats depend on the now-lost illusion that a new, individual view can come into being and release us from clichéd perception. The avant-garde, in Jameson's view, is impossible, because it depends on the myth of the artist as individual stylist.

Jameson is not alone in thinking that the bourgeois subject is dead, and the heroic artist along with it. Roland Barthes's seminal essay "The Death of the Author," for example, argues along similar lines, claiming that our idea of the individualist author is a myth of the bygone modern era:

> The *author* is a modern character, no doubt produced by our society as it emerged from the Middle Ages, influenced by English empiricism, French rationalism, and the personal faith of the Reformation, thereby discovering the prestige of the individual, or, as we say more nobly, of the "human person."[8]

With the death of the mythical author, Jameson and Barthes both see a new emphasis on socially-determined codes of meaning. Instead of individual artists regenerating language with unique feats of style, they see artists capable only of working within established symbolic codes. Unable to make "an original gesture" the postmodern artist (or "scriptor," in Barthes terminology), can only "mingle writings." Even when the scriptor "seeks to *express himself*, at least he knows that the interior 'thing' he claims to 'translate' is itself no more than a ready-made lexicon."[9]

Barthes sees the mingling of writings from existing cultural matrices as the inevitable mode of postmodern writing. For his

---

[7] Frederic Jameson, "Postmodernism and Consumer Society," *The Continental Aesthetics Reader*, ed. Clive Cazeaux (London: Routledge, 2000) 285.

[8] Roland Barthes, "The Death of the Author," *Critical Theory Since Plato*, ed. Hazard Adams (New York: Harcourt Brace Jovanovich, 1992) 1131.

[9] Barthes, "The Death of the Author," 1132.

part, Jameson departs from Barthes's view only by colouring it with the dark tint of political melancholy. Whereas artists of the historical avant-garde would quote traditional texts in an attempt to parody them, postmodern writers have, in Jameson's view, seen the futility of the avant-garde project. They "no longer 'quote' such texts, as a Joyce might have done … they incorporate them."[10] They have lost the faith that there is a fresh way of seeing that avant-garde work can restore:

> Pastiche is, like parody, the imitation of a peculiar or unique style, the wearing of a stylistic mask, speech in a dead language: but it is a neutral practice of such mimicry, without parody's ulterior motive, without its satirical impulse, without laughter, without that still latent feeling that there exists something *normal* compared with which what is being imitated is rather comic.[11]

No drawing of moustaches on the Mona Lisa can save us now. In Jameson's pessimistic view, we are doomed to empty acts of repetition.

I do not dispute the death of the author, nor do I make any claims for the revival of parody. But I do wish to draw attention to two examples of work by writers I am calling critic-pasticheurs—literary critics working through pastiche—because this work seems to me to accomplish exactly what Jameson sees as impossible. Their work uses postmodern pastiche to accomplish both the linguistic and the institutional projects of the avant-garde. It defamiliarises via pastiche, and in the process challenges the established modes of critical writing.

The Critic Pasticheur and Defamiliarisation
Who, then, are the critic pasticheurs? Two will serve as my examples here: David Kellogg and Benjamin Friedlander. Both are American literary critics and, perhaps not coincidentally,

---

[10] Jameson, *The Political Unconscious*, 283.
[11] Jameson, *The Political Unconscious*, 284.

poets. Both have written works of literary criticism that are, in whole or in part, deliberate imitations of pre-existing source texts. Their works don't set out to parody those source texts: rather, they imitate them, using pillaged phrases and sentence structures as means of creating new insights.

The opening of Kellogg's essay, "The Self in the Poetic Field," offers a compact example of what the technique looks like. It is composed of a pastiche made up of (in Kellogg's words) "a line by line rewriting, with a few sentences removed, of J.D. Watson and F.H.C. Crick's 'A structure for Deoxyribose Nucleic Acid' published in the journal *Nature* in 1953." The original Watson and Crick essay begins like this:

> We wish to suggest a structure for the salt of deoxyribose nucleic acid (DNA).
>
> This structure has novel features which are of considerable biological interest. A structure for nucleic acid has already been proposed by Pauling and Corey (1). They kindly made their manuscript available to us in advance of publication. Their model consists of three intertwined chains, with the phosphates near the fibre axis, and the bases on the outside. In our opinion, this structure is unsatisfactory for two reasons: (1) We believe that the material which gives the X-ray diagrams is the salt, not the free acid. Without the acidic hydrogen atoms it is not clear what forces would hold the structure together, especially as the negatively charged phosphates near the axis will repel each other. (2) Some of the van der Waals distances appear to be too small.
>
> Another three-chain structure has also been suggested by Fraser (in the press). In his model the phosphates are on the outside and the bases on the inside, linked together by hydrogen bonds. This structure as described is rather ill-defined, and for this reason we shall not comment on it.[12]

[12] J.D. Watson and F.H.C. Crick, "A Structure for DNA," *Nature* (April 2, 1953): 737.

Kellogg's essay makes only minor variations:

> I wish to suggest a structure for contemporary American poetry (C.A.P.). This structure has novel features which are of considerable critical interest.
>
> A structure for poetry has already been proposed by Eliot. He has kindly made his manuscript available to the world for the last eighty years. His model consists of an enveloping tradition, with the dead near the centre, and the individual talent on the outside. In my opinion, this structure is unsatisfactory for two reasons: (1) I believe that the material that provides the poetic structure is the living community of readers, not the dead. Without the stack of coffins, it is not clear in Eliot's model what forces would hold the structure together, especially as the variously interpreted bodies near the centre will repel each other. (2) The self of the poem is extinguished along with the poet.
>
> Another dynamic structure has been suggested by Bloom. In his model the dead are on the outside and the living individuals on the inside, linked together by Freudian anxieties. This structure is rather loosely described, and for this reason I shall not comment on it.[13]

The goal, here, is far from parody. Kellogg is not out to mock the ambitions of scientific inquiry, nor does he wish to cast any doubts on the validity of the source-text. Instead, his project, here and in the remainder of the essay, is to defamiliarise our usual ways of looking at literary history, and the relation of the poet to his or her work.

Benjamin Friedlander's project is more ambitious. In *Simulcast: Four Experiments in Criticism* he undertakes a massive rewriting of source texts. Here, as in the opening of Kellogg's essay, his goal is not parody *per se*. Instead of seeking to undermine the authority of a source text, he sets out to follow

[13] David Kellogg, "The Self in the Poetic Field," *Fence* 3.2 (Fall/Winter 2000-2001): 97-8.

the verbal contours of his texts as a means of discovery. He outlines his experimental critical project as follows:

> I describe these works as experiments because all four are based on source texts and thus inaugurate a species of criticism in which the findings only emerge after struggle with predetermined forms. Sometimes this struggle took shape as an exercise in translation, not unlike the re-creation of a sonnet's rhyme-scheme and metre. Often, translation was impossible, and the struggle resolved itself instead in an act of controlled imagination—not unlike the sonnet's original creation. In each case, the production of my text had less in common with the ordinary practice of writing an essay than it did with the composition of metrical verse [the book's] somewhat scandalous methodology [involves] the creation of criticism through the strict recreation of an earlier critic's text (or, more precisely, through as strict a re-creation as the discrepancy between my source text and chosen topic would allow). Thus, my "Short History of Language Poetry" follows the arguments (and even wording) of Jean Wahl's *A Short History of Existentialism*, while "The Literati of San Francisco" takes Edgar Allan Poe's *Literati of New York City* as its template ... Although I was predisposed in each of these pieces to certain arguments and conclusions, I willingly abandoned these when they became incompatible with the critical approach demanded by my source.[14]

What is particularly interesting here is the way that Friedlander's work embraces postmodern notions of the writer and works against traditional notions of authorship.

Friedlander's book is not the product of his informed, critical reflections on his topics prior to writing. In fact, sometimes the book's assertions are, as he says, at odds with his own convictions. He does not record his observations, does not "paint" the landscape of his pre-existing literary knowledge. There is no bourgeois individual intelligence creating insight

14 Benjamin Friedlander, *Simulcast: Four Experiments in Criticism* (Tuscaloosa: University of Alabama Press, 2004) 1-2.

through heroic reflections. Hesitating to call the book's often-stimulating insights the assertions of a critic or author, one falls back on the old, New Critical idea of the book's *speaker*, here. But even this idea seems to imply the creation of a consistent character who might hold the views on offer, and this is not what happens in Friedlander's work. There is a strange sense in which the assertions of *Simulcast* belong to no personality, to no character possessing traits or existing prior to the text itself. We don't so much have a speaker as a Barthesian scriptor. The scriptor, after all, isn't just defined as the combiner of existing discourses, but as a creature simultaneous with the text itself. As Barthes puts it:

> The Author, when we believe in him, is always conceived as the past of his own book: the book and the author take their places of their own accord on the same line, cast as a *before* and an *after*: the Author is supposed to feed the book—that is, he pre-exists it, thinks, suffers, lives for it; he maintains with his work the same relation of antecedence a father maintains with his child. Quite the contrary, the modern writer (scriptor) is born simultaneously with his text; he is in no way supplied with a being which precedes or transcends his writing, he is in no way the subject of which his book is the predicate; there is no other time than that of the utterance, and every text is eternally written here and now. This is because (or: it follows that) to write can no longer designate an operation of recording, of observing, of representing, of "painting."[15]

The technique is clearly the product of the postmodern world of the scriptor and of pastiche. But unlike the emptiness of Jameson's postmodern pastiche, this work results in a kind of defamiliarisation.

Indeed, both Kellogg and Friedlander turn to their source-texts as critical tools to take them away from their own instinctive thoughts about literature, and force them into new insights different from their own critical predispositions. The

---

[15] Barthes, "The Death of the Author," 1132.

project shares a great deal with the creative works of the Oulipo, which used deliberate, systematic forms of writing, carried through with some rigor, to break past habitual modes of composition and thinking.

What makes the work of Kellogg and Friedlander particularly effective is their turning to source-texts from discourses at a remove from the dominant norms of critical prose in our time. Kellogg leaves the humanities behind and seeks out a scientific source-text, while Friedlander turns to temporally remote, belletristic criticism (Poe), or to a philosophy deeply out of fashion in the academy (Existentialism). The discourses are alien enough to break our usual norms of thinking, but familiar enough to generate insights that are still comprehensible, if not uncontroversial, to readers embedded in our current discursive environment. As the critic Vincent Sherry once said of the intertextual poetry of John Matthias, which draws from arcane historical source-texts "on the one hand, the pedagogue offers from his word-hoard and reference trove the splendid alterity of unfamiliar speech; on the other, this is our familial tongue, our own language in its deeper memory and reference."[16] Critic-Pasticheurs like Kellogg and Friedlander offer us an estrangement of criticism based on the revival and re-examination of disused discursive strategies. Their work, then, is simultaneously postmodern pastiche and avant-garde linguistic regeneration.

The Death of the Critic
The critic-pasticheur doesn't just accomplishes the linguistic goals of the avant-garde: he accomplishes the avant-garde's institutional goals as well. Unlike the historical avant-garde, though, the critic-pasticheur doesn't challenge the institutions of autonomous art. Rather, he challenges the institutions and

---

[16] Vincent Sherry, "The Poetry of John Matthias: 'My Treason and M y Tongue,'" *Word Play Place: Essays on the Poetry of John Matthias*, ed. Robert Archambeau (Athens, Ohio: Ohio University Press/Swallow Press, 1998) 29.

assumptions of professional criticism, and does so through the use of postmodern pastiche.

It is a deeply embedded tenet of criticism that the critic must be a knowing subject standing behind his or her methodologically-grounded truth-claims. The critic has, in this view, a method or technique that can be applied consistently to texts. The method yields results that the critic stands behind as a matter of professional pride and integrity. This idea has something approaching official status in the academy. In 1966, for example, the American Association of University Professors declared that the professional knowledge-worker is:

> guided by a deep conviction of the worth and dignity of the advancement of knowledge, recognises the special responsibilities placed upon him. His primary responsibility to his subject is to seek and to state the truth as he sees it …[17]

In this view the critic is an earnest and sincere subject, standing behind his written words. The speaker of the book is identical with the author: indeed, the author stands in relation to the words of the book in the "author-God" position so thoroughly debunked by Barthes.

When Friedlander calls his methodology "scandalous," the scandal to which he refers can only be a scandal of professionalism. When he chooses to abandon the "arguments and conclusions" that he personally believes in order to follow the textual contours of his sources, he strikes a blow at the very idea of the critic as a knowing subject standing behind his words. He undermines the idea of critical writing as the presentation of existing and established knowledge. Instead, he proposes the critic's work as a matter of generating new and challenging insights through the defamiliarisation of habitual modes of thought.

---

[17] Bruce Robbins, Secular Vocations: Intellectuals, Professionalism, Culture (London: Verso, 1993) 36.

The answer to the question of whether avant-gardism is still possible under postmodern conditions must, then, be yes. But in this latest iteration of the avant-garde impulse, some of the primary actors are not artists but critics.

Johanna Drucker

Neon Sigh :: Epistemological Refamiliarisation[*]

Infinitely dense, the porous papers flame with headlines ripped from every narrative ever written. Hyperbolic claims rise fast as trapped memory and shoot through the roof of belief. Mined and ready, from a rich, almost inexhaustible vein, the permanently expandable archive understands itself to be aware, waking slowly to the real impossibility of what that means. Goodbye, we sigh, to old Dubai, the deal's over, suspended, done. Haunt the refugees, their terror dreams unfold. The world turns a blind dark eye on the ceiling that threatens to come down. A hundred years war, or more, the plagues and pestilences, hissing sibilants of destruction, ride out with fierce intensity, laying waste.

"Epistemological defamiliarisation," the phrase given currency by the work of Russian theorist-critic Viktor Shklovsky, among others, remains emblematic of the attitude of the early 20th century avant-garde. Made even stranger when rendered in transliteration as *ostrananie* the concept still seems a potent tenet in an otherwise moribund legacy of self-styled political or activist work. Or does it?

Cast a glance backwards. The romantic movement practically defined itself by following William Blake's insistence

* Special thanks to Andrea Douglas for her comments on this piece. She raised the issue of exoticisation, as well as providing the Special Victims Unit reference. And to Jerome McGann, for continual exchange around issues of modernism and contemporary art.

that art should open the doors of perception. In ensuing culture wars, however, a rallying cry of "épater le bourgeoisie" situated the visionary experience within a social frame where it narrowed to a shock attack on moral propriety and the repressive decorum of an often hypocritical social order. The concept of "novelty" drove the twin engines of commodity marketing and art world publicity along parallel and related tracks. Strangeness, abstraction, even the conceptualism of Moreau or Redon were terms on which distinctions among class-based practices became articulated as much as they were aesthetic exercises in expression of hitherto-unimaginable thought forms. By the mid-20th century, esoteric practices are famously defined in Adorno's terms as the very foundation of resistance to the numbing formulae of culture industries and administered thought. Familiar territory. But the critical apparatus of subversion and critical resistance are still invoked as if the difficulty inherent in odd shaped representations is itself sufficient to provoke thoughtful insight. But what are the alternatives? If making-strange has become the all-too-familiar, shall we unlink aesthetic experience and knowledge, knowing, ways of seeing as thinking? Or reformulate the terms on which it occurs?

Flash forward to the present. Thomas Hirschhorn, "Superficial Engagement," a massive stuff-and-overload installation at Barbara Gladstone in February, 2006. Images of fashion, war headlines, mutilated bodies from the front lines of conflict, and geometrically abstract metaphysical paintings by Emma Kunz. David Joselit describes the way Hirschhorn's installation works within "Fashion-driven cycles of consumption" and image-glut, to expose the lie of our "American world of euphemism." What media refused to do in the news, this work did in its presentation, Joselit would have us believe.[1] But is this true? Or is the lurking assumption on which the display of mutilated bodies works itself based on an

---

[1] David Joselit, "Thomas Hirschhorn," *Artforum* (March 2006): 285-286.

unacknowledged legacy of modernism's own foundation in claims to the autonomy of the image. Even now the way the photographs Hirschhorn displays are embedded in a mass of other things, a huge mess and excess of images, language stripped from headlines about the war in Iraq, mannequins perforated with nails and screws which we are invited to add to with the power tools that lie ready to hand, even now these images are radically decontextualised, lifted out of the necessary narratives that connect them to the real circumstances of which they are documentary evidence. The metaphysical paintings, with their geometric abstractions, can be read as the sign of art as escapism, of visual images of transcendence and other-worldly-preoccupation. But they could also be read as the answer to the problem posed by the "just showing" approach to visual images. For Kunz's metaphysical works are meditations, they are not images of something abstract, they are the record of a meditative practice. Ritual value is inscribed in performance, activity. The value of images in a religious setting is not their iconography, but the way they are activated in and serve as provocation for ritual practices. Like church architecture or the recitation of the liturgy, the power of religious imagery is in its capacity to interpolate the subject into a relation with a discourse of belief. So we can read Kunz's work as a genuine alternative to the simple presentation of visual images, or we can imagine them (as I think Hirschhorn, mistakenly does) as paintings of escapism, symptomatic of the escapism generated daily across all zones of visual culture, fine, mass, and mediated.

Looking at the ways Hirschhorn's installation does or doesn't succeed tells us a great deal about the state of contemporary fine art and cultural criticism. Next door, at Lurhing Augustine, a show of paintings of artists by artists. The institutionalisation of visual art discourse within the spaces of Chelsea, themselves all an unapologetically deliberate investment strategy (more than SoHo, even which had at least a whiff of pioneer innocence and courage about it, some risk, which in the Chelsea leverage deals of capital investment in real estate was never even a trace element) is inescapable. The MFA mills crank and this year's hot young things attempt their MTV entry into the arena with ever-upped-ante scale products. We know all this.

But Hirschhorn's installation (he's not a newly minted art school grad, but a veteran artist with a long history of culture-jamming work) can't just be bracketed out of consideration because of its location. Something else has to be said about it beyond the obvious preaching-to-the-converted effect of using gruesome images in a manner that could be construed as opportunistically gratuitous or, alternatively, effective in their check on our collective escape from reality. Obviously we can't just "respond to the work" as if its situation–historical as well as cultural/geographical–had no bearing. One friend compared these images and the overwhelming in-your-face stuff-ness of the installation to the regular numbing exploitation of Special Victims Unit, *Crime Scene Investigation*, night time dramas combining fashionable, glam stars and hideously explicit imagery. The domestication of violence into consumable entertainment performed nightly by these television shows seems at once similar to and distinctly different from Hirschhorn's attempt to bring the reality of the current war— our war, America's ongoing violent invasive war—into visual form, make it present through those images.

Can it be done? And are Hirschhorn's gestures successful? What does this tell us about art now and modernism's legacy? What critical issue comes to the fore in debating the efficacy of such complicated, contradictory work? Can we still learn anything at all from works of art? Are either defamiliarisation or epistemology within the current purview of aesthetic experience? And if so, is that question itself so laden with moral value that it cancels itself out. Hirschhorn's didacticism is not political. The work is insufficiently analytical. They show something. But how does their presence expose assumptions about what the power of mere display is within the frames of already well-circumscribed art practices and venues? The juxtapositions in this installation should be about embodiment and entanglement. Could they be a call to action? First we have to recognise the extent to which image alienation has become so rote we don't even see *how* we see—and thus have no way to access what we do not know, and, in the political sense, need to, and in the human sense, might want to, in order to act.

I'll cycle back to the critical term I'm proposing: refamiliarisation, after a glance at certain points of important contrast and comparison. But refamiliarisation suggests a critical and aesthetic move to lower novelty value, and return images to the embedded conditions of production, shift them away from commodity status and into meaning, recovering a sense of the referent within the real, that has been emptied out of all public and political discourse over the last forty years. (Maybe longer. Maybe always? Was it different in Rome? The Medici's Florence? Hitler's Germany?) I only see what I know, in the historical frame of post-WWII aggression and its relation to economic booms, imperialist rhetorics, and the historical decay of the activist left into a "new" academic investment in the very "symbolic" that simultaneously seemed to melt into vaporous air, become those awful floating signifiers that post-structuralism taught us to identify only to turn us into purveyors of empty belief. Not all is lost, but to formulate a foundation for critical knowing as a practice we have to look at the legacy of modernism and conceptualism and in particular, their relation to language and narrative.

***

The administration says No Way and the senate figures caution themselves with figures snatched off telephone poles and voter polls. All the wiring went underground sometime in the last quarter of the century. After that? Infrastructure rendered invisible erases the connecting lines. Our dots are misplaced, small pins on a map drawn by an earlier empire. Under the skin of superficial boundaries, water flows, with air, and other forms of seepage, wetting the damp underbelly and hot sands with fetid tears. We did not see them, no, the teen said, shrugging his thin shoulders while the dancer's body hung in the wind, undone, utterly, a small strip of flesh against a violent sunset sky. The kids were meaner than she thought, hitting the table with their sighs.

Let's start at the hinge-point of modern to late-modern, a moment of substantive transformation in belief systems, when the advent of conceptualism, accompanied onstage by pop and minimalism, shifted the ground of fine art production from work to text, from studio to idea, and from a demarcated territory of practices defined by materials and disciplines to a dialogic condition of procedures and exchanges: the 1960s with all its attendant cultural baggage and clichés.

Pop's bright icons flashed. *Five words in neon*, Joseph Kosuth's self-referential conceptual work borrowed the signage technology of bars and diners. Bruce Nauman, a bad boy, highly irreverent, and not-quite-categorisable as either conceptual or pop artist, made playfully sly works employing the same glowing gas tube medium. *The True Artist Helps the World by Revealing Mystic Truths (Window or Wall Sign)*, 1967, rendered in neon is an irresistible work. The title is so pointedly and poignantly funny in its acknowledgement of the pretentiousness of traditional beliefs and the hollowness left by throwing them away. Any sign will do, window or wall, and the role of the artist is generically defined. We can read this piece even better by putting it in relation to two others, close in time, the kinetic flashing, punning *Suite Substitute* (1968) and double-entendre *Run From Fear, Fun from Rear* (1972). All eschew the elite intellectual cool of high conceptualism, swapping in a vernacular tone. *Suite* and *Run* are trivial and silly, they are just fun, goofy, seriously unserious. The willingness to change register redeems Nauman, keeps him from sanctimonious pieties of pretentious intellectualism.

Modernism may have had its *indépendants*, anti-salonistes, dada player's, avant-garde breakers-of-form and rejecters-of-tradition, but the unapologetic and unframed appropriation of commercial and industrial methods, images, and language became the signature gesture of 20th century late modernism. Gone was the angst, the romantic yearning for the sublime, replaced by a wry engagement with the absurdly ridiculous and blatantly commercial-industrial. In a word, "pop," that playful vernacular idiomatic smart-game of art flirted seriously with its once-terrifying nemesis—mass culture. Nauman is not Picasso, taking mass-made materials into the frame of art to show how unshakable was the separation of high/low, a formalist inventor. And he is not the conceptual arch-humorist Duchamp, naming, signing, gesturing, framing exposing the strategies of art making to make agile motions of intervention and *détournement* avant-la-lettre in his punning games and twists of phrase and reference frame.

Nauman's pop-conceptualism went way beyond these modern dalliances and like the work of the greats—Warhol, Rosenquist, Lichtenstein, Oldenburg–launched a full-scale all-out liaison with the mass culture universe. This wasn't a one-time act of appropriation or a limited borrowing of stuff for the sake of formal novelty (cubism). Nor was it an act of superiority according to old paradigms in which the culture industries were held in high disdain. The oppositional attack vanished (or was banished) with pop's vibrant games. Nauman signals that change and embodies it, with his still shocking but none-the-less darkly amusing Clown Torture videos, his coyly inaccessible underground chambers with their cameras reporting on the nothing that happens, and other smartly innovative interventions in the normative modes of art and media production.

Hardly a display of Frankfurt School critical theory, Nauman's aspirations sit in the limbo hinge zone, right on the edge between older modes mid-century high-modern distance from all manner of things mass and mediated and the coming post-modern enthusiasm for a cool and distanced use of the materials of the culture it criticises. Nauman just knows that neon looks great when it flashes, that it catches the eye and holds it in the dynamic on-off display of vivid simple lines arcing across dark space. His boyish jokes continued for decades, with pokes in the eye and an instantaneous erection as a greeting. These works have the political savvy of a bar joke (i.e. none) combined with a capacity to disarm. It's funny, after all, that abrupt sign of silly hostility or virility, right there, bonk! in your face, uncensored, unedited, kind of dumb and great at the same time. But something else is also at work in Nauman's engagement with language, a hint at the beginnings of a story returning to the stage. A tale waits to be told and, in its telling, will reconnect these works with their situations and circumstances. The language Nauman uses isn't that of high conceptualism. It's vernacular, popular, and funny.

Nauman was willing to be flatfooted and dopey in his literalism (the photograph of the word being waxed in "Waxing Hot" or the photo of the artist devouring letters in "Eating my words") at a time when conceptual artists' engagement with language was often couched in the most esoterically sophisticated philosophical terms. Both Kosuth (above mentioned) and Mel Bochner made a self-conscious display of their Wittgensteinian credentials. The idea is a machine that makes art. Sol Lewitt's condensed image of conceptual production betrays its links to the industrial system through the specific image of its metaphor. The idea of art as idea, Kosuth's version, shifted the material ground out from under the work. That was the crucial sixties move—onto the conceptual high ground. Production values can't compete. Art is nothing in relation to mass material culture, its mediated frenzies and production capabilities, a tiny marginal boutique activity that validates certain ideological concepts the way the gold standard works its efficacy in the economic systems of symbolic exchange. Conceptualism wasn't invented in the 1960s. Even before Duchamp, the symbolist painters Odilon Redon and Gustave Moreau were passionate artists of ideas, as was Dante Gabriel Rossetti (as Jerome McGann is never weary of reminding us). Idea-based art gave the lie to realism in the 19th century while engaging in elaborate visual artifices. Idea-based art attempted to diminish the claims of visual, optical practice in the 1960s, by swapping in language as if it had no material presence or character. The difference is profound. 1960s conceptualism is not monolithic. If Kosuth found in language a near-immaterial (in his mind) way to make an art of ideas, then Nauman recharged that idea with a vibrant materiality so that his language pulsed and blinked and assaulted its viewers with a constant reminder of the mediated condition of all expressions of form. Once that insistence comes back into the picture (literally, as the way these objects are made, metaphorically, as into the frame of critical apprehension), then the historical and cultural circumstances of production aren't far behind.

The language games of conceptualism were far from the field of political battle. The Wall of Resistance, a striking counter-war project organised by artists protesting the Vietnam war, was one of a series of actions that showed the cracks in the belief system about the way abstract and esoteric work could function in any "political" sense. Does the aestheticisation of language-as-image in conceptualism and pop coincide too conveniently with a shift in public discourse? Narrative had long been eliminated within the modern approach to visuality and image making, and the passing of reference from language is only a later phase of this attempt at a visuality of "plenitude" or "full presence" as we were once wont to say. This issue of narrative will recur, as a way to ask about the role of image making, fine art, and the reference frame of so-called "symbolic" forms.

In the days of 1960s Pop, it seemed like mass culture was a great new playground of fun and games. Counter-culture saturated the mainstream even as advertising, television, print magazine publication, high-end print technology—all saturated the landscape of daily life with an unprecedented level of visual artefacts. All seductive, all gorgeously produced, the slick magazine and televisual standards raced past the old techniques and technologies of fine art like a Ford Mustang passing a 1930s Oldsmobile. The analogy doesn't hold, except to demonstrate that fine art would need to struggle after the mid-20th century with new problems. How to define its superiority in conceptual terms, not production terms on the one hand, and on the other, to capture sufficient capital to embody, in sheer material force, the status of a highly industrially produced object. From the advent of modern industrialism, and its accompanying capability for rapid and high-volume image production, fine art had cornered a market on hand-made, well-crafted, unique objects. Rarefied commodities, individually traced, with a signature of the artist's body-as-hand.

Fine art still struggles to be and not to be of the mass culture, and to exist as a commodity different from the others, a thing distinct and yet among the ideologies. How, precisely, works of art can embody such complex negotiations is what makes them continually interesting. How can they show the ways our image-culture works?

The making-strange and laying-bare-the-device foundations of modern critical art seemed to offer a means of aesthetic intervention. The defamiliarising exercises still work. But only sometimes. Art zones operate in their own self-defining realms. The rules of engagement are structured and defined, and yet one of the rules is that they are always up for grabs. Nothing can tell us quite what we need to know, except that shock doesn't do it. As someone commented, fully weary with the irony of the observation, in the 1910s the proto-surrealist Jacques Vaché could be outrageous by suggesting that the greatest gesture of aesthetic radicalism was to pull out a gun in a crowd and start shooting, but in the 1990s in America, these actions had become such pathetic banalities that they only showed how futile such aesthetic intervention had become.

***

Disbelief, a daily utterance, skims over the heads of the crowd. Consumable idol, heroic tale, promotes the lone voice singing in the manufactured wilderness. American contractors conduct their business under the stage, the apparatus as usual utterly concealed. Modernism asked us to expose the workings. When there were workings that could be exposed. Quantum networks, unexplained influences at a distance, just like the daily wireless conversations. What could be stranger? Calling home at all hours from anywhere on earth, or above it. Flying as we do through an Ethernet sky. Beam me—where? No one will ever love you like—sometimes I feel like a nut sometimes—Two days later they asked themselves why they had let the Bloat go on uninterrupted. Pink stripes in a Las Vegas night club black shirt, face flushed with excess, he stood in front of them and sucked the air from every corner of the room, proposing a single category of critical engagement—transcendent, ahistorical, universal, totalising in its mechanistically conceived economic determinism: The Commodity. And we were to do what with the neo-Nazi in his white shorts, arms above his head, under arrest, swastikas tattooed on the maggot-white flesh?

Something ugly, exploitative and utterly, as per his title, superficial is evident in Hirschhorn's work. The obvious things to say—that the image of transcendence is belied, that the availability of documentary evidence about the war breaks the hygienic lies of media reporting, that the excesses of stimulus barrage are difficult to counter with any sense of the real as a referent—can and have all been said. To be confronted with something that isn't *just* product, but that has a hint of idea-about-production, that stops us, gives us some, any kind of pause and reflection, has to be worthy of at least attention.

But all images come to us embedded and entangled. Looping in the iterative streams of association and reference. Modernism's autonomy was never much more than a rhetorical stance, a momentary bracketing out of "other" matters so that form might have its classical say (Mondrian, Kandinsky, Twombly) or romantic expression (Pollock). The legacy of visuality as self-evidence is persistent, perniciously so, even after and in spite of all the postmodern, post-structuralist insistence on contingency.

Here we come back to the crux of our legacy. What did the moderns put aside? Modernism's crux, from the point of the crucial break with salon and academic traditions, was to render narrative and story unwelcome as aspects of visual art. The branding of narrative as kitsch, of vignettes and sentimental tales as beneath consideration, the disdain and scorn for O. Rijlander's *Fading Away*, that extremely popular multiple-negative manipulated photograph of a dear one dying young surrounded by family members of miscellaneous generations (a demographic study worthy of the best focus group marketing team), the rejection of Rossetti and the pre-Raphaelites, the bracketing-out of Morris and Moreau– all because the pictorial was to gain its identity through rejection of literary references. By claiming self-sufficiency through full presence, without recourse to the alluded-to and referencing narratives, images floated free of the class-based conditions of production they supported, the myths of un-alienated labour, rarefied talent, and individual talent got embodied most particularly in the practices of abstraction and conceptualism.

Hirschhorn seems to be trying to counter this. He clearly wants to insist on the impossibility of a circulation of images without accountability. The concept of contingency, promoted with the post-modern critical domain as an antidote to modernism's once-proud and once-unchallengeable concept of autonomy, was a move towards the recontextualisation of images within historical and current systems of meaning production. In a contemporary frame we add the cognitive, constructed, and constitutive approaches to perception as physiological, embedded and embodied. Hirschhorn's viscerally repelling images remind us that an image is in fact of something, in the flesh and real, a fact we are all too liable to forget. If we identify, and we do, with circumstances of meaning production, with images as extensions and projections of self into referent and back, with the physicality of perceptual frames and the ability to understand what Mark Hansen has rescued from Bergson as "affection" –all that attends to the experience of seeing as it resonates through embodied perception—then—Hirschhorn's work is germane. The argument it might be making is for recognition of embodiment, a refamiliarisation rather than a de-familiarising.

Neon signs. Neon sigh. The exhaustion factor of contemporary art is balanced by its vitality, but in that period of late 1960s, early 1970s, something rather profound occurred. Under the general rubric of conceptualism the grounds of art making shifted from production values to ideas. But on a sociological level, other changes were institutionalised. Look at Nauman. He's not toppling icons in the public square, he's playing in his room. Call it suburbanisation. He was a boomer kid, an art school trained and MFA-type artist, a new phenomenon of the post-war era, licensed and normalised into the art system of shows, galleries, museum retrospectives and coffee-table monographs. That system was all invented in the last decades of the 20th century and then naturalised to seem like it had always been. Within its frames, mythic rhetoric prevails. The publicity apparatus relies on the language of resistance, transgression, and critique, the familiar shibboleths of academic thought.

Not coincidentally, but importantly, the period at which conceptualism insists that language is a means of dematerialisation of art into idea (it's not), other important shifts in the way public discourse works, is mediated, and operates in contemporary culture are taking place. Public discourse has ceased to have any referent in the real. What does that mean for those of us who believe in the power of the symbolic? The efficacy of language and representation are instruments of belief, not mere expressions of it. Culture inversion, too much heat generated off the street, rising only to be trapped in an upper atmosphere. Hypocritical collapse.

Somewhere between Nauman's neon and Hirschhorn's excesses the fate of art in the current era seems to have been rerouted through a dystopic server. The deformance engines of contemporary life wreak havoc on the finer sensibilities. Aesthetic sensations explode. Shatter effect might be the image-equivalent of a dirty-bomb, except that drawing such analogies participates in a similarly (repulsive, to my mind) gratuitous superficiality as other exploitative sensationalisms. Bloody crime scene photos of the victims of explosions. Hands blown off. Feet shattered. Bodies mangled. All on display. Where does he get them? Doesn't take them himself. The endless circulation of all stuff, of course, internet life, that streaming zone, dip in and help yourself. The display exoticises through decontextualisation. We need to refamiliarise ourselves with the conditions of their production. Not just see these images, but know how and why they come into being. Confront our current impotence with a modest attempt at competence, not shock effect, but a slower, more deliberate reading of our own complicity with the existence of these images.

The dawn chorus went wild, birds showing off everywhere, while the cables ran fast under the suburban ground, lighting the way with their hot lines of feed. We lay on the couch in the afternoon and wondered how the season had advanced so far so fast. Nothing ventured, nothing lost. The ides of this month register as taxation in the next, lost days, unproductive and untouchable. If we march for impeachment, losing site of our credit ratings, the sun will set just the same. Boldness in the face of safety—you bet! The terror industries prevail, always outstripping their mark. Some markets seem inexhaustible, weighted and freighted with infernal return. Bite the hand that feeds you, hard. Immunity communities, a bond within and without the flesh, renew their promises nightly in the recycling systems of belief.

Bonita Rhoads and Vadim Erent

An Aesthete's Lost War: Lyotard and the Un-Sublime Art of New Europe

It is a critical commonplace to observe that, following the procession of one ascendant modernist art movement after another, today the cluttered multiplicity of artistic production institutes no single prevailing orientation. Incorporating bio-tech experiments in genetic manipulation (Critical Art Ensemble) as readily as ancient Chinese traditions of fire-work display (Cai Guo-Qiang), the contemporary art environment assimilates figurative and abstract painting right along with computer programming, encompasses daguerreotypy as much as mobilography (cell phone photography). What's identified then as the formal and conceptual repertoire of postmodern art is more truly a restive aggregation, ramified with contending styles, techniques, devices. What's more, at no point in history have so many resources been devoted to the institution of art: museums, galleries, curators, collectors, journals, art departments and art professors. Never, accordingly, have so many artists been generating this much art to satisfy so avid a demand. Clearly, that's all good news for those publishing the art books and sitting on the museum boards. The boisterous heterogeneity of creative postmodernist output, as some chroniclers proclaim, may even be a fine thing for the public. Yet there's plenty of bad news to report, if we heed the equally vociferous reproach of experts, primarily those pointing at the subsumption of the whole sprawling conglomerate of art production and consumption within the post-industrial culture complex. Postmodern art, as the customary paradox goes, has shouted down the master-narratives of modernism with its unprecedented diversity of voices only to get muffled in corporate domination.

This Frankfort School-variety of denunciation is certainly involved in the vigorous indictment against contemporary art levelled by one of postmodernism's most influential theorists. Jean-Francois Lyotard's unfavourable estimation of postmodern art practices appears, at first glance, irreconcilable with his affirmative appraisal of the postmodern condition of incredulity. As Lyotard has famously diagnosed it, the contemporary loss of faith in "a discourse called philosophy" is an instance of 'good riddance.' With our former confidence in the visionary principles of the Enlightenment now in crisis, the French philosopher judges that we have rightly dispensed with our affiliated anticipations of universal peace, fellowship and social justice. Fredric Jameson sums up Lyotard's schematisation of contemporary scepticism as a collective resignation to the fact that,

> the older master-narratives of legitimation no longer function in the service of scientific research—nor, by implication, anywhere else (e.g., we no longer believe in political or historical teleologies, or in the great "actors" and "subjects" of history— the nation-state, the proletariat, the party, the West, etc.).[1]

In other words, since we no longer bank on theology or metaphysics, dialectical materialism or the wealth of nations, we're irreverent towards transcendental signifieds and ironic in the face of transcendental signifiers. We perpetually acknowledge the contradictions of multinational capitalism but

---

[1] Fredric Jameson, Foreword to Jean-François Lyotard, *The Postmodern Condition: A Report on Knowledge*, trans. Geoff Bennington and Brian Massumi (Minneapolis: University of Minnesota Press, 1991) xii.

we no longer expect the tension of these contradictions to spark the fire of salvation. Not having achieved the liberation promised by the forward march of instrumental reason, we instead have liberated ourselves from the delusion of liberation itself. And, for Lyotard, this postmodern caginess towards grand-narratives and their subsequent de-legitimisation is so positive a development that he can proclaim: "Postmodern knowledge is not simply a tool of the authorities; it refines our sensitivity to differences and reinforces our ability to tolerate the incommensurable."[2]

Yet, Lyotard, announcing the final demystification of legitimising myths in the postmodern present, might be premature. In his equally canonical yet contrarian view of our discouragement under late capitalism, Frederic Jameson suggests that it is more accurate "to posit, not the disappearance of the great master-narratives, but their passage underground as it were," a subterranean strata in the culture from which these "buried master-narratives" persist in exerting an "*unconscious* effectivity" on our contemporary thinking and being.[3] It is also possible to suggest that this subterranean passage, this repression of the meta-narrative drive, comes back on the other side of psycho-social organisation as the return of the repressed in other areas of collective activity. One important case to consider in this regard, we believe, would be the chief partisan of scepticism himself. The repressed seems to reanimate for Lyotard in the field of aesthetics and, more specifically, in the guise of high modernism. Indeed, it is our argument that, in Lyotard's analysis of contemporary culture, the modernist painter's grasp at sublimity perversely becomes in itself a key legitimising scenario. As Lyotard writes: "The sublime is perhaps the only mode of artistic sensibility to

---

[2] Jameson, Foreword to *The Postmodern Condition*, xxv.
[3] Jameson, Foreword to *The Postmodern Condition*, xii.

characterise the modern."[4] That is to say, the sublime becomes the transcendental aspiration of a continuous negative dialectics in the development of Western art whose "fundamental task," as Lyotard will evangelise it, is "that of bearing pictorial or otherwise expressive witness to the inexpressible."[5] Ironically then, Lyotard's campaign against the grand-narrative's constitutional demagogy will ultimately result in his own articulation of a master-narrative by other means. But let's back up to consider the turns of Lyotard's reasoning more narrowly.

Plotting postmodernist production as a disappointing instalment in the trajectory of modern art history, Lyotard quite unabashedly favours what he sees as the rigorous modernist partition upholding what Peter Bürger calls the "autonomy of art" from the "praxis of life." Of postmodern art and its proclivities, he proclaims: "This is a period of slackening."[6] And throughout his article, "Answering the Question: What is Postmodernism?," Lyotard bluntly advocates the escalating brinkmanship of modernist subtraction which propelled bourgeois art from aestheticism to impressionism to contemporary art via the avant-gardes. It's a familiar chain of events—Cezanne flattens the impressionists, Picasso and Braque attack Cezanne, Malevich disposes of figuration, Duchamp breaks with painting, etc.[7] Extending this conventional sequence of art historic accretion-by-attrition, Lyotard then calls on the postmodern visual arts to take up position as the subsequent instalment in the series of consecutive insights which, he contends, has been progressively maiming the master-narratives of Western painting. It should therefore be clear that while Lyotard champions the "postmodern condition" of apprehensiveness towards

4 Jean-François Lyotard, *The Inhuman: Reflections on Time*, trans. Geoffrey Bennington and Rachel Bowlby (Stanford, California: Stanford University Press, 1991) 93.
5 Lyotard, *The Inhuman*, 93.
6 Lyotard, *The Postmodern Condition*, 71.
7 Lyotard, *The Postmodern Condition*, 79.

knowledge, when it comes to culture he is no unconditional enthusiast of the merely postmodern. Art practices which abandon modernist principles leave Lyotard deeply troubled. Whether such counter-modernist tendencies in contemporary art are advanced in the name of postmodernism or against it, these are to Lyotard equally seen as reactionary attempts to reverse the legitimate enterprise of advanced art production, namely that the sole content of art ought to be art itself, or rather "the task of art remains that of the immanent sublime."[8]

It follows that postmodernism in art, for Lyotard, is viewed as "undoubtedly a part of the modern" and must therefore, as he specifies it in even more emphatic terms, indicate "not modernism at its end but in the nascent state, and this state is constant."[9] Carried to its conclusion, the perpetual modernism that Lyotard summons here is further defined as the project: "To make visible that there is something which can be conceived and which can neither be seen nor made visible: this is what is at stake in modern painting."[10] It is thus in inescapably grand-narrative terms that Lyotard identifies the sublime as the supreme anti-narrative criterion for painting, invoking not only the Kantian sublime and its inferential manifestation in "formlessness, the absence of form" but also within the scriptural commandment ("Though shalt not make graven images") since this is Kant's example of "the most sublime passage in the Bible in that it forbids all presentation of the Absolute."[11] One can hardly imagine more transcendental precepts erected to guide the proper *ex minimis* progression-by-privation in the development of modern art. So long as painting points to the sublime, writes Lyotard, it "will therefore avoid figuration or representation," and, not hesitating to indicate even the most extreme teleology for artistic production, he

---

8 Lyotard, *The Inhuman*, 128.
9 Lyotard, *The Postmodern Condition*, 79.
10 Lyotard, *The Postmodern Condition*, 78.
11 Lyotard, *The Postmodern Condition*, 78.

continues: "It will be 'white' like one of Malevich's squares."[12] Lyotard's references to the Kantian invocation of the Mosaic prohibition and to Malevich's sacred squares (which were exhibited hung icon-like, "v krasnom uglu" — at the *beautiful corner*" of a room), together with his enthusiasm for Barnett Newman's representation of the sublime in such work as *Stations of the Cross*, all additionally point to his predilection for a theologically-inflected art of exactly the kind explicitly rejected by the avant-gardes — what the futurists heckled as "the Solemn, the Sacred, the Serious, the Sublime of Art with a capital A."[13]

Nevertheless, it is by employing the generic avant-gardist thrust of the manifesto and its militaristic (heroic) idiom that Lyotard agitates against that strain of postmodern art which would topple the modernist sublime. "Let us wage a war on totality," he writes, "let us be witnesses to the unpresentable."[14] These are fighting words, not to mention they're also the concluding words of *The Postmodern Condition*, so the stakes are obviously high; the anti-totalitarian course of culture itself, manifested in the "unpresentable" of sublimity, is on the line. Lyotard revisits these stakes in "Representation, Presentation, Unpresentable," collected in *The Inhuman*. Here, the threat unleashed by postmodern art production is further defined as "a loosening of the tension between the act of painting and the essence of painting, whereas this tension has persistently motivated one of the most admirable centuries of Western painting."[15] It is this 'loosening,' this 'slackening' which Lyotard claims leads to "deresponsibilising the artists with respect to the question of the unpresentable."[16] By contrast, Lyotard's imperishable modernism is one where: "The

12 Lyotard, *The Postmodern Condition*, 78.
13 Filippo Tommaso Marinetti, cited in Caroline Tisdall and Angelo Bozzolla, *Futurism* (New York: Thames and Hudson, 1996) 101.
14 Lyotard, *The Postmodern Condition*, 82.
15 Lyotard, *The Inhuman*, 127-8.
16 Lyotard, *The Inhuman*, 127.

postmodern would be that which, in the modern, puts forward the unpresentable in presentation itself."[17] That is to say, Lyotard promotes a revolving aesthetic revolution with the notion of the sublime at its core and various art practices as so many orbiting aesthetic manifestations representing the unrepresentable in endlessly original "new presentations, not in order to enjoy them but in order to impart a stronger sense of the unpresentable."[18] Otherwise, Lyotard forcefully cautions, postmodern art production "brings with it the corruption of the honour of painting, which has remained intact in spite of the worst demands of States (make it cultural!) and the market (make money!)."[19]

If the honour of painting presumably survived the catastrophes of the first half of the 20th century intact, it is no small imputation to suggest that it is under the threat of annihilation today. But Lyotard detects just such a danger in the eclecticism of postmodern art production, its reactivation of the figurative, its lack of squeamishness in the encounter with popular culture. He writes:

> As for the "trans-avant-gardism" of Bonito Oliva and the similar currents one can observe in the USA and Germany (including Jencks's "postmodernism" in architecture, which the reader will do me the favour of not confusing with what I have called "the postmodern condition"), it is clear that behind the pretext of picking up the tradition of the avant-gardes, this is a pretext for squandering it. This inheritance can only be transmitted in the negative dialectic of refutations and supplementary questionings. To want to get a result from it, especially by addition, is to arrest this dialectic, to confine the spirit of avant-gardist works to the museum, to encourage the eclecticism of consumption.[20]

---

[17] Lyotard, *The Postmodern Condition*, 81.
[18] Lyotard, *The Postmodern Condition*, 81.
[19] Lyotard, *The Inhuman*, 128.
[20] Lyotard, *The Inhuman*, 127.

Squandering by addition rather than progressing by deduction, certain postmodernist artists have, in other words, disregarded the sacred modernist tenet—art's autonomy from socio-political, economic and cultural spheres. Transgressing this consecrated border between high art and low culture, they have thereby reduced the aesthetic and social values of the spiritual aristocracy to the culture of mass entertainment and consumption, equated art with kitsch. Furthermore, the art of "addition" allows for the resurgence of figurative realism plus the unprecedented introduction of pop-cultural iconographic devices. Taken together, such infractions fritter away the contemporary artist's modernist "inheritance," relegating "the spirit of avant-gardist works to the museum." Of course, it goes without saying that the art of the avant-garde was cloistered in the museums long before these alleged postmodernist 'betrayals.' But Lyotard is not talking about actual artworks; it is rather the spirit of the work which is now being abandoned, confined, withdrawn from cultural circulation. Objecting to the art which now ranges freely in its place, Lyotard reiterates the standard criticism of postmodernist dissolution:

> What is called on by eclecticism are the habits of magazine readers, the needs of the consumer of standard industrial images—this is the spirit of the supermarket shopper. To the extent that this postmodernism, via critics, museum and gallery directors and collectors, puts strong pressure on the artists, it consists in aligning research in painting with a de facto state of "culture" ...[21]

Simply put, the "spirit of avant-gardist works" has been reduced to "the spirit of the supermarket shopper."

Warhol was probably the first target of this kind of critical indignation, attracting quite the identical protest, namely what we might label the "supermarket" affront. As far back as 1963, in her review, "Pop Art at the Guggenheim," Barbara Rose

---

[21] Lyotard, *The Inhuman*, 127.

writes: "I find his images offensive; I am annoyed to have to see in a gallery what I'm forced to look at in the supermarket. I go to the gallery to get away from the supermarket, not to repeat the experience."[22] Such a view assumes the art gallery and museum as safe havens from the vulgarity of instrumental "means-ends" relations in the real world. More, Rose's position normalises the bourgeois practice of relegating art (with the artists' consent) to the cathedral, the palace, the museum, where the public can confront the sublime, the infinite, the *il y a* (there is) rather than have its tastes offended. But the offence, the annoyance, the indignation that Warhol inspired was, of course, right in line with the avant-garde's project, which included among its favourite intentions the determination to *épater le bourgeois*. While perhaps today bourgeoisie "can no longer be *'épaté,'*"[23] at the time, the critics of pop-art were certainly susceptible to the provocation. Clement Greenberg, the high priest guarding the temple of high culture from low brow infiltrations, identified the threshold as the one demarcating the avant-garde from kitsch. He never accepted the unexpected turn of advanced art to pop-art, calling it a "multitude of fashions, vogues, waves, fads, manias."[24] In an amazing revision of the spirit of the avant-garde, Greenberg actually wrote: "Not that the avant-garde ever really meant revolution. [...] The avant-garde's principal reason for being is, on the contrary, to maintain continuity: continuity of standards of quality—the standards, if you please, of the Old Masters."[25] And that is of course blatantly wrong. The avant-garde's raison d'être was revolutionary through and through. Its project was to dethrone the institution of art itself from its overbearing

22 Barbara Rose, cited in Benjamin H. D. Buchloh, *Neo-Avantgarde and Culture Industry: Essays on European and American Art from 1955 to 1975* (Cambridge, Mass.: MIT, 2000) 21-2.
23 Antone Compagnon, *The 5 Paradoxes of Modernity*, trans. Franklin Philip (New York: Columbia University Press, 1994) xiii.
24 Clement Greenberg, "Avant Garde Attitudes" [1969], *On-line Picasso Project*, 30 Aug. 2005 <http://csdll.cs.tamu.edu:8080/picasso/OPPv2ArchivesArticle?id=18>
25 Greenberg, "Avant Garde Attitudes."

postures as an autonomous sphere. Thus LEF (New Left Front) and Mayakovsky called to "throw Pushkin off the steamboat of Modernity." In this regard, Mayakovsky's insistence that his commercial work for Agitprop, the Soviet propaganda and advertising agency, was of the highest creative quality (and he really considered it some of his best work) anticipates Warhol's vulgar soup cans.

The customary question then remains whether contemporary art, voided of transcendence, can represent anything other than commercial and consumer values. Or is Lyotard correct to urge a postmodern art which evolves ceaselessly into modernism, pushing forward into the past? Certainly, one pervasive critique of the arts today amounts to the diagnosis that no art practice is capable of withstanding its integration in the culture complex of late capitalism, its participation in the cash nexus of image production and consumption. Or rather, from a more worldly perspective, might we say that today the uninhibited interpenetration between "art and life" has simply demolished modernism's former pretensions to autonomy from commercial and political spheres? In that case, pop-art's arrival as the *post-avant-garde* can be viewed as yet another bracing shift to candour, in the sense that the pop-artist openly owns up to complicity with the market, passing up the heroic stances of the modernist artist silhouetted against the backdrop of mass culture (read heroic Pollock vs. transvestite Warhol) while also foregoing the avant-gardist artist's offensives against the institutions of art. Is it the case, then, that pop-art simply accepts both the culture and the institutions of art, works with and within them? Or can the full severity of Lyotard's reproof apply: that pop-art obstructs the negative dialectics of art-historical advancement, thereby assaulting the sublimity indispensable for the anti-totalitarian polity?

Surely, Jameson is right to say that pop-art is not unambiguously critical of consumer society.[26] Nevertheless, it at least possesses a critical agenda directed against the late modernism of abstract expressionism. In simple terms, pop-art is out to get Pollock. Abstract expressionism at the time was fully enshrined in American universities. Action painting was academically-sanctioned art. While the abstract expressionists represented the unrepresentable sublime, pop-art typified the visual media, the everyday rhetoric of mass production and mass culture. Still, there is a gut sense in which the liberal viewer feels that Warhol just ought to be critical of Coke and of Campbell's Soup. Otherwise, how can we like him? (Jameson sounds disappointed: Warhol is not a critic of Coke). But, of course, Warhol's work is celebratory; it simply is not melancholic because, well, because actually, as Warhol insists on showing us, everybody loves Coke. Indeed, Warhol precisely commented on the egalitarian socio-economics of our passionate bad taste and enthusiastic mass consumption when he wrote that the very rich and the very poor alike drink Coke. Pop-art may not refine us but that's because it is too democratic. Appallingly, it's with us, it's on our side; it, with its viewer, consumes images. Spectacle and spectator, breachless in this cooperative obsession, both are consuming mass icons and mass culture in unison. Moreover, for both art viewer and artwork, the consumption is that of the pre-consumed. At once a found object, the soup can or coke bottle is not a found object in itself, chanced upon in a state of aesthetic innocence, but an object already aestheticised, already art, already consumed. These postmodern *nature morte* are undigested like the seventeenth century Dutch still-lives of game, fowl and fish, and so they are raw, but, simultaneously, as Campbell Soup cans, they are pre-fabricated, pre-packaged, pre-pared, half-cooked, half-digested (they are conjointly the raw and the cooked).

[26] Fredric Jameson, *Postmodernism, or, The Cultural Logic of Late Capitalism* (Durham: Duke University Press, 2003) 158.

Certainly the concatenated ecstasy of consumption in Warhol's art is legendary. Fascinated with the real world around him and with its fascinations, he tirelessly represented them. In this, Warhol presides over the first art movement that displays reality wholly as culture, exhibits mass culture as first nature. If we take the Barthesian paradigm of the sign as a formula, we can say that pop-art grasps the very sign of mass culture as a signifier, not so much to de-mythologise it from its civic connotations and retail naturalisations, but to re-signify it within another register, an art-code, in which the accord of the sign is split and its dizzying ambiguity revealed—is this sign ironic or not? Take Warhol's dollar paintings. Is this $ an ode to US currency or is it highly ironic?

Is this a critical statement on the contemporary conflation of art and money, art as financial currency, art as capital investment? Or is it a vulgar transgression precisely against the cultivated autonomy of the artistic sphere, valorising the collaborationist position of the artist in the realms of exchange value, in this case celebrating art as wealth? Confronted with this dilemma in Warhol, Bürger suggests that such content "contains resistance to the commodity society only for the person who wants to see it there."[27] Still, in the $ paintings we can see Warhol's conceptual development from Jasper John's paintings of symbolic *things*, the American flags and practice targets, which remain visual onomatopoeias of emblematic objects that could really be encountered in the world. By contrast, Warhol presents the pure sign, a dollar sign (as opposed to an actual dollar bill). And he is even willing to sign dollar bills. Not turning *everything* into art (like the Russian futurists) but *anything*. Such a seizure of the *anything* was, in turn, to influence the whole cadre of appropriation artists who follow after Warhol: Levine, Richard Prince, Kruger, Sherman. And so, pop-art consummates the total incorporation of life and art, of art and media, the full aestheticisation of late capitalist

[27] Peter Bürger, *Theory of the Avant-Garde*, trans. Michael Shaw (Minneapolis: University of Minnesota Press, 1984) 61.

production and everyday existence. That is to say, we've arrived in the artful modernity of which the futurists dreamed but the life here doesn't rise to art. Rather, art is engulfed by the world and is worldly. Everything is down to earth, is on display and up for sale; whence the transcendent?

On top of Letna Hill, overlooking the Vltava River and the Prague city centre, stands the seventy-five foot Metronome created by Vratislav Karel Novak. This prominent, kinetic sculpture was erected in 1991 to inhabit the vast base (vacant for thirty years) formerly occupied by the colossal sculptural ensemble that included the largest ever (30m) effigy of Joseph Stalin—it stood facing Prague, surveying the city, daunting it. In an age when "contemporary public art has turned to the monumental abstraction as its acceptable icon,"[28] the abstract, streamlined, constructivist arm of the Metronome certifies the Czech nation's official passage from the repressive era of compulsory socialist realism to the democratically-sanctioned

[28] W.J.T. Mitchell, *Picture Theory: Essays on Verbal and Visual Representation* (Chicago: University of Chicago Press, 1995) 376.

modernism. Every aspect of the Metronome can be seen to defy the totalitarian sublime of the Stalin statue it supersedes. Built for eternity, the long-ago annihilated Soviet monolith, in its granite permanence and dinosaur monumentality (the thing was so massive and sturdy it could not be disassembled and had to be blown up with explosives) is still contrasted with the perpetual movement of the modish, up-to-date Metronome. The teleological temporality of proletarian revolution affirmed by the Stalin figure is accordingly rebuked by the pure, "neutral" passage of time through which the metronome marks out the incessant tempo of history. As the arm sways from one side to the other, it charts the skies offering the infinity of the universe as a contrast to and commentary on the Stalin assemblage, a parable of a fallen colossus: the messianic sublime of Communism is trumped by the infinite sublime of time's "natural" current. Indeed, this inhuman, metronomic indifference to history does not differentiate between human events; it is equally impartial to tyranny and to democracy. Its function is not even to keep track of time—that is the work of the public clocks (the medieval Prague Orloj just below makes an obvious counterpoint)—it signifies only sheer time, marks its continuance. A prominent public spectacle, the Metronome thus serves to iterate and reiterate in perpetuity the plain indubitable fact of time marching on. It offers both Praguers and tourists the relief of conciliation. It says "time changes everything" but it does not moralise or memorialise, or mourn, or protest. And, so, the Metronome's commentary on the history of the site and on the course of history itself is concentrated entirely within its meta-narrative, formal, art historic registers, signalling the shift from one aesthetic exponent of the sublime to another, from the triumphal idiom of socialist realism to the negative dialectics of abstract modernism.

A postmodernist perspective on the Metronome suggests an additional critical issue. Seen in relation to Claus Oldenburg's superlative rescaling of trivial objects (a titanic safety-pin, a behemoth button, a building-sized lipstick), the Metronome employs the same technique of monumentalising a diminutive contrivance. Oldenburg's surrealistically immense gadgets and utensils deterritorialise their surroundings by dwarfing their vicinity in a newly imposed relativity of scale.

Monumentalising the mundane, as it turns out, ironises monumentality itself as a category. Novak's gigantic Metronome, on the other hand, succeeds in symbolically magnifying the instrumental function of this tempo-setting device while projecting it onto the surrounding city. That is to say, while the tempo assimilates all historical epochs within its "neutral-natural" time flow, it, nevertheless, somewhat to the contrary, simultaneously suggests the enforcing rhythm of the new capitalist order in a manner reminiscent of the chronometer's introduction into the workplace to quicken the pace of performance, escalating the labour-rhythm of production, tightening work discipline on the shop and factory floor. With the fall of the Communists, the meat-lines would disappear ("meat-line" was, incidentally, the unofficial epithet used for the Stalin statue's double file of granite subordinates lined up behind the dictator) but the Czech citizenry would definitely have to pick up their pace in the rate of production (and in their consumption).

Such artistic collaboration with the ascendant ideological and economic order seems an inevitable outcome in most every critical account of the contemporary culture of multinational capitalism. Our analysis of the Metronome attempts to illustrate specifically how opposition to one repressive aesthetic paradigm, such as state-sanctioned socialist realism, may simply lead to the rigid valorisation (à la Lyotard) of yet another potentially hegemonic and co-opted aesthetic persuasion. Today, we could easily claim that it becomes unproductive, even conformist, to counter the figurative gigantism of the totalitarian past with abstract modernist monumentality. The negative dialectics of aestheticism and formalism and the whole plastic research into the sublime has ended up yielding very "positive," very profitable results in the field of commercial manipulation. The avant-garde, irregardless of artists' intentions, serves, in the words of Thomas Crow, "as a kind of research and development arm of the culture industry."[29] Or, as W.J.T. Mitchell bleakly observes: "Oppositional movements such as surrealism, expressionism, and cubism have been recuperated for entertainment and advertising, and the boldest gestures of High Modernism have become the ornaments of corporate public spaces."[30] In such an environment, Lyotard's insistence on the "constancy" of modernist principals and his call for the permanence of revolutionary returns to the formalist concerns of the ineffable, the unrepresentable and the sublime, appear downright reactionary.

Czech artists and intellectuals who have almost overnight witnessed the institutional change of guard from communist culture ministry to late capitalist culture industry, from obtuse government propaganda to the ubiquitous colonisation of public attention by commercial advertising, have had to recalibrate their conceptual positions in response to these developments. Some of the most interesting interventions are therefore engaged in multidimensional, multimediational critiques that address the heterotopic postmodern condition of this new society. Two recent examples of public art, both created by Czech women artists who have achieved prominence since the Velvet Revolution, Milena Dopitová and Lenka Klodová, are exemplary in their capacity to contend critically with a multiplicity of issues, provoking certain intransigent authoritarian strains of their nation's recent history while also addressing the present commercialisation of spirituality, in artworks that shift gracefully and slyly from the transcendent to the banal, from sacred to supermarket.

Milena Dopitová's photographic series of Prague mothers negotiating the urban landscape with their children, *Come, I'll show you the way through Paradise—Prague Madonnas*, was a commissioned work, approved in its proposal stage for exhibition in the Czech Republic's pavilion at the 2000 World's Fair in Hanover. Originally, the photographs were to involve

29 Cited in Mitchell, *Picture Theory*, 376.
30 Mitchell, *Picture Theory*, 376.

quite an engaging conceit; this serial presentation of contemporary metropolitan maternity would duplicate yet also counterpoise a cycle of Czech medieval Madonnas on display at the pavilion entrance. As conceived, Dopitová's project was thus to hold up a 21st century mirror to the "eternal" themes evoked by Marian imagery: the sanctity of maternal love, solicitude, compassion and self-sacrifice. Additionally, we can suppose that the Czech artist, in executing her project, must have been governed by some sense of accountability to national pride. Presumably a World Exposition country pavilion implies a prestigious honour and patriotic opportunity to represent the contemporary state of Czech arts and to be seen in connection with the nation's established art heritage as well, in this case the medieval Madonnas. However, upon review by the Czech General Commissioner, the inclusion of Dopitová's series was vetoed and Pavel Mára's photographic nudes were chosen as a replacement.

That the officials responsible for the Czech Pavilion rejected the commissioned series, preferring to install Mára's nude Madonnas alongside the medieval prototypes, immediately suggests some transgressive ingredient in Dopitová's *Prague*

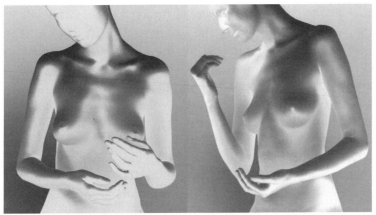

Madonnas. But what? Appraising Dopitová's photo-vignettes of urban maternity, one can hardly help but judge them as the least likely candidates for official censorship of any kind. Every predictable rationale for suppression—obscenity, sensuality, radical political or subversive ideological content, violence, crudity—appears serenely absent. On the surface, Dopitová's images look to be studies in ordinariness. Was the provocation possibly the sheer lack of it? To accentuate the puzzle, Mára's nudes, the usurpers in this cultural parable, with their aloof sexuality and lithe, unclad torsos, must be seen as the more conventionally indecent by comparison. But clearly, they satisfied the officials' idea of how photography could properly correlate to the art heritage of the national past, and of how contemporary art could refurbish the values of religious art, rendering these in updated forms, serving old wine in new skin.

With the startling chiaroscuro of black and white photography, and the contrast further intensified by the reverse-negative effect (*à la* Man Ray), Mára endows his nudes with an auratic radiance, flooding them in an otherworldly glow. More precisely, the reverse-negative printing invests these Madonnas (depicted as delicate female torsos) with the capacity to radiate light forth as if from inside, a contrivance that serves to dissolve the typical opposition of body and soul, casting flesh as lustrous spirit; the halo is interiorised. Quite literally then, this series *illustrates* (in the sense of illuminating) the spiritual condition of the hallowed Marian corpus. With Mára's incandescent images of the Holy Mother bathed in divine light on the one side, let us now turn to consider the *pulp media*-style photographs from Dopitová's rebuffed series. By comparison with the Virgins that replaced them, Dopitová's portraits would seem to offer unexpectedly mundane tableaux of Prague mothers and children in various sites throughout the city, engaged in mostly routine activities—shopping, eating, working, playing (although, in one deviating instance, a mother is shown begging). It follows that one of the features that must have disqualified these quotidian Madonnas to the officials was precisely the 'unspectacular' look of the photographs, a lack of 'high art' indices, their absence of any evident transcendence marking mother and child as archetypes of a sacred relationship.

Or, to state it more bluntly within the art-historic continuum that is our focus, it is from the plainly secular, materialist, heterodox, ambidextrous position of postmodern production that Dopitová sets out for an encounter with the sacrosanct iconography of Christian art. Unlike the Mára Madonnas, these earthbound portraits have cast off any attitude that could let them double (without irony) as devotional, cult objects or align them with the patrician programs of modernism. Instead, this series works in the tradition of appropriation art (once again Warhol, Levine, Prince, Kruger, Koons, Sherman), adopting the feel of the industry photograph while applying mass-cultural devices of production. The Photoshop layering which allows fields of the photographs to be rendered in colour while seamlessly joined to other elements in black and white, introduces into this work an element of postcard triviality. Or, rather, taken altogether, the portraits have the look of photo-reportage for a popular parenting magazine. None of this is to say that Dopitová's series on contemporary motherhood fails to address the original context of religious art. On the contrary, the photos are interweaved with updated re-enactments of familiar episodes and iconography from the life of the Virgin: the Annunciation, Flight into Egypt, the Pietà, Virgin *Lactans*, etc. Yet, even while Dopitová (no stranger to feminist thematics) evokes this Marian imagery, she is reformulating it, even profaning it, perhaps more effectively than by a direct assault, precisely through the seemingly casual attitude of her adaptations and the discretion of her transformations. Let's consider some of her specific compositional strategies.

The iconography of Christian art commonly positions the Virgin Mother as a background for the Christ Child, a straightforward enough structural allusion to her supporting function in the *vitae domini*. But the *Prague Madonnas*, presented mainly as middle-class modern women, some chic, urbane, and evidently professional, have other functions, other things to do. While some still hold onto a child and provide the chromatic ground for its figure, these mothers are multitasked, engaged simultaneously in shopping, talking on cell phones, hailing a cab. It is in photographs like these that the rapprochement of two art registers (sacred and postmodern) begins to create an additional antagonistic relationship between them. Thus, for example, in one picture the mother is holding the child while leaning in the opposite direction to speak into her phone. The effect is of a precarious balance/unbalance between attachment and autonomy of mother and child. Pictorially, the child is not at the centre, neither is he centred on the ground of the mother, neither then is he at the proverbial centre of the universe, his mother's or the viewer's. That is to say, Dopitová subtly represents women, rather than their dependents, as the primary subjects of their own maternity. In this regard, it is interesting to apply to Dopitová's *Madonnas* what Julia Kristeva wrote of Giovanni Bellini's fifteenth century Madonnas. Kristeva calls on the viewer to "behold the distance [...] separating the bodies of infant and mother in his paintings."[31] Kristeva then continues

31 Julia Kristeva, *Desire in Language: A Semiotic Approach to Literature and Art*, ed. Leon S. Roudiez, trans. Thomas Gora, Alice Jardine, Leon S. Roudiz (New York: Columbia University Press, 1980) 247.

her analysis of one typical Bellini painting by pointing out that the Madonna figure—"head, face, and eyes—flees the painting, is gripped by something other than its object," and this elsewhere space beyond the canvas is what Kristeva labels the *maternal jouissance*, that enjoyment within the mother and exclusive to her, which remains forever inaccessible to the child even through corporeal contact.[32]

This implies that, in manipulating the image of ideal maternity epitomised in the Madonna, Dopitová slyly exhibits mothers who are not exclusively characterised by children but rather are women with children. We have mentioned that in some of the portraits these women appear chic, elegantly dressed, professional. In others, however, they appear simply capable, unromantic—the manner in which they tend to the needs of children is not sentimentalised by Marian attitudes of adoring solicitude but is shown practically (though not harshly) as a matter of expedience and efficiency—a question of getting the job done—for example, the mother propping the child's penis while the boy is peeing in the park, the mother serving

[32] Kristeva, *Desire in Language*, 247.

her young son a hotdog from a paper plate. Still, these are innocuous enough representations unless seen as versions of the sacred relationship between Holy Mother and Infant Christ. The subtitle of the series, *Prague Madonnas*, is therefore crucial to the visual impact of the works. As postmodern translations of the doctrinaire typologies in religious art, we ask whether Dopitová's series may be related to such high profile art scandals as Andres Serrano's 1989 *Piss Christ* and Chris Ofili's 1996 collage with elephant dung, *The Many Faces of Mary; Representing the Virgin*, which generated controversy throughout New York when displayed in the publicly funded *Sensation* show at the Brooklyn Museum. Our answer: we think so. Although in far less excrementally obvious ways, we believe Dopitová's work was likewise judged profane, as crap or dung hurled on the transcendent. In other words, by rejecting Dopitová's Madonnas, the Czech Pavilion commissioner protected the representational sanctity of motherhood; censuring the mundane, de-sublimated image, he defended the otherworldly status of the holy family and, by extension, the ideal of every family. Indeed, it can be argued that in Western cultural history, the Marian cult of maternity contains the ultimate reassurance of a conduit between secular and sacred. As Kristeva writes: "theology defines maternity only as an impossible elsewhere, a sacred beyond, a vessel of divinity, a spiritual tie with the ineffable godhead, and transcendence's ultimate support."[33]

In contrast to the immaculate Mára Madonnas that represented the Czech Republic in Hanover, Dopitová's mothers are thus maculated by the mundane realities of errands and chores. Moreover they fail to rise above their environment or to refine it even in terms of their desires, which, clearly, are manufactured by advertising. One of the tableaux shows a mother and baby daughter under a sexy billboard advertising cosmetics with a typical slogan asserting female value as

33 Kristeva, *Desire in Language*, 237.

feminine beauty: *"Já za to stojím"* — *"I'm worth it."* Yet another tableau shows the same chic, youthful mother shopping for shoes. Her child is to the side of the scene, watching her sizing a shoe, trying on its potential image. As with pop-art, it is impossible to determine whether the subject, here the mother, is reduced or celebrated in the role of consumer. Are these women empowered and liberated, are they sexy, are they sold, or both, caught up in the ricochet of consumption by which the consumer is at the same time also another product?

And how does the image of *blessed mother qua consumer* provoke the traditional cult of motherhood? It is once again in the context of the cult of motherhood with its "luminous serenity of the unrepresentable,"[34] and its prominence in the history of Western art that Lenka Klodová's May 2005 series, *Vitězky (Winners)*, takes a decisively transgressive turn.

Winners was presented this spring as part of a public, open air exhibition on the Letna "Art Wall," which extends alongside the Vltava and its adjoining highway. Four artists chosen by a Prague city commission were given opportunities to fill the stone alcoves built into the River Wall originally to brandish communist propaganda at drivers, tram-riders and pedestrians. Klodová's series, the first displayed, consisted of billboard size photographs of heavily pregnant women athletes impossibly competing in such Olympics-type sports as javelin throw, high jump, gymnastics, running, shot-put and soft-ball. It is significant that the art in this exhibition occupies a public space formerly delegated for government propaganda; set in the embankment within the stone frames left by the communist regime, the work thus retains an ambience of the demagogy and coercion of state-sanctioned programs and paradigms. At the same time, these placards also occupy a global public sphere saturated by advertisement; the name of the series, *Vitězky* (literally, women winners) clearly puns on the worldwide ubiquity of the sportswear mega-brand *Nike* (Nikē

---

[34] Kristeva, *Desire in Language*, 243.

in Greek mythology being a goddess of victory). Or rather, to put it in more general terms, the icon of an athlete, like the image of the worker, the soldier or, indeed, that of the mother, has certainly been one of the most favoured of propagandist rhetoric. Art which has rendered the athlete's image in the service of politics spans the ideological spectrum from ancient republicanism to fascism and communism, in the last century from Alexander Rodchenko to Leni Riefenstahl et al.

The identification of propaganda with advertising in Klodová's series is therefore as apt as it is common. One enterprise sells ideology, the other sells a product but, while propaganda sells the product of ideology, advertising sells the ideology of a product, and both do it (as Barthes has shown) by the operation of naturalisation, or the mythologisation, of a sign. In a gesture that ironises such contemporary myth-making, Klodová first grafts the two registers into one image. The *Winners* are at once national heroes (Olympians) and next they are the modern divinities of lifestyle (*Nike* ads). Yet, in an absurd next step of hyper-accumulation-signification, Klodová endows these heroes/icons with yet another super-signifier, the master-narrative of maternity. The resultant tripartite-hybrid presents a kind of monstrosity, a freakish shorthand of a contemporary predicament—a mutant trapped in the postmodern matrix of ideology, marketing, and sentimentality. The resultant freighted female athletes, awkward, bizarre, disfigured figures of hyper-pastiche fall out of every conceivably desirable value system. It is as if, metaphorically, the ideal of maternity and the image of pregnancy here serve to disfigure the icons of political ideology and consumerism. In the present age of mass media politics, marketing and communications, in which the message of the image is increasingly focused, focus-grouped, motivated and market-targeted, the ambiguity of Klodová's *Vitězky* thus engaged the Prague public with a contemporary hieroglyph compressing and expressing our present cultural abundance and cultural impasses. When the series was on display, one could actually recognise fellow tram-riders who were encountering the *Vitězky* for the first time by the progression of confusion, astonishment, amusement and reflection evident in their expressions.

It is helpful to ascertain the work of these two Czech artists in relation to the historical avant-gardes which attempted to break the spell of aesthetic autonomy and, with it, the reign of abstract formalism by reactivating the impact of the narrative and the figurative in art. Then as now, the enterprise of the ineffable does not provide the necessary crudity to engage the authoritarian power of ideological or economic hegemonies. Nevertheless, the historical avant-gardes have also failed by their own definition since the "intention of the historical avant-garde movements was defined as the destruction of art as an institution set off from the praxis of life."[35] But the accumulated work of these movements remains an inexhaustible, explosive source of conceptual vitality for today's artists and intellectuals. The work of pop-art precisely revisited the techniques and

[35] Bürger, *Theory of the Avant-Garde*, 83.

devices of the preceding avant-gardes (some critics identified it with neo-dada) albeit with a diacritics of its own. The artists who have inherited pop-art, the sots-art practitioners (Komar and Melamid, et al.) in the east, as well as the appropriation artists, Levine, Kruger, Sherman, in the west, have in their turn recalibrated the procedures developed by Warhol and Co., deploying these decisively against the symbolic orders and the industries of image production and consumption, forming an essential precedent in the reanimation of the historical avant-gardes' program of engagement in the praxis of life.

Cindy Sherman, who (incidentally) had a major retrospective at Prague's Galerie Rudolfinium in 1998, appears a particularly productive influence for the generation of artists that includes Dopitová and Klodová. Sherman's *categorical blurs* (Rosalind Kraus's term for images transgressing the borders of gender and anatomy)[36] together with her mass-media thematics can be seen in both Dopitová's and Klodová's series, which also share Sherman's strategy of total appropriation, not simply confiscating individual images but parasitically inhabiting the whole signifying system, invoking the entire gamut of an industry's image repertoire. Thus while Dopitová and Klodová collude with Lyotard's doctrine of unravelling master narratives of their totality, their strategy is not in presenting the sublime otherness in its incommensurability with the vulgarity of mass culture, but in inhabiting the mass-cultural systems of representation and pressuring, manipulating, sabotaging these regimes from the inside. Furthermore these artists recognise that the discourse of the ineffable and the sublime is itself a master-narrative which has been appropriated by the image industry and they press on with the work of undoing transcendent, utopian paradigms exemplified, in this particular case, by the figures of Holy Mother and Victorious Olympians.

Intervening in the global culture and transgressing the transcendental, Dopitová and Klodová at the same time engage

---

36 Rosalind Kraus, *Bachelors* (Cambridge, Mass.: MIT, 2000) 13.

the contingent, situational, site and context specific mini-narratives with critical, deconstructive gestures which are the precondition of effecting the local cultural environment. This is an existential attitude that is quite different from the position assumed by Lyotard. Lyotard is a militant aesthete (*let us wage a war*), battling against the tyranny of popular culture to save the honour of the sublime. Lyotard's call to war in the name of the ineffable is underpinned by a reverse class consciousness: the self consciousness of the spiritual aristocracy organised against the vulgarity of mass culture. Lyotard articulates this explicitly when he refers to the "intellectual class" of artists and philosophers, a membership which certainly carries with it a measure of responsibility to the public. But Lyotard also identifies a beyond of that responsibility, a calling outside of public discourse. The artists' ultimate duty, Lyotard writes, is to answer the question, "What is it to paint?" just as philosopher is responsible to the question "What is thinking? The public is not necessarily the interlocutor on this question."[37] The phenomenological whirligig of thinking about thinking and painting about painting does, inevitably, intimate the transcendental and the sublime, and so this demarcation between the public and the philosopher-artist is yet another formulation of the autonomy of art from the marketplace of life.

The work of Dopitová and Klodová, which is being produced right on the geo-political cusp where authoritarianism surges into late capitalism, follows a different orientation, that of prodding the public, plumbing the issues, discoursing with the media, baiting the conventions. Of course, this very art is funded by the institutions and regimes it interrogates, which at first glance seems to confirm Lyotard's sense that art cannot be both engaged and also resist its context anymore. Yet there are moderators in this debate who are willing to draw the lines less dogmatically, who chart our historical coordinates in less extremist topographies, and who

---

[37] Lyotard, *The Inhuman*, 128.

look to the interstices for areas of possibility. For example, in his conversion with German artist Hans Haacke, sociologist Pierre Bourdieu discusses the place of the artist in contemporary culture, in relation to the public as well as to the state. Bourdieu insists that a true latitude exists for art at this moment: "A public system leaves a very large margin of freedom, but one must still make use of it"[38] even while he regrets that it is not exploited often enough: "Unfortunately, citizens and intellectuals are not prepared for this freedom in relation to the state."[39] To our mind, the provocative public art created by Dopitová and Klodová strikes out precisely for those enterprising borderlands towards which Bourdieu gestures: "artists, writers, and scholars, who hold in trust some of the most exceptional accomplishments of human history, must learn to use against the state the freedom that the state assures them."[40]

---

[38] Pierre Bourdieu and Hans Haacke, *Free Exchange* (Stanford: Stanford University Press, 1995) 75.

[39] Bourdieu and Haacke, *Free Exchange*, 73.

[40] Bourdieu and Haacke, *Free Exchange*, 72.

Mairéad Byrne

Avant-Garde Pronouns

People don't get no time to feel and spend them intelligence. The most intelligent and innocent are poor, are crumbled and get brutalised. Daily. —Bob Marley

When Louis Armand invited me to contribute to this volume of essays, I went out on my front porch to consider the implications. Why me? How did he find me? Can a member of the Curriculum Subcommittee of the Instruction Committee be avant-garde?

A recent publication, *Séance* (Make Now, 2006), connects committees and the avant-garde. I know what it is to *avoir séance*, to be *en séance*, to *faire une longue séance*, to *prendre séance*, and even, eventually, to *lever la séance*.

I know the inexorable sadness of pencils. But avant-garde?

If not avant-garde, then how about historian of the avant-garde? Preserver of the avant-garde? Can Roethke's institutional dust, "finer than flour, alive, more dangerous than silica," be mixed with the intoxicating vim of the avant-garde? On Tuesdays, Wednesdays, and Thursdays, I sprinkle news of the avant-garde over the heads of students. I assign manifestos as homework, or did—until a student fingered that particular absurdity. I offer helpful directions:

TO READ ANTONIN ARTAUD'S *ALL WRITING IS PIGSHIT*

STAND
outside the RISD Library on Benefit Street with back to front door

CROSS
Benefit Street *[look right look left look right again]*

CLIMB
College Street to Prospect

TURN
right and proceed up ramp or steps to Brown University's Rockefeller Library

ENTER
through revolving doors *[to conserve heat]*

PRESENT
identification at security desk

CONSULT
Josiah for Mary Ann Caws's *Manifesto: A Century of Isms*

TRANSCRIBE
Call Number [CB 427.M287 2001] &

NOTE
location of available copy/copies

PROCEED
to appropriate floor for circulating copy *[consult list by elevator]*
OR Reference Room *[for use in library only]*

PROCURE
book &

CARRY
to coin/card copier on 1st or 2nd floor

COPY
pages 460-1

RETRIEVE
& fold, roll, or otherwise temporarily store, pages

RETURN
book to Reference Desk or cart

READ/LEAVE/READ

CONSULT
teacher if confused

The avant-garde tradition is still exemplary. Saying *pigshit* in the classroom is bracing. Saying *all writing is pigshit* is fun in 101. Oxymoron is an excellent pedagogical pivot but sooner or later the see-saw dips. What David Lloyd calls "the unexpungeable melancholy of the pedagogical scene" (263) describes the constitutive exemplarity of pedagogy whereby subject matter and teacher are inexorably bound to fall short and be shed by the student, who is primed to outstrip both.

The subject, in some sense, must necessarily be smaller than the student. Making an example of the avant-garde requires great sophistication, or crudity. Cutting the avant-garde down to size to fit Tuesdays and Thursdays, for example, may not yield the controlled explosion or distributed tremors a teacher desires. David Lloyd concludes:

> What this meshing of the aesthetic and the political within the field of pedagogy implies is that any sustained attempt to rethink the nature and function of cultural education from a radical perspective must entail a simultaneous critique of the political culture of representation. In the absence of such a critique, radical pedagogy will continue to reproduce, at the "microscopic" level of its implicit practices, the processes of

116

ideological interpellation that its explicit tendency seeks to disrupt.[1]

As a teacher, I am a handler of avant-garde traditions. I don powerful avant-garde gloves to manipulate explosive avant-garde materials. I work to learn more. Every year brings increments. I build an avant-garde nest-egg.

As a poet, I am a little bit avant-garde. I have avant-garde stones in my pocket which I finger from time to time. But I'm not likely to be part of the advance party of anything. I don't even like parties. In a war situation I'd probably hide.

Can an Irish poet be avant-garde? Perhaps—if s/he emigrates.

I'm too post-colonial to be avant-garde. I know a little bit about the avant-garde. I myself am slightly avant-garde. Susceptible to avant-gardism. I let down my avant-garde. I enjoy one glass of wine a night & am moderately avant-garde.

Can a mother be avant-garde? Show me examples.

Under the starry sky, I think about my fellow poets in Providence. Wendy Walters over there on Lindy. Can a 21st century artist be avant-garde? Can an African-American be avant-garde? Mike Magee in Cumberland. Can a man with a big house be avant-garde? Mike Gizzi. Brian Kim Stefans. Brian is quite avant-garde, for a traditionalist. Robert Creeley is avant-garde. He has gone ahead of us all.

I go in for my binoculars. Back out on the porch, I train them on the grassy plain beyond the city walls where Ron Silliman's 160-strong standing army of North American poets on active avant-garde service is encamped.[2] I see their fires, way back

---

[1] David Lloyd, "Kant's Examples," *Unruly Examples: On the Rhetoric of Example*, ed. Alexander Gelley (Stanford: Stanford University Press, 1995) 276.

[2] In "The Practice of Art," the afterword to Dennis Barone and Peter Ganick's *The Art of Practice: Forty-Five American Poets* (Potes & Poets Press, 1994)—although it may appear to the preface to *In the American Tree* (National Poetry Foundation, 1985), Silliman observes "That more than 160 North American poets are actively and usefully involved in the avant-garde tradition of writing is in itself a stunning thought" (377).

there in 1994, ringing the city. I am a little bit bourgeois too, a necessary condition for avant-gardism.[3] I have a porch. I have binoculars.[4]

I wonder about the condition of the avant-garde army's camping gear; and feel slightly oppressed.

***

Not long ago I was wading manfully through Jed Rasula's *Syncopations* while lying in bed when suddenly I got stopped in my tracks:

> The canon, like any bureaucratically administered organisation, takes its directives from licensed operators. The formal and legal requirements for operating canonical mechanisms are analogous to those for obtaining an aviator's license. Next time you read Ashbery, listen for the sonic traces of disconnection and detachment ...[5]

Whoa! Did Jed Rasula just say you??? "Next time *you* read Ashbery ..." I do a quick spot check. Look to my right. Look to my left. There's no-one else here except my 8-year old daughter Clio and my cat Vincent. Jed Rasula is talking to *me*. Jed Rasula assumes he has an audience. Jed Rasula is confident in his audience (he doesn't know it is me). Jed Rasula is *chummy*: "Next time you read *Ashbery* ..." Not John Ashbery. Or the poet John Ashbery. Just Ashbery. I go straight downstairs to my library where the poetry books are alphabetically arranged,

3 See Paul Mann's *The Theory Death of the Avant-Garde* (Bloomington and Indianapolis: Indiana University Press, 1991) 81: "The avant-garde was launched by the bourgeoisie and is locked into a decaying orbit around it; it was born with the bourgeoisie because the bourgeoisie had to externalize its opposition in order to better contain it."

4 I don't actually have binoculars.

5 Jed Rasula, *Syncopations: The Stress of Innovation in Contemporary Poetry* (Tuscaloosa: University of Alabama Press, 2004) 159.

more or less, and pluck Ashbery off the shelf. *Next time you read Ashbery.* I'm doing it, Jed!

Ron Silliman is stunned by the thought of the 160 North American poets "actively and usefully involved in the avant-garde tradition."[6] I'm stunned by Jed Rasula's assumption of audience. And who's to say he doesn't mean that *you* in the plural? I check the book's due date. See—it's also been taken out (from Brown University's Rockefeller Library) by someone else, five months ago.

In my bedroom, Jed and I lie in easy confab chewing the fat about Ashbery. It is 6.30pm on Sunday the 29th of January 2006. My cat Vincent is plumped at my feet and my daughter Clio is on the floor beside me, building a Dutch-roofed hotel for dolls out of a large cardboard box. Ashbery is there too. Every now and then I dip in to listen for the sonic traces of disconnection and detachment Jed mentioned.

I want to tell him, "I'm not too sure what you mean about the sonic traces, Jed." "I am full of pride," my daughter says, beaming over her house: "Now that is what I call a *roof*." I want to say: "Would you look at that, Jed," and laugh companionably. But I'm not sure Jed Rasula means me in that *you* after all. He may have me mixed up with someone else.

I wrote a poem:

JED RASULA
So Jed Rasula dropped by & he was rapping about his Auntie Meggie who was a musher in the Iditarod I don't know how many times & actually took the Red Lantern in '95 after a whole saga of attempts to cross the Burled Arch of Nome. First try was in '78 & she scratched in Rohn. I mean she had barely left Wasilla. Okay she was a Rookie. Next time was '79, it would've been the southern trail but she scratched in Ophir citing a sick team and her leader did die. A double intussusception Jed said. In '80 she made it to Cripple. That was a northern year. 497

6   Ron Silliman, "The Practice of Art," *The Art of Practice: Forty-Five American Poets,* eds. Dennis Barone and Peter Ganick (Connecticut, Potes & Poets Press, 1994) 377.

miles to Nome. Closing in. She had knee surgery in '82, something brewing since '79 Jed said, so she didn't get back on the trail till '85 when she scratched in Anvik. In '89—I guess maybe she had to have surgery on the other knee—she scratched in Grayling, citing a soft trail. 429 miles to go so she shaved 68 miles off her best to date. That was a southern year. Then finally—this is the killer—in '92 she scratches in Unalakleet citing a sore thumb. Only Shaktoolik, Koyuk, Elim, Golovin, White Mountain, and Safety to go, 229 miles Jed said. But she never gave up. It was incredible Jed said. She should've got the Most Improved Musher Award. But she got the Red Lantern in '95. No gold. Just a plaque. For stick-to-itiveness. 17 days 6 hours 2 minutes & 5 seconds it took her, Jed said. In the Iditarod you know there's a lot of money at stake. In XXXIII the top 30 shared $705,000, with Robert Sorlie alone taking $72,067. There were 7 females, with Jessie Royer, DeeDee Jonrowe & Aliy Zirkle in 9th, 10th, and 11th place, Jessica Hendricks 15th, Melanie Gould 23rd, Diana Moroney 27th and Harmony Barron 29th. By the time you get to 29th you're talking only $2,193. But Jessie Royer got $35,511 and DeeDee walked away with $29,244. DeeDee finished in 9 days 8 hours 49 minutes & 42 seconds in '98. And 9 days 11 hours 24 minutes and 7 seconds in '95. That's fast. Sorlie's not that fast. Auntie Meggie was a sport, Jed said. It wasn't about the money. But she had a dog that later won the Lolly Medley Golden Harness Award. That's like the Yale Younger for dogs. We were enthralled listening. Jed said Meggie's achievement was remarkable, exemplary, significant, instructive, and singular, while not without precedent. Where is she now we all wondered. Dead Jed said.

Despite the assured *you*, the Rasula of *Syncopations* is usually sceptical about audience, to a tortuous extent. Ragtime it ain't:

A real wild card now is the audience. For one thing, audience is no longer identical to readership. The boost in orality provided by the growth in poetry slams has certainly had some spillover effect, creating new readers, but American culture is being drained of literacy skills at a considerable pace. Curiously, this may result in a growing audience for published poetry as the very act of reading becomes more archaic, specialised, attaining a certain antiquarian glamour. There will be increased urgency on the part of readers to identify themselves to one another ...[7]

The poetry audience has exploded with Slam but let's not look at that. Instead let's look at this little secret society of book-lovers which may or may not emerge in reaction to Slam. I mean, what is this??? Who cares about the glamorous antiquarians! Slam poets already publish books and CDs, for which there is a committed audience. Surely that's a viable focus of interest?

Slam doesn't fit Rasula's definition of poetry:

> Poetry [Slam?] is fundamentally esoteric, in several senses: it [Slam?] is socially insignificant (although, as symbolic capital, poetry [Slam?] must exist the way gold bars exist in Fort Knox, in a precarious affiliation with currency standards) and therefore represents an uncommon or esoteric enterprise; but it [Slam?] has a long tradition of obscurity and obscurantism, and its [Slam's?] legendary affiliations with the muse tradition suggest than poetry [Slam?] is esoteric with respect to mind or psyche as such.[8]

And Rasula's definition of poetry doesn't fit my experience:

> As esoterica, poetry's value is at once inscrutable and beside the point. As public enterprise, on the other hand, poetry is now caught in a conspicuously widening culture gap (or series of gaps). Insofar as it is deeply invested in literacy and in the knowledge criteria of literate culture, poetry is bound to seem antiquated, esoteric, scholastic, and casually intimidating even when it purports a more populist orientation. As an active component in oral culture, poetry is periodically rekindled into prominence, even if only at the level of affective immediacy. There is a third zone, an interface between orality and literacy, that is more emphatically visual in the venues of electronic media. There is obvious potential here for the inauguration of

[7] Rasula, *Syncopations*, 32.
[8] Rasula, *Syncopations*, 36.

new poetic enterprise, one in which poetry might conceivably rival film. Not a serious rival, maybe, since poetry's investment in the word will limit its semiotic appeal in the long run.[9]

Perhaps Rasula is right. His insights, as Bruce Andrews says on the back cover of the book, are penetrating and unique. Maybe poetry is esoteric. Yet it is a boldness for me; it is how I connect to people of all ages, at every level of society accessible to me. And right now, Jed's talking to me.

***

Can a woman be avant-garde?

***

Can a woman be avant-garde? Hell, yes. The term may be a bit military. But women serve in the armed forces now. It may be a bit French. But plenty of women are French. Even among Ron Silliman's standing army of 160-plus North American poets "actively and usefully involved in the avant-garde tradition of writing" (377), there are many women, camped out there in 1994. To borrow a strategy from Silliman, you (yes!) have:

> Lorine Niedecker. Barbara Guest. Kathleen Fraser. Bernadette Mayer. Rosmarie Waldrop. Nicole Brossard. Anne Waldman. Hannah Weiner. Fanny Howe. Lyn Hejinian. Ann Lauterbach. Alice Notley. Maureen Owen. Beverly Dahlen. Mei-Mei Berssenbrugge. Abigail Child. Rae Armantrout. Kathy Acker. Susan Howe. Johanna Drucker. Lynne Dreyer. Leslie Scalapino. Laura Moriarty. Rachel Blau DuPlessis. Patricia Dienstfry. Theresa Hak Kyung Cha. Tina Darragh. Carla Harryman. Marjorie Welish. Joan Retallack. Fiona Templeton. Cole Swenson. Eileen Myles. Erin Moure. Diane Ward. Jean Day. Karen McCormack. Gail Scott. Harryette Mullen. Erica Hunt. Julie Patton. Norma Cole. Mary-Margaret Sloan. Dodie

[9] Rasula, *Syncopations*, 36-7.

Bellamy. Jessica Grim.[10] Eileen Agar. Claude Cahun. Leonora Carrington. Suzanne Césaire. Lise Deharme. Marcelle Ferry. Léonor Fini. Valentine Hugo. Frida Kahlo. Nelly Kaplan. Mariam van Hirtum. Jacqueline Lamba. Mary Low. Dora Maar. Lee Miller. Nora Mitrani. Joyce Mansour. Meret Oppenheim, Mimi Parent. Valentine Penrose. Kay Sage. Toyen. Remedios Varo. Unica Zürn. Bonna. Emmy Bridgwater. Hannah Höch. Annie Lebrun. Gisèle Prassinos. Alice Rahon. Edith Rimmington. Dorothea Tanning.[11] Jen Bervin. Gwendolyn Brooks. Erica Carpenter. Brenda Coultas. Alison Croggon. Toi Derricotte. Kristen Kaschock. Amy King. Rachel Loden. Sheila E. Murphy. Nourbese Philip. Sina Queyras. Adrienne Rich. Lisa Robertson. Kim Rosenfield. Muriel Rukeyser. Rebecca Seiferle. Ntozake Shange. Juliana Spahr. Jane Sprague. Gertrude Stein. Stephanie Strickland. May Swenson. Stacy Szymaszek. Catherine Walsh. Susan Wheeler. Harriet Zinnes.[12]

That is some block of tofu. Pure protein. And there's plenty more in the deli that came from.

Kenneth Goldsmith has a very good answer to the question: What's the difference between poetry and visual art? This question comes up frequently in Visual Poetry. If it works within the economy of poetry, it's poetry, Kenny says. If it works within the economy of visual art, it's visual art. This formula can also be applied to the question *What is poetry*? Or *What is the avant-garde*? If it is editorially—or self-identified—as avant-garde, it's avant-garde.

Women are quintessentially avant-garde. They are forever bursting their own boundaries, producing, from their own bodies, perfect forms for manipulating the future. I'd go as far as to say that in order to be quintessentially avant-garde one

[10] *Moving Borders: Three Decades of Iinnovative Writing by Women*, ed. Mary Margaret Sloan (Jersey City, N.J.: Talisman House, 1998).

[11] Martine Antle, "Women of the Avant-Garde 1925-1985," graduate course, Romance Languages and Literatures Department, University of North Carolina at Chapel Hill. http://www.unc.edu/courses/fren330/

[12] From my own bookshelves. Ihave no idea if these women are avant-garde. I scooped them into my big tin basin but it immediately sprang leaks.

must be a woman (quintessence and economy are not the same thing, of course). When women poets and artists are defined by the relevant economies of time, space, nationality, language, art form, genre, etc., as avant-garde, they become doubly avant-garde (just as artist-mothers are double-bearing). They are avant-avant garde.

While it is definitely possible for a man to be avant-garde, in any one or more of the many definitions and interpretations of the term, according to the respective economies involved, it is impossible for a man to be avant-avant garde. I am reminded of an Irish artist I once knew intimately who, when it snowed or rained hard, and we were walking, put me out in front of him so he could find shelter. That is often the position of women, artists or otherwise, in relation to the avant-garde.

I asked Jane Sprague if she believed in the existence of the avant-garde. She said yes. Later, speaking about community, she said that she had revised her concept of community and understood it now more in terms of a network. At some level, I still see the avant-garde as a phalanx of Roman soldiers moving crab-like through the dark. But it could be a constellation. It could be a web. It could be an Olympic torch passed from generation to generation, between cultures, much as Irish painter Michael Mulcahy, in the 1980s and 1990s, with his own sword and bata fada,[13] travelled the roads of Connemara, the streets of Dublin, and the bóithríns[14] of Inis Oirr, in some sort of sympathy with Artaud.[15]

---

[13] Long stick; also penis.
[14] Little roads.
[15] In 1937, Artaud journeyed to Ireland with his Cuban sword and "St. Patrick's" walking stick, which he wanted to return to the Irish. He spent much of his time isolated in hotels and guest-houses in Galway, Inis Mór, and Dublin where— out on the streets—he was beaten up. He could find no resting place for the stick, which he then lost, before being deported and institutionalized. See Stephen Barber, *Antonin Artaud: Blows and Bombs* (London and Boston: Faber & Faber, 1993) 73-96. St. Patrick was not, in any case, Irish but was brought to Ireland as a captured slave, probably from Wales.

As with madness, when one participates in the economy of the avant-garde, institutions emerge.

***

In a *Voices & Visions* video documentary on Langston Hughes, George Houston Bass identifies Hughes's commitment as follows:

> There are two important traditions out of middle-class Black America. There is the bourgeois tradition of narcissism and escapism. And there is the service tradition. Hughes comes out of the service tradition.[16]

I too identify with the service tradition, which seems to me today to have a clarity and urgency which the avant-garde tradition does not.

***

In 1843, Daniel O'Connell, leader of the Repeal Association for the Repeal of the Act of Union (1801) which dissolved the separate Irish Parliament, called for a series of mass meetings to demonstrate the strength of popular support. Here is what O'Connell ordered:

> I want a Repeal meeting either at Clonmel or Cashel or Thurles. I want to see from 60,000 to 100,000 Tipperary boys meeting peacefully and returning home quietly, to adopt the petition [in favour of Repeal] and to organise the Repeal rent.[17]

---

16 *Voices and Visions: Langston Hughes.* South Carolina Educational Television; Annenberg/CPB Project (New York: New York Centre for Visual History, c. 1988).

17 Oliver McDonagh, *The Emancipist: Daniel O'Connell 1830-1847* (New York: St. Martin's Press, 1989) 227.

What O'Connell got was more than 40 monster meetings held at the rate of two a week for seven months, blanketing the country and attracting audiences each of which represented a sizable proportion of the entire country. Seven meetings in May attracted crowds of 300,000 each. Attendances of half-a-million people were regularly reported in the summer months.[18] The lowest estimate of attendance at the August 15th meeting at Tara is 800,000. The population of Ireland at that time being just over 8 million, [19] it is probably safe to say that the vast majority of those 8 million people attended a monster meeting between March and September 1843, probably many times over. Now that's a crowd. And they got a show: "It was a giant's theatre, and virtually a year long play."[20]

O'Connell spoke at 31 of the meetings, "Walled by wide air and roofed by boundless heaven," as Bulwer Lytton writes, going on to describe the trajectory and impact of O'Connell's voice:

> It glided easy as a bird may glide.
> To the last verge of that vast audience sent,
> It played with each wild passion as it went:
> Now stirred the uproar, now the murmurs stilled,
> And sobs or laughter answered as it willed.
> Then did I know what spell of infinite choice
> To rouse or lull has the sweet human voice.[21]

O'Connell was a great orator and his subject was a matter of life-and-death to his audience who "shouted, groaned, laughed, scorned or exulted, according to their cues."[22] Two years later, another great orator, Frederick Douglass, visiting Ireland,

[18] McDonagh, *The Emancipist*, 234.

[19] The 1841 Census of Ireland recorded the population as 8,175,124. By 1851, as a result of the Famine, the population had declined to 6,553, 574. In 1861, the figure was 5,798,564, and the decline continued into the 20th century.

[20] McDonagh, *The Emancipist*, 229.

[21] Cited in McDonagh, *The Emancipist*, 229.

[22] McDonagh, *The Emancipist*, 230.

addressed approximately 40 meetings ranging in size from 100 to 5,000[23]—much smaller crowds than O'Connell's but still large, by poetry standards. Douglass's subject was slavery. Although his audiences of middle-class Protestants and Quakers had a moral rather than a mortal interest, they too were passionately involved as contemporary newspaper reports, parenthetically recording their *Great shouts of ha-ha, Loud cheering, Great cheering, Loud laughter and cheering, Tremendous cheers, Great applause, hear hears* and *oh ohs*, attest.

Poetry audiences, by contrast, seem remarkably dead. It may be a mistake to associate this deadness with civility. The audience may just be dead. And the responsibility is obviously the poets' as, somewhat uniquely, the poetry audience is composed principally of practitioners of the art, and their families, poetry readings being much like karate tournaments in that respect. Except that karate tournaments are big.

The numbers are not good in poetry. In an interview in *Contemporary Literature*, Paul Muldoon said:

> I think in the overall shape of things, there's a problem with poetry and its place in the world. A few people read it. Maybe only a few people have ever read it. Not many people were reading John Donne. Five hundred people made Byron famous overnight. Tennyson was selling thousands of copies of books, but so was Rod McKuen.[24]

There's also my own epic poem on the subject:

POETRY
The perfect art form for those who dislike crowds.

23 Mairéad Byrne, "The Lion & The Tiger: Frederick Douglass in Ireland, 1845-1846," *The Freedom Talks: Reflections from Rhode Island Scholars* (Providence: Rhode Island Council for the Humanities, 2004) 32.
24 Paul Muldoon, Interviewed by Lynn Keller, *Contemporary Literature* 35. 1 (Spring 1994): 28.

If things are bad with poetry, they're abysmal with the avant-garde, the pre-requisite and defining feature of which seems to be the ability to shrink an audience. Alan Lareau, in his study of literary cabarets of the Weimar Republic, in various ways identifies "intimacy and coziness"[25] as the natural habitat for *Kleinkunst*, or small art. Schall und Rauch, which could accommodate 1,100 people in its "gigantic tunnel"[26] failed ultimately because, whatever the excuses, the performers weren't good enough for an audience this size. Trude Hesterberg's Wilde Bühne had more success in "[finding] a modern, relevant voice for the stage and [developing] a contemporary art form," partly because "whereas Schall und Rauch had held an impossible 1,100 viewers, Hesterberg's locale seated just 127 in armchairs at tables."[27] Nevertheless, the Wilde Bühne lasted only three years, vanquished by inflation.

The account of the shooting star of the earlier Cabaret Voltaire, founded in Zurich by Hugo Ball and Emmy Hennings, which opened on 5 February 1916 and closed in July, is also salutary:

> At first the performances offered traditional, though sophisticated, literary cabaret fare of poetry, chansons, and classical music. The group's international composition, their growing interest in modern music, and the readings of their own unpublished works were refreshing contributions to the cabaret tradition. But not until later did the cabaret begin to be truly experimental; the term Dada does not surface in Ball's diaries until two and a half months after the cabaret's opening (here as a name for a journal, not for an artistic movement). In time the presentations became more innovative, as Ball realised that conventional poetry was generally ineffective in live performance. The group began to explore futurist and cubist ideas, including phonetic and simultaneous poetry, but just as

---

[25] Alan Lareau, *The Wild Stage: Literary Cabarets of the Weimar Republic* (Columbia, SC: Camden House, 1995) 12.

[26] Lareau, *The Wild Stage*, 24.

[27] Lareau, *The Wild Stage*, 70.

the radical experimentation began, the cabaret closed. Dada art, however, subsequently blossomed in various gallery soirees in a more exclusive but also more radical style.[28]

So do we need a different way of counting, as Paul Mann suggests, quoting Charles Bernstein?

As a poet, you affect the public sphere with each reader, with the fact of the poem, and by exercising your prerogative to choose what collective forms you will legitimate. The political power of poetry is not measured in numbers; it instructs us to count differently.[29]

I understand what is being said here but would argue strongly in favour of retaining the conventional method of counting:

There were six people in the audience; three of them left after the first reader; they were her family. So it was just Jimmy and me. Afterwards we went for ice-cream.[30]

The regulatory language in the Bernstein quotation is a law unto itself. I can think of things I'd sooner do than exercise my "prerogative to choose what collective forms [I] will legitimate." My Muse says *Write this—now*; that's pretty much the only instruction I get. It's not esoteric. Anyway, I want to be able to count in the old way: assets, pulses, the number of thousands at Akhmatova's funeral, the clothes on the Emperor.

In what sense does the *Wikipedia* definition work?

The *vanguard*, a small troop of highly skilled *soldiers*, explores the *terrain* ahead of a large advancing army and plots a course for the army to follow. This concept is applied to the work done by small bands of *intellectuals* and *artists* as they open pathways through new cultural or political terrain for society to follow.

---

28 Lareau, *The Wild Stage*, 12.
29 Cited in Paul Mann, "A Poetics of Its Own Occasion," *Contemporary Literature* 35 (1994): 242.
30 Interview with self.

Can a radical artist, like Langston Hughes, who deals in large numbers, be avant-garde?

Is Duke Ellington, who said *the people are my people* and who made it all happen on a very large scale for a very long time, avant-garde? Bebop is bebop and Duke Ellington is Duke Ellington. Can the avant-garde be also a magnificent enterprise, bound not only in bonds of intimacy, friendship, marriage and sexual relationship, to the development of an art-form but also in bonds of service to the development of an audience?

Jed Rasula says no, that: "Apart from the Black Arts Movement, the avant-garde has rarely been linked to populism, even when (as in the case of Dada) it's been resolutely anti-elitist."[31] On the other hand, he describes the artist class in America as being essentially enervated, and redundant:

> that segment of the population traditionally prepared for administrative and leadership roles in the dissemination of ideas and values, the liberal humanists, find themselves masters of a forum that no longer exists (or has been exiled to the storage room in a museum). Those of us trained in the legacy of philosophical counterpoint and rhetorical ingenuity, whose sensibilities have been indexed by education to an itinerary of salient cultural moments (in art, architecture, music, literature), have literally no one to talk to but ourselves.[32]

Matinée audiences in Dublin (or *mattinny* as we called them), at one time, and maybe still, shouted up at the hero on the screen, or the pantomime dame, when danger threatened: *Look behind you!* I want to shout *Look behind you* too. Not from a *post* to an *avant* which is no different to the *garde*,[33] or which is the

31 Rasula, *Syncopations*, 181.
32 Rasula, *Syncopations*, 188-9n6.
33 My argument in "Wildflowers for Ted and Steve," http://maireadbyrne. blogspot.com/2006/02/wildflowers-for-ted-steve-speaker.html, a conciliatory bouquet offered to Ted Kooser and Steve Evans, on the occasion of the latter's borrowing of the former's language in "Free (Market) Verse," serialized in three online instalments during the week of 30 January 2006, http://www. thirdfactory.net/freemarketverse.html.

"outside of the inside, the leading edge of the mainstream," as Paul Mann says (*Theory Death* 13). Nor from parts unknown to the *post* which is itself the anxiety-dream of the avant-garde, one in which enough life-insurance has finally been bought. But *Look behind you Professor! Look behind you masters of rhetorical counterpoint and philosophical ingenuity!* There is a very large country at your disposal, one infinitely large, in fact, without borders, though not without connection to the avant-garde. It is the country of poverty, where our assets are infinitely useful, infinitely applicable.

***

My front line is the intersection of Academy and Chalkstone on the west side of Providence, where I live. My zone of comfort is a seam. There are many *they*s. There are the *they*s up ahead on whom our eyes are fixed. The *they* who organise everything. The *they* of Big Brother. The numbskulls who pull the levers in our heads. The *they* in relation to whom we feel powerless. But, if we have not removed ourselves, we are surrounded by *they*s even more powerless. Who do not enjoy the privileges of education, status, mobility, income, publication opportunity, telecommunications, and office space which we[34] consider inadequate.

> The *vanguard*, a small troop of highly skilled soldiers, explores the *terrain* behind a large advancing army and plots a course for escapees to follow. This concept is applied to the work done by small bands of intellectuals and artists as they *open pathways* through new cultural or political terrain for *as many people as possible*.

My avant-garde are the children on the school bus, who lead me out, and for whom I lay down what I've got:

---

34 I want a new we.

THE AVANT-GARDE

Every morning I smile enough to break my face
up at the children in the grimy windows of the school bus.
I bust a gut to make them break into a smile.
I wave. I jump down & up. I mouth
have a nice day & when
the bus stops at the lights I run
to catch it up & jump
up & down & wave & grin
enough to break my face & crack
theirs open one more time.

Coda

But then, while Kenny Goldsmith lives, can the avant-garde
ever die?

Ann Vickery

From Being Drafted to a Draft of Being: Rachel Blau DuPlessis and the Reconceptualisation of the Feminist Avant-Garde

The avant-garde is a movement that seeks to break with the past, to articulate its dissent in the face of the current social order and, as Ezra Pound so famously put it, "Make it New." It would seem to fit hand in glove with the poetics of feminism that also characterises itself as subversion or resistance, and which seeks to engender social change. Both have had militant overtones in their manifestoes and in their struggles against an identified enemy. Yet the avant-garde and feminism have had a troubled history and been far from good comrades. To add fuel to the fire, both are coming increasingly under attack as critical formulations. Jed Rasula, for example, argues "The term 'avant-garde' should be retired,"[1] while Paul Mann views the avant-garde as complicit in the very forces it seeks to oppose, indeed, that it has been vital to a neutralising culture industry."[2] Linda Alcoff notes that following post-structuralism, "feminists

---

[1] Jed Rasula, *Syncopations: The Stress of Innovation in Contemporary American Poetry* (Tuscaloosa: University of Alabama Press, 2004) 194.
[2] Paul Mann, *The Theory-Death of the Avant-Garde* (Bloomington: Indiana University Press, 1991) 78-79; 92.

cannot demarcate a definitive category of 'woman' without eliminating all possibility for the defeat of logocentrism and its oppressive power." Accordingly, an effective feminism can only be "a wholly negative feminism, deconstructing everything and refusing to construct anything."[3] In a further step, postfeminism would have gender identity as something simply to be transcended rather than critiqued. Alternatively, avant-garde poetry has been condemned for too quickly jettisoning the humanist subject, Romana Huk contending that the subject is "too often pre-emptively dismantled or deconstructed as being from the get-go a shifting, pronominal illusion that vanishes into the larger cultural text."[4] This essay investigates the implications of this "bad history" and considers how a re-conceptualisation of the avant-garde might open up possibilities for a feminist aesthetics, and potentially recuperate both for today's critical usage. I will illuminate such an undertaking through a brief overview of Rachel Blau DuPlessis's career, as a writer who has sought to bring together the concerns of the women's movement with a highly experimental aesthetics.

In the 1970s, second-wave feminists turned specifically to literature as a political tool through which to articulate female experiences previously marginalised as private, trivial, or taboo. Kim Whitehead notes that the women's movement (occurring between 1972 and 1982) privileged poetry as a transparent autobiographical mode in which language could be stripped and made accessible to ordinary women. In this respect, there was an emphasis on newness of *content* rather than newness of *form*. Whitehead adds that a feminist poet called on a sense of an "ongoing, surviving self" where "through the lyrical 'I'—she understands the necessity of self-assertion to survival, and the necessity for some sense of

---

3 Linda Alcoff, "Cultural Feminism versus Poststructuralism: The Identity Crisis in Feminist Theory," *Signs* 13.3 (1988): 417-18.
4 Romana Huk, "In AnOther's Pocket: The Address of the 'Pocket Epic' in Postmodern Black British Poetry," *Yale Journal of Criticism* 13.1 (Spring 2000): 26.

subjectivity that withstands the storms of division and marginalisation." The poem was an instrument then, in which the feminist poet developed a distinctly "feminist combination of *subjective* and *collective* voice in poetry."[5] In *Naked and Fiery Forms: Modern American Poetry by Women: A New Tradition*, Suzanne Juhasz defined feminist poetry as:

> A poetry whose poet speaks as a woman, so that the form of her poem is an extension of herself ... A poetry that seeks to affect actively its audience ... A poetry that is revolutionary because by expressing the vision of real women it challenges the patriarchal premises of society itself.[6]

As DuPlessis notes, such poetry encourages a reading of confluence between the subjectivity of the enounced and that of the enunciation, as the poem's speaker. The "I" of the poem seems depict the poet, generating a humanist illusion of totality and presence. She adds: "There is an illusion of sincerity, authenticity, and expressive presence created by the poem."[7]

A further ingredient was a sense of moral urgency to such poetry. To understand this urgency it is worth noting that Erica Jong, a fellow classmate of DuPlessis's at Barnard in the 1960s, recalls a creative writing class in which the male teacher and his male guest insisted that "women can't really write."[8] However, the feminist movement's reliance on the lyrical "I" was problematic for DuPlessis in being grounded on gendered foundations that cast women in the role of beautiful and silent muses. She notes that she did not want "the perfection of lyric,

5   Kim Whitehead, *The Feminist Poetry Movement* (Jackson: University Press of Mississippi, 1996) xix.
6   Suzanne Juhasz, *Naked and Fiery Forms: Modern American Poetry by Women, a New Tradition* (New York: Harper & Row, 1976) 205.
7   Rachel Blau DuPlessis, "Marble Paper: Toward a Feminist 'History of Poetry,'" *Modern Language Quarterly* 65.1 (March 2004): 103.
8   Rachel Blau DuPlessis, "Reader, I Married Me: A Polygamous Memoir," *Changing Subjects: the Making of Feminist Literary Criticism*, ed. Gayle Greene and Coppelia Kahn (New York: Routledge, 1993) 99; cited subsequently in-text as "Reader."

the separation of lyric, the selectivity of lyric, the purity of lyric."[9] Yet there seemed no alternative, no way to move into "a real poetic career": "I'd now say … that the positions available for me to take up as a woman writer—inside language and inside the mechanisms of poetry, and outside its various apparatuses and institutions of culture—were unsatisfactory to me."[10] Through the newly published British edition of William Carlos Williams's *Paterson*, she began to see how representation of "experience," at least, might be complicated and radicalised. Attracted to their "extensive, encyclopaedic, all-over experience," she would focus on *Paterson* and Ezra Pound's *Pisan Cantos* for her 1970 dissertation. These modernist writers were more institutionally acceptable than Emily Dickinson or Virginia Woolf (DuPlessis notes that studying their work would in the mid-60s have been considered a gesture of professional suicide) but de-politicised through the teachings of New Criticism. She also became part of a small uptown poetry group interested in surrealism, dada, and prose poetry and began subscribing to forums of innovative writing like the journal *Caterpillar*. Of course, movements like surrealism tended to see women as mediums than producers. And while attracted to the abstractions of New York School, its poets were still largely reacting to the heroics expounded by "core" male artists like Pollock and de Kooning.

Increasingly DuPlessis felt herself polarised between woman and artist and, one might add, between revolutionary and public intellectual ("Reader," 99). In *A Theory of the Avant-Garde*, Peter Bürger argues that avant-gardism is not purely aesthetic in orientation but also attacks the institution of art.[11] DuPlessis's

[9] Rachel Blau DuPlessis, "On Drafts: A Memorandum of Understanding," *Onward: Contemporary Poetry and Poetics* (New York: Peter Lang, 1996) 145; cited subsequently in-text as *OD*.

[10] Rachel Blau DuPlessis, "Haibun: 'Draw your/Draft,'" *H.D. and Poets After*, ed. Donna Krolik Hollenberg (Iowa City: University of Iowa Press, 2000) 114-15; subsequently "Haibun."

[11] Peter Bürger, *The Theory of the Avant-Garde*, trans. Michael Shaw (Minneapolis: University of Minnesota Press, 1984).

battles as a poet-critic (who undermines the distinctions between writer and interpreter) have been highly tactical. As Toril Moi has demonstrated in her study of Simone de Beauvoir, the effective voice of dissidence also requires a certain submission in order to accumulate enough cultural capital to speak out and be heard. If the woman avant-gardist does not first play the movement's muse, then she does time as the dutiful daughter. To some degree, the latter also holds true for the feminist. Both feminist and avant-gardist must undertake a careful balancing act between institutional recognition and inciting change. DuPlessis became one of the first three women preceptors in the English Department at Columbia, joined the just-formed Columbia Women's Liberation movement in the late 60s, and in 1974 became an editorial board member of the nascent academic journal, *Feminist Studies*. Her activist profile and the radical essay form she used in "For the Etruscans" (1979) and "Family, Sexes, Psyche" (1979) were not received well by all sectors of the academy.[12] Although she was already well-known as a feminist critic, DuPlessis was granted tenure at Temple but not promoted from Assistant Professor, "something definitely intended as an insult".[13] She would be promoted soon after the publication of *H.D.: The Career of That Struggle* (1986) which quickly followed *Writing Beyond the Ending* (1985).[14] Both volumes had standard modes of argument and tone and took up the *telling* of innovation rather than its *doing*. Perhaps due to academic pressures, DuPlessis's criticism has continued to take

---

[12] *Feminist Studies* sought to combine academic and political objectives. DuPlessis would be co-author of a statement of purpose for *Feminist Studies* which stated: "feminism has the potential fundamentally to reshape the way we view the world. We wish not just to interpret women's experience but to change women's condition. For us, feminist thought represents a transformation of consciousness, social forms, and modes of action." Cited by DuPlessis in "Reader, I Married Me," 104.

[13] Rachel Blau DuPlessis, e-mail to the author, 2 June 2006.

[14] Rachel Blau DuPlessis, *H.D.: The Career of That Struggle* (Bloomington: Indiana University Press, 1986); *Writing Beyond the Ending: Narrative Strategies of Twentieth-Century Women Writers* (Bloomington: Indiana University Press, 1985).

two divergent paths, some of it creatively crossing genres while other parts embody the more traditional form for scholarly work.

How a feminist politics and avant-garde aesthetic might be brought together would only begin to be apparent when she met Objectivist poet George Oppen. In 1965, she sent him a paper on *Paterson* and they began to correspond. In Oppen, DuPlessis found a mentor, not so much a father figure but rather, as Oppen himself put it, an *"oncle."*[15] While she was still resisting the implications of being a woman poet, she notes that "from the earliest moments of our conversation, we seem to have talked about male and female, that is about gender in poetry" (*LRBD* 120). Moreover, they shared a post-Holocaust identity. DuPlessis notes that "the struggles around social justice, tolerance, and especially feminism were brightened for me, by a light, an aura from Judaism." Like her father, Jewish identity would be "a thick burden from the past" although she was brought up as "an explicit secular humanist in the Ethical Culture movement."[16] Oppen suggested to her that the poet must strive for "Pure vividness in poetry, pure confrontation—." Furthermore, writers cannot construct a social ethic "unless we know, finally, what we want."[17] For Oppen, an image is encountered, not found: "There are things/We live among 'and to see them/Is to know ourselves.'"[18] Or, as he says in a letter to DuPlessis, "There are certain things, appearances, around which the understanding gathers. They hold the meanings

---

[15] George Oppen, "Letters to Rachel Blau DuPlessis," ed. Rachel Blau DuPlessis, *Ironwood* 24 (1984): 126; cited subsequently as *LRBD.*

[16] Rachel Blau DuPlessis, "Circumscriptions: Assimilating T.S. Eliot's Sweeneys," *People of the Book: Thirty Scholars Reflect on their Jewish Identity,* ed. Jeffrey Rubin-Dorsky and Shelley Fisher Fishkin (Madison: University of Wisconsin Press, 1996) 136.

[17] Cited in Rachel Blau DuPlessis, "Objectivist Poetics and Political Vision: A Study of Oppen and Pound," *George Oppen: Man and Poet,* ed. Burton Hatlen (Orono: National Poetry of Foundation, 1981) 134; from a letter by Oppen to DuPlessis, 24 January 1969; cited subsequently as *OP.*

[18] George Oppen, *Collected Poems* (New York: New Directions, 1975) 147; cited subsequently *CP.*

which make it possible to live, they are one's sense of reality and the possibility of meaning."[19] The ground of such a poetics is inclusive and strives towards the numerousness of being. Rather than prescribe an idea or thought, one occupies it. The image becomes known only through this active attention, an ongoing meditation that attempts to read and reread the image in all its possibility. For Oppen poetry "which is of any value is always revelatory. Not that it reveals and could reveal Everything, but it must reveal something ... *and for the first time* ... it is a knowledge which is hard to hold, it is held in the poem, a meaning grasped again on re-reading" [italics added] (*SL* 133). The Objectivist ethos rethinks experience as cumulative and perspectival. Comprehension is achieved not through transparency but through return. In this return of attention, this continuing focus on ordinariness, there is the possibility of discovering the new.

DuPlessis would write of Objectivism that such a poetics begins "with the person, not the word, that is, with sincerity" (*OP* 125). It therefore shares a key principle with second-wave feminism (in the discourses of both feminism and Objectivism, sincerity becomes inter-related with notions of authenticity or truthfulness). However, Peter Nicholls suggests that the Objectivist understanding of sincerity is consonant with Emmanuel Levinas's who argues that the ethical subject is "the risky uncovering of oneself, in sincerity." Nicholls suggests that sincerity for Objectivists, as with Levinas, is not so much directed to inner feeling as bound up with a concept of laying oneself bare or vulnerable to what lies beyond one's borders. Another aspect of Objectivism is the role of affect. Attempting to describe the meditative nowness of his poetics, Oppen wrote, "It can really not be thought about because it contains the thought, but it can be felt. It is what all art is about" (*SL* 90). Affect too is central to feminism in moving a person toward change.

---

[19] George Oppen, *The Selected Letters of George Oppen*, ed. Rachel Blau DuPlessis (Durham: Duke University Press, 1990) 123; cited subsequently *SL*.

DuPlessis's first collection, *Wells*, was published in 1980 but contains poems from across the previous decade or so.[20] Written in 1971, "A Poem of Myself" rejects the idea of unified subjectivity, ending with the line, "Come in, come in, I say to all the fragments." While pared down by Oppen, DuPlessis felt that it showed her "a positive and solid mirror of what I could do." A 1976 poem, "Voyaging," would also be trimmed by Oppen but this time, signalling her growing self-confidence, DuPlessis disagreed with the transformation (although she would still dedicate it to him). DuPlessis was, however, still grappling with the question that Oppen posed: "How to be good. The trap which has engulfed most women poets" (*LRBD* 123). Oppen himself was not adverse to falling into this trap, remarking in a 1969 letter, "You're a nice girl, you know" (*LRBD* 129).[21] DuPlessis's powerful poem, "Memory," focuses on female experience, dramatising a resistance of cyclic return:

My mother stands on the lawn
saying "I have wasted my life"
but never saying that again

[...]

she turned to me;
what ash-tongued
comforting that then tries no

20 Rachel Blau DuPlessis, *Wells* (New York: Montemora Foundation, 1980; http://www.durationpress.com/archives).
21 Oppen's views on women's capacity to write poetry were ambivalent. In "Technologies," he wrote of "feminine profusion" as "inartistic," "inelegant," and "Which cannot grasp/The world/And makes art//Is small." This drew the wrath of Denise Levertov who appropriated his image of the hawk and had it howl back in a poem, "Nothing matters, timor mortis conburbat me." In a conversation with L.S. Dembo, he noted, "There are times one is infinitely grateful for the feminine contribution, and times one just has to fight about it[sic]." He would add, "'What's the use of yelling that? What the use of saying that?' That's what nice women say to us, women as nice as Denise Levertov is, but sometimes one objects." Dembo, "The 'Objectivist' Poet: Four Interviews," *Contemporary Literature* 10.2 (1969): 209.

o no you haven't
(wasted)?

Cleaning "for Thrift," laughing
do you want this,
do you remember
this dress? I don't even remember.
I am living in the dumbness
of time
over.
No recollection
little words o
no o
no.

[…]

The ink is black.
The paper is burning.
Everywhere illegible tissue-thin
Ashes no, no not full ones
no recollection
swirly in the wavy war of heat
like pieces of a one-letter alphabet.

The house grows darker. My first poem
was "Memory."

[…]

Every day
seemed to have nothing
wasted "My life is wasted"
house hill no recollection
grow darker.
A woman
choosing   the choices
that were
and that's really all it was
moment by moment

nothing except the fact
that everyone always
had chosen;
as, to be born.

The reference to "chosen" suggests that certain identities—such as gender and Jewishness—are inescapably thrust upon us and have their own heritage. The last stanza plays with the irony of limited choices, yet the poem itself enacts resistance to the "nothing" or waste that culture has sometimes characterised and accordingly, devalued women's lives. The poem is especially powerful in demonstrating how the mother's summation of her own life, once voiced, places an unbearable burden of guilt on the daughter for being part of that structure of family and domestic responsibility that has consumed her mother's life. The metaphoric reference to "ash" makes parallels between this and the burden post-Holocaust Jews must bear in remembering the "nothingness" and waste of so many lives of the past generation.

"Memory" maps out many of the themes and strategies of DuPlessis's major serial poem *Drafts*. The phrase, "no recollection" is particularly ironic in a poem about memory, suggesting that memory itself is faulty. There is the focus on "little words," broken down even to the grief of "o," the symbolic par excellence of "nothing." This is a poem about female experience but also about the breakdown of voice and the inability to relate words accurately back to experience.

Another poem, "Voice," refuses the feminine role of silence yet acknowledges being fragmented. There is already the play between self-assertion and its undercutting that will occur in *Drafts*:

split now
no longer
whole never again
perfect like a daughter—

The cracked throat
sounding
itself

my voice the
voice that no longer
fears (but does)
(fear) the necessity
to speak.

Besides integrating Oppen's Objectivism into her own poetics,
DuPlessis began constructing a gynocentric tradition of avant-
garde cultural production, looking to both Classical and
modernist writers and artists as non-hegemonic legacy. Later
poems in *Wells* are dedicated to Sappho, Dickinson, Woolf, and
Georgia O'Keefe. She also explored the possibilities of a
mythopoetic tradition which was very much in keeping with
feminist poetry of the era. Such a project re-read and reclaimed
female figures who defied expected roles or laws of the state as
stories that could inspire twentieth-century women.
Accordingly, the female muse in "I dream of women" is cast in
symbiotic relationship with the woman poet: "We cannot make
contact, yet we have created each other." Mirror images of each
other, there is a sense of a democracy that is homosocial in
nature: "We touch our finger tips as equals." Yet precisely
because muse and woman poet are mirror images of one
another, there is no room for difference; the new republic is one
of uniformity. In fitting with the eroticisation of writing, this
democratic revolution is through sexual desire although the
passion is not yet acted upon: "We could kiss each other. It
would be no surprise." The good girl therefore does not break
the heterosexual contract underlying the lyric. There is, as yet,
no orgasmic rupture. DuPlessis also revises the myth of Psyche
into one of androgyny, whereby man gives birth and the
woman has a phallus feminised as the "lace of her foreskin." In
such playful reversal, difference remains within Cartesian
dualisms. In "Eurydice," DuPlessis celebrates the woman who

refuses the Orphic calling and retreats further underground. Oppen himself affirmed such a vision, "maybe there is an underground stream of poetry which will seem, sometime, to have been the river of poetry" (*LRBD* 131). Oppen's adoption of the exile position, his attempt to find leverage out of a marginal place, was greatly appealing to DuPlessis. In this mythic topos, the hidden force of "wells" and "undertow" are given a utopian charge as against their traumatic loadings in the earlier poems which more directly touch on matters of personal and social history.

While poems in *Wells* are still overt, they exhibit an opening of form, beginning to experiment with homophonic play as this excerpt from "Medusa" demonstrates:

> she weaves a woven
> To webble the wobble words.
> A—
> gnomy
> hey nonny nonny

As in *Drafts*, there is also the use of the little word, "A," also used as a prefix to transform the "ignominy" surrounding the myth of Medusa and to slide it more lightly to nursery rhyme and even, semiotic babble. DuPlessis seems to merge the underground practice of the avant-garde with a feminine pre-symbolic.

After writing "Eurydice" in the mid-70s, someone alerted DuPlessis to H.D.'s poem of the same name resulting in what she called "a talismanic moment of connection" ("Haibun," 116). Later she wrote of that period, "I needed a woman, a poet, and a modernist, and I needed her badly" ("Reader," 103). This need overcame her frustration with what she termed H.D.'s "romantic thraldom."[22] While DuPlessis may have been attracted to the earlier poet's midrashic-like chains of meaning,

---

[22] Rachel Blau DuPlessis, *The Pink Guitar: Writing as Feminist Practice* (New York: Routledge, 1990) 20; cited subsequently *PG*.

H.D.'s symbolist and transcendental poetics would no doubt have jarred with the objectivist-inflected materialism of her own poetics. Burton Hatlen suggests that DuPlessis sometimes engaged in "a deliberate 'misreading'" of H.D., whereby the misreading opens up new, creative dimensions of H.D.'s text.[23] DuPlessis certainly agrees that H.D. was recuperated in quite specific ways by herself and other second-wave feminist poets or poet critics such as Alicia Ostriker, Beverly Dahlen, Adrienne Rich, and Barbara Guest: "We influenced her work, how it was read, what parts of it were read, why it was interesting. We made it matter for this generation" ("Haibun," 117).

Susan Rubin Suleiman contends that "if women are to be part of an avant-garde movement, they will do well to found it themselves."[24] Recoveries of past women writers like H.D. arguably say more about the way in which late twentieth-century feminists defined their own avant-gardism than what was actually occurring in the modernist era. In generating a foundational narrative of origins, DuPlessis and her contemporaries compiled a historical avant-garde that included Gertrude Stein, Virginia Woolf, Emily Dickinson, Mina Loy, Marianne Moore, Laura Riding, Lorine Niedecker, Gwendolyn Brooks, and Barbara Guest. Recuperated one by one, these poets were viewed as lone stars ("one of the stars…in that tiny firmament," as Marianne DeKoven characterises it)[25] rather than part of a constellation. Such an individualist, piecemeal strategy meant that women remained situated as marginal players to the male-dominant movements and consistently read through a narrative of alterity rather than centrality. If the avant-gardist is cast as outsider, then the innovative woman writer is the double outsider, existing in what Susan Rubin

---

23 Burton Hatlen, "Renewing the Open Engagement: H.D. and Rachel Blau DuPlessis," *H.D. and Poets After*, ed. Donna Krolik Hollenberg (Iowa City: University of Iowa Press, 2000) 139.

24 Susan Rubin Suleiman, *Subversive Intent: Gender, Politics, and the Avant-Garde* (Cambridge, Mass.: Harvard University Press, 1990) 32.

25 Marianne DeKoven, "Gertrude's Granddaughters," *The Women's Review of Books* 4.2 (1986): 12.

Suleiman calls a "double margin." The resulting picture of women in the modernist avant-garde (setting forth a discrete series of avant-garde women writers and, in so doing, reproducing the canonical strategies of New Criticism) has since been contested following the influence of cultural studies in modernist studies. While critics like Janet Lyon have begun to demonstrate the significance of the salon as a site of female cultural power, there has also been a shift in studies of H.D.'s world to Bryher's promotion of the avant-garde or their joint forays into the world of experimental cinema.[26]

In viewing past women avant-gardists as "pioneer Katies," to use William Carlos Williams's term,[27] the late twentieth-century avant-gardist could distinguish herself as being part of a *collective* female formation (for, as Paul Mann suggests, the previous avant-garde is retained as precisely that which is left behind, reiterated as history or lesson)(40). DuPlessis's next collection, *Tabula Rosa* (1987) featured promotional blurbs by Kathleen Fraser and Susan Howe. All three writers, as well as Beverly Dahlen and Frances Jaffer, were associated with *HOW(ever)*, a broadsheet journal that reflected the specifically female community from which it sprung in featuring *only* women's experimental poetry and art.[28] In its title, *HOW(ever)* signalled a break with the cultural dominant in sounding an alternative or "however" to a primary proposition. It also foregrounded the journal's affiliation to a modernist female avant-garde (having been sourced from Marianne Moore's quip in "Poetry" and echoing one of H.D.'s titles in its abbreviated form of *H(er)*). Yet while *HOW(ever)*'s editors set out to bring

---

26 See Janet Lyon, "Josephine Baker's Hothouse," *Modernism, Inc: Body, Memory, Capital*, ed Jani Scandura and Michael Thurston (New York: New York University Press, 2001) 29-47; Susan Stanford Friedman's more recent work, including *Analyzing Freud: Letters of H.D., Bryher, and Their Circle* (New York: New Directions, 2002); and Susan McCabe, *Cinematic Modernism: Modernist Poetry and Film* (Cambridge: Cambridge University Press, 2005).

27 William Carlos Williams, *In the American Grain* (New York: New Directions, 1956) 178.

28 Men were allowed to contribute reviews and critical material but rarely did so.

women scholars and writers not affiliated with institutions together, they were largely unsuccessful in breaking the institutional structure already in place.

Steve Evans characterises the nexus of innovative women writers emerging out of the 1970s as a "feminist counter-public sphere,"[29] a term Rita Felski coins to describe the public discourse of feminists who do not "claim a representative universality but rather offer ... a critique of cultural values from the standpoint of women as a marginalised group within society."[30] In his grouping, Evans includes the writers Alice Notley, Bernadette Mayer, Hannah Weiner, Nicole Brossard, Fanny Howe, Rosmarie Waldrop, and Kathleen Fraser. However, such writers might be thought of as participating in a "host of competing counterpublics" for Brossard was a central member of Quebecoise feminism whose linguistic innovations were motivated substantially by the call for regional freedom. Notley and Mayer participated in a formation invested in New York School generationalism. The group of writers central to the *HOW(ever)* project wrote alongside and participated in other avant-garde formations such as Language poetry, although they were often excluded in any institutionalising gestures (such as Ron Silliman's landmark anthology, *In the American Tree* (1986)[31]). They are perhaps best viewed then as a quasi-public sphere, a useful demarcation of Ruth Hoberman that captures the fluidity between separatism and women groups who work with mixed-gender counterpublics.[32]

29 Steve Evans, "After Patriarchal Poetry: Feminism and the Contemporary Avant-Garde: Introductory Note," *differences: A Journal of Feminist Cultural Studies* 12.2 (2001): ii.

30 Rita Felski, *Beyond Feminist Aesthetics: Feminist Literature and Social Change* (Cambridge: Harvard University Press, 1989) 167.

31 Ron Silliman, ed. *In the American Tree* (Orono: National Poetry Foundation, 1986).

32 Ruth Hoberman, "Women in the British Museum Reading Room during the Late-Nineteenth and Early Twentieth-Centuries: From Quasi- to Counterpublic," *Feminist Studies* 28.3 (Fall 2002) 489-521.

HOW(ever)'s merging of linguistic innovation and feminist politics occurred simultaneously with poststructuralism's critique of a realist naturalisation of language and the transparent transmission of knowledge. As Rosi Braidotti discerns, poststructralism's textual poetics was largely through the metaphor of the feminine:

> From ... Derrida's injunction that in so far as it cannot be said that the "feminine" functions as the most pervasive signifier; [to] Foucault's bland assertion that the absence of women from the philosophical scene is constitutive of the rules of the philosophical game, to Deleuze's notion of the "becoming-woman" marking a qualitative transformation in human consciousness—the feminisation of thought seems to be prescribed as a fundamental step in the general program of anti-humanism that marks our era.[33]

French theorists like Hélène Cixous argued that the feminine was the sphere of the unconscious or the pre-symbolic and for women linked to the body: "More so than men who are coaxed toward social success, toward sublimation, women are body."[34] For Cixous and Julia Kristeva, the feminine enabled a revolution in language. However, many feminist critics have noted that poststructuralism tends to focus on how male avant-garde writers have explored the feminine. Elisabeth Frost points out that Kristeva even excludes women from the avant-garde project by asserting that women are "psychologically unsuited the use of semiotic disruptive rhythms or sounds because the risk of psychosis is greater for women than for men."[35] As Sianne Ngai discerns with much astuteness, in embracing the feminine, the feminist poet is now obliged to

33 Rosi Braidotti, *Nomadic Subjects: Embodiment and Sexual Difference in Contemporary Feminist Theory* (New York: Columbia University Press, 1994) 140.
34 Hélène Cixous, "The Laugh of the Medusa," *New French Feminisms: An Anthology*, ed. Elaine Marks and Isabelle de Courtivron, trans. Keith Cohen and Paula Cohen (New York: Schocken Books, 1981) 257.
35 Elisabeth A. Frost, *The Feminist Avant-Garde in American Poetry* (Iowa City: University of Iowa Press, 2003) xxii.

negotiate, or take account of, a tradition which is dominated by male modernists.[36]

As I have suggested with the later poems of *Wells*, DuPlessis was both attracted to and troubled by using the feminine for feminist avant-garde practice. Her second volume, *Tabula Rosa*, has the leading epigraph, "She cannot forget the history of poetry/because it is not hers":

21. lay dee   hist! story
    l'idée   mystery
    lay dés   My hystery

...

25. Milk of the culture's teeming
           HU
   gushes at my   NGRY weaning.
          A   ("Crowbar")

Here, DuPlessis entertains the possibility of an alternative space to the history of the lyric that has positioned woman as the "lady" ideal. The alternative is "hystery," a positive make-over of what has been culturally cast as the negative, a space of madness and mystery. There is, however, an attempt to bring together essentialism with culture through the metaphor of motherhood. As with second-wave feminism, there is the revising of words to emphasise a feminine presence and the excerpt is underwritten (here quite literally) by anger. Hank Lazer points out that such "underwriting" adds a financial or economic resonance to DuPlessis's text and one might extend this to the notion of draft, an "overdraft" being an economic situation where the sum exceeds a viable balance.[37] DuPlessis's work then is an overdrawing of or act of excess in culture's

---

[36] Sianne Ngai, "Bad Timing (A Sequel). Paranoia, Feminism, and Poetry," *differences: A Journal of Feminist Cultural Studies* 12.2 (2001): 18.

[37] Hank Lazer, *Opposing Poetries, volume 2: Readings* (Evanston: Northwestern University Press, 1996) 57.

system (and part of this excess is affect). Elsewhere, she would argue, "I leave as an open, and perplexing question whether there is a female difference within what has been called a 'feminine' position and relation to language. If there is, I am playing it; if there isn't, I am sometimes playing it anyway."[38] Yet what happens to this excess is open to conjecture:

How to be that which is unspoken how to speak that which is
"repressed" elusive anyway tangential different
Impending space different enough how to write that which
is/ is

unwritten.[39]

In "Language Acquisition," an essay she wrote around the same period as she began *Drafts*, she is more critical of the feminine: "It is odd to read of things 'maternally connoted' or to hear that we may 'call the moment of rupture and negativity' which conditions and underlies the novelty of any praxis 'feminine' when this still leaves a little in the air what the specific relations of a woman writer to the semiotic register could be" (*PG* 87). Theorists like Braidotti and Nancy Hartsock have also questioned the deconstruction and "death" of the subject at the very point in history where women "are beginning to have access to the use of discourse, power, and pleasure."[40]

Not only deeply problematic in both its exclusion from the social and the dominance of male modernists in its tradition, the feminine could be said to perpetuate gender codes that associate women as being more adept at certain kinds of expression and roles than others (precisely the problem DuPlessis experienced in having the lyric as the foundation for

[38] Cited in Lynn Keller, *Forms of Expansion: Recent Long Poems by Women* (Chicago: University of Chicago Press, 1997) 253.
[39] Rachel Blau DuPlessis, *Tabula Rosa* (Elmwood: Potes & Poets Press, 1987) 72; subsequently *TR*.
[40] Braidotti, *Nomadic Subjects*, 140.

feminist poetry). Ngai points out the difficulty of moving beyond such a model:

> A familiar question thus returns: how does one develop a critique of sexual difference without referring to the binary terms whose reiteration would seem to affirm and reinforce the system of "sexual difference" itself? Since the feminist critics constantly faces a situation in which the basic presuppositions of the sex-gender system are not only posited but potentially re-entrenched, "by the practical context of [her own] invention in them," the enterprise of critique threatens to become a paranoid economy, with the question of "complicity" at its very centre.[41]

Precisely through identifying the patriarchal and phallogocentric as objects of attack, literary feminism re-affirms their centrality in culture and language. The avant-garde also has this dilemma of being secondary. In seeking rupture and separation, it necessarily defines and reinforces the force of that which it opposes. Wishing to strike out toward a different future, the avant-garde is tied to past and present, hyper-aware of and caught by its own temporality.

DuPlessis would become increasingly wary of archetypal or psychoanalytical-inflected explanations. For the feminist avant-garde poet, poetry can only be, as DuPlessis states, "provisionally/complicit resistance" (*TR* 73). With her serial poem, *Drafts*, DuPlessis moves beyond the "otherness" which, as she notes in "Manifests,"[42] remains in the binary system, to writing "otherhow" — as "the multiple possibilities of a praxis" (*PG* 154). DuPlessis's title self-consciously echoes Pound's *Drafts & Fragments of Cantos CX-CXVII*. In "Draft 1", DuPlessis writes, "CANO, can o, yes no/conno-/tations of impurities."[43] This also invokes Virgil's concept of arms and the man ("Arma virumque cano") and foregrounds Pound's militant agenda for

41 Ngai, "Bad Timing," 19.
42 Rachel Blau DuPlessis, "Manifests," *Diacritics* 26.3-4 (1996): 49.
43 Rachel Blau DuPlessis, *Drafts 1-38, Toll* (Middletown: Wesleyan University Press, 2001) 4; cited subsequently as *Toll*.

avant-garde change. Yet to be drafted is to be called up to battle by a social regime to act on its behalf. Rather than have agency in one's aggression, an army draftee is devolved of agency, rendered complicit in supporting and being absorbed in a monolithic order. The revolutionary struggle is revealed as maintaining hegemony rather than articulating the non-hegemonic.

Significantly, the last words of Pound's *Drafts* is one of defeat, "That I lost my centre/fighting the world./The dreams clash/and are shattered—/and that I tried to make a paradise terrestre."[44] While the long poem enabled openness and flight of impulse, Pound desired mastery, and increasingly invested *The Cantos* with an imperative tone. Furthermore, as Peter Nicholls suggests, issues of myth, politics, and ethics were merged unproblematically together by being projected back onto an idyllic and remote past.[45] Pound not only saw social process as unilateral—"The whole tribe" as coming from "one man's body" (708) but also endowed *The Cantos* with a masculine show of force in the hope that it "burst thru" to luminous images of paradise. These, he saw as cohering, "even if my notes do not cohere" (797). For Pound, judgement was unassailable, having been found in linguistic precision itself. Oppen would note that, "Pound's ego system, Pound's organisation of the world around a character, a kind of masculine energy, is extremely foreign to me."[46] He also found its epic nature difficult to stomach: "I suspect we all admit to ourselves—or I will admit to myself   that I read the *Cantos* in fragments   as fragments" (*SL* 249-50). Discussing poetic practice with DuPlessis, he suggested that what was needed was "courage, not 'audacity'—Pound's word—but plain courage. To say what it's like out there ... out here" (*SL* 122).

---

[44] Ezra Pound, *The Cantos* (London: Faber & Faber, 1975) 802.

[45] Peter Nicholls, "On Being Ethical: Reflections on George Oppen," *The Objectivist Nexus: Essays in Cultural Poetics* (Tuscaloosa: University of Alabama Press, 1999) 243.

[46] Cited Dembo, "The 'Objectivist' Poet," 170.

DuPlessis seems to agree, wanting a poetry that was specific to its time and cultural history, that could speak of the "now" that "plunges into every object." Beyond Pound, *Drafts* invokes Oppen's notion of draft as air in "The Occurrences":

Limited air   drafts
In the treasure house moving and the movements of the living
Things fallsomething balanced Move
With all one's force
Into the commonplace that pierces or erodes

The mind's structure but nothing
Incredible happens
It will have happened to the other
The survivor   The survivor
To him   it happened (*CP* 206)

For DuPlessis, the "limited air" was that of the lyric tradition and the teachings of New Criticism which had seen a distilled air, purified of Otherness. In contrast to the consoling order that Pound arguably sought, she wanted a poetry that was disorderly, messy, excessive, contrary, and—following Walter Benjamin—that would involve waste, debris, social detritus, or the taboo. Yet she would be still be attracted to the encyclopaedic impulse of the long poem "in which the writer invents a new and total culture, symbolised by and announced in a long work" (*PG* 17) "get[ting] everything in, inclusively, reflexively, monumentally" (*PG* 9). She would attempt to combine this with a methodology of radical particularism. Politicising the draft of air, it becomes breath, a person in the act of doing. The act of writing is no longer an act of being drafted, but the very draft of being.

Drafts begins in *Tabula Rosa* in its second section. It takes as its cue Beverly Dahlen's serial poem *A Reading* although it distances itself from Dahlen's more Freudian approach. DuPlessis notes that the first drafts were written on a notebook bound in marbled paper given to her by Fraser. Inspiration and the material for *Drafts* then is drawn from the dialogue and support of a surrounding feminist avant-garde. Excluded from subsequent collections of *Drafts*, "Writing" might be seen as Draft #0, a textual degree zero, containing the supplement, the marginal, and the lost. In "Writing on 'Writing,'" DuPlessis notes that she wanted to "take herself as central yet in all her otherness, to try writing otherness when it is sometimes felt, or stated repeatedly, that otherness is the opposite of writing, although it may inspire writing" (*TR* 84). Taking the space of negation heralded in "from The 'History of Poetry,'" she simultaneously begins a commentary of it:

Marginalia without a centre? No beginning, No. No
One word one   ending? No, because form
"word" kkhkkhgggh   at all times is instilled. O noble
Koré   la la   that ongo-
Threaded into the dyad ingness that entrance into speaking
                                                                              (*TR* 77)

DuPlessis uses parallel columns to establish a midrashic dialogue between self and writing. Yet within this dyadic structure, she attempts to refuse definitive openings and closure, promoting instead a model of the middle and the continuous. This is partly achieved by splitting phrases and words by line breaks but also by ironic repetition ("One word one"). It is also achieved through the non-sense of song ("la la") and pure sound ("kkhkkhgggh"), which reflect at once the dyadic structure of mother and baby and also the collapse of a singularity of self that occurs upon parenting. Here, the emotional complexity of love, responsibility, and frustration is conveyed both through and between language's segmentation.

"Draft 1," appearing in *Tabula Rosa* with "Draft 2," turns on the issue of "both/and," specifically in terms of negation and affirmation. It begins with the "N" of No which is repeated on the next line, then echoed pictorially with a small N within a larger N. Visually the doubled pictorial N looks like mountain peaks, emblematising the sublime horizon of writing (as she notes further in the poem, "theater of the/ page cream space peaks" (*Toll* 6)). The second half of the poem contains a doubled pictorial Y. which tactically mirrors the N. while visually suggesting the female body. DuPlessis saw *Drafts* as undertaking the promise of "Writing" in offering an alternative to poetry. In contrast to the iconic, static form of "postcard poetry" (*Toll* 4) with its "lyric hit" and recognisable markers of "beauty" and "perfection," she wanted to "reconfigure what [poetry] can do, how it is regarded, and what its scope and meanings are." In calling her emergent serial poem, "Drafts," DuPlessis stages them as a work-in-progress, not so much "unfinished" in themselves (each "Draft" may be read and is often published initially as a separate, complete text in itself) but as constantly linking to, dissembling, and revising one another. As such, there is also a shift in focus from product to labour—a flagging of their own temporality. DuPlessis notes that the *Drafts* are "freshly drawn and freely declared" (although this is a fiction); their completion are always provisional. *Drafts* also involves "the pull or traction on something" and therefore are an "examination from the ground here, not elsewhere" (*OD* 145).

Drafts makes manifest, then, rather than being a manifesto or declaration. Its poems are performative, reiterating the past in order to "make it anew." The poetics of returning attention, of occupation over time, reveals "a seam opening inside existence" (*OD* 151). While focused on the constitution of the self and thus following the orientation of much feminist poetry, it undercuts the articulation of a definitive self, revealing the fictionalisation of subjectivity. The opening *Drafts*, for instance, returns to *Wells*:

Silences are the reaches of discourse

(rich incipit's big initials)

         walled
There is a yes and a no   up

welled   (*Toll* 9)

In *Drafts*, DuPlessis seeks to make poetry "not remembering//but constructed of Memory/time going forward athwart" (*Toll* 231). It questions the autobiographical imperative: "The poem is not you. Except as if you are/yourself in doubt//impeded clarities repeated." Elsewhere she would ponder: "Is this writing or memory? Projection or repetition?/Real or unreal? The memoir of me, or anti-memoir/Against my real life?"[47]

The long poem mimics memory as an expansive and flexible medium. In a letter dated 21 March 1975, Oppen advises DuPlessis to "stop writing poetry. Write prose. Without telling yourself that prose has to be different from poetry, or longer, or anything else" (*SL* 301). Yet in doing so, she moves away from Oppen who would confess, "I write such godawful prose that I am not tempted to prose procedures" (*SL* 317). In *Drafts*, DuPlessis combines narrative and lyric elements, crosses genres (documentary, report, ode, elegy, autobiography, midrash), creates palimpsests, uses gloss, creolisation, over-writing, multiple fonts, punning, and word-hinges, all of which contribute to a sense of the text as being at once inclusive (polyvocal, multi-cultural, and symphonic) as well as filled with gaps, hesitant, and conflicted. Blacked-out patches of text in "Draft 5: Gap," "Draft 52: Midrash," and "Draft 68: Threshold" remind the reader of the overlay of social censorship that regulate such tracings of the past.

DuPlessis argues that the memorialising function in poetry has generally singled out female figures to be surrounded by the male gaze (*OD* 144). In looking at cultural material, *Drafts* performs a commentary while also foregrounding that material's *historicality*. Peggy Kamuf notes that this is different from historical context; once a work's context has subsided "into archival compost," it "has a relation as well to a future, by

---

[47] Rachel Blau DuPlessis, *Drafts: Drafts 39-57, Pledge, with Draft, Unnumbered: Précis* (Cambridge: Salt, 2004) 39.

which it remains always to some extent incomprehensible by any given present. She contends, "What we still call literature … would be the reserve of every present, instituted meaning and thus the possibility of its transformation, that is, the possibility of a future."[48] At the same time as this utopian potential, there is a sense of the melancholy in *Drafts*, a mourning for a particular set of identifications and histories, primarily those such as gender and Jewishness which relate to DuPlessis's own cultural matrix ("Draft 22: Philadelphia Wireman" mourns a local or geographically proximate figure whose history remains unknown). This goes hand in hand with the belatedness of the contemporary avant-garde which has, in the wake of poststructuralism's various deconstructions (of history, the subject, and gender), a different understanding of its temporality and potential force to the modernist avant-garde. DuPlessis's disorderly excesses of memory and its gaps of forgetting, following her "both/and" non-dialectical model, is resonant with Kamuf's historicality.

Furthermore, DuPlessis's process of return enables *Verwindung*, a Heideggerian term which Gianni Vattimo uses to signify transformation through distortion.[49] This is perhaps similar to Charles Altieri's notion of a "tilt" of subjectivity.[50] In both the focus is on movement (consonant with Objectivism) rather than opting for a choice between one or the other version, or of falling back onto a narrative of progress. Recurrence then generates difference as plenitude rather than dialectic. DuPlessis conceives return through yet another strategy in her use of the fold. Introduced as a structural

[48] Peggy Kamuf, *The Division of Literature, or, the University in Deconstruction* (Chicago: University of Chicago Press, 1997) 164. This would tie in with Giorgio Agamben's concept of the 'new' "as that which cannot be experienced except as unknown, as emerging only in an 'estrangement' that removes from the most commonplace objects their power to be experienced."

[49] Gianni Vattimo, "Verwindung: Nihilism and the Postmodern in Philosophy," *SubStance* 16.2 (1987): 7-17.

[50] Charles Altieri, "Avant-Garde or Arrière-Garde in Recent American Poetry," *Poetics Today* 20.4 (1999): 629-53.

principle in 1993, each new draft (beginning with "Draft 20") corresponds in some way to an earlier one. This fold would be repeated again, such that "Draft 39" would have "Draft 1" and "Draft 20" as its donor drafts. The connection between poems might be sensuous, formal, intellectual or allusive, but in making the connection change the potential meaning of each. DuPlessis argues that the fold might be seen as "ethical indistinction" (*Toll* 234), foregrounding the space of poetry as "the in-between." Certainly much of *Drafts* is about thinking through the relationship between the "out-there" to the "over-here" (*Toll* 234) as there is in negotiating "it" (the poem, experience) and "me." The generative qualities of the fold is emphasised by the pun "foaled" (*Toll* 142) and throughout *Drafts* there is a focus on the process of writing as mothering. The text resists authorial control and there is much play on its alterity, on its various gaps and absences, its em spaces (the reversal of "me") (*Toll* 40) and the mother's need to "stay mum" ("mum's the word," *Toll* 142).

However, the systematic grid imposed on *Drafts* sometimes seems to undercut its openness as text. Just as Hank Lazer has argued that the directions given by DuPlessis on how to read an earlier poem "Megaliths" were an error in privileging a particular way to read (down each column, then across both), a grid impels the reader to look at particular parts in the manner of puzzle-solving their connections (42). Certainly it disrupts the reading habit to read chronologically or from front to back in the form of a book. *Drafts* foregrounds the illusory nature or impossibility of a completely "free form" in other respects. There is the dating at the end of each draft, which reinforces the poem as being not simply an aesthetic article but also historical utterance. DuPlessis's extensive footnoting also sets up an institutionally correct system of acknowledging source material. As with the grid, the footnotes might be seen as privileging a particular way in which a Draft can be read, with their emphasis on the existence if not importance of authorial intention. While DuPlessis uses footnoting as an ethical gesture to acknowledge the cultural and aesthetic underpinnings of a poem's germination, such extensive and formal footnoting nevertheless signals the cultural capital of *Drafts*. Furthermore, the latest collection of *Drafts* (covering Drafts 39-57 and an unnumbered Draft) is subtitled "Pledge" and most of its *Drafts* end with a dedication, often to fellow writers and scholars. Arguably, all these mechanisms have the opposite effect to strategies of shock or disturbance (the more traditional avant-garde objectives) in that they provide the reader with cues as to how to navigate the text and how it should be positioned within the poetic field. That said, DuPlessis is still playful with these devices and their effects, even incorporating Caroline Bergvall's mis-citation of "historical dread" as "historical dead" into "Draft 25" (*Toll* 163).

"Draft Unnumbered: Précis" seems like a conclusion to *Drafts* not only in ending the collection of *Drafts 39-57*, *Pledge*, but also in briefly capturing the nature of each Draft hitherto and being situated outside the numbered process that marks *Drafts*'s seriality. Yet DuPlessis views it as a "benchmark set at the apparent centre of [the] project" and continues to produce more Drafts.[51] As avant-garde text, *Drafts* is "Exploration not in service of reconciling self to world, but creating a new world for a new self" (*PG* 19). While it does a thoroughly poststructural turn in its deconstruction of experience and history, *Drafts* seeks to cross the divide between an aestheticisation of subjectivity and ethical materialism, to reveal the subject as a being in-process and multitudinous even while interpolated through particular cultural hegemonies. It is emblematic of the ways in which contemporary experimental women writers reconceptualise both feminism and the avant-garde, demonstrating how the belatedness of both formations (and, of course, their uneasy fit) generate responses including but also over and beyond negativity, the paranoid or melancholic.

---

[51] Rachel Blau DuPlessis, "An Interview with Jeanne Heuving," *Contemporary Literature* 45.3 (2004): 405.

Esther Milne

The Affective and Aesthetic Relations of Epistolary Presence[*]

Introduction
Within the technological imaginary, developments in communication systems are often represented as a series of decisive shifts and abrupt breaks. The new technology emerges, it seems, out of nowhere, escaping the tentacles of historical materiality. Devoid of a past and promising a future perfect, this narrative of progress helps serve global commodity relations in its uncritical celebration of the new. As a response to these socio-technological representations, this paper argues that the relation between old and new media is more complex than is often assumed by contemporary media theory. Narratives of change are dramatically complicated by the striking continuities between different communication systems. What follows teases out some of these continuities by exploring how geographically distributed postal networks produce affective and aesthetic relations of intimacy.

This is not, however, to deny the problematics encountered by critical historiography. The historical approaches of poststructuralism, for example, have offered a rejoinder to a certain universalising version of history that wants to erase

[*] Sections of this paper were originally published in *Fibreculture Journal* 1.2 (2003) as "Email and Epistolary technologies: Presence, Intimacy, Disembodiment."

difference. In its effort to see difference where hitherto there had existed the smoothness and functionality of structuralism, poststructuralist media theory celebrates rupture and aporia to reveal the disjunction of history and its representation.[1] Yet even as "discontinuity" has been a useful conceptual framework though which to understand activist poetics and avant-gardism,[2] it is quite remarkable that some of these rhetorical strategies can end up confirming that very methodology and ideology they wish to confound. That is, while arguing for historical rupture against the totalising view of historical seamlessness, these kinds of studies may be seen actually to rejoice in the unbroken narrative of history.

Presence

Intimacy, affect and aesthetics are always intertwined at the level of technology. As an avant-garde strategy, for example, the practices of mail-art are enabled by the material conditions of the postal exchange.[3] In turn, the economies of this exchange are underpinned by the dance between absence and presence: writing a letter signals the absence of the recipient and, simultaneously, aims to bridge the gap between writer and recipient. As William Decker puts it, "exchange of letter sheet thus articulates and substantiates the central paradox of epistolary discourse: that the exchange of personally inscribed texts confirms even as it would mitigate separation."[4]

"Presence" has emerged as a major focus for researchers and artists of digital culture, computer networks and new medical, communication and entertainment technologies.[5]

[1] See Friedrich A. Kittler, *Discourse Networks 1800/1900,* trans. Michael Metteer (Standford: Standford University Press, 1990).

[2] Louis Armand, *Solicitations* (Prague: Litteraria Pragensia, 2005) 214.

[3] See Annmarie Chandler and Norrie Neumark (eds.), *At a Distance: Precursors to Art and Activism on the Internet* (Cambridge, Mass.: MIT/Leonardo Books, 2005).

[4] William Merrill Decker, *Epistolary Practices: Letter Writing in America before Telecommunications* (Chapel Hill: University of North Carolina Press, 1998) 46-7.

[5] Luisa Paraguai Donati and Gilbertto Prado "Artistic Environments of Telepresence on the World Wide Web," *Leonardo* 34.5 (2001): 437-442; Matthew

Presence refers to the degree to which geographically dispersed agents experience a sense of physical and/or psychological proximity through the use of particular communication technologies. In areas as diverse as virtual reality, video conferencing, MUDs (multi-user domain), newsgroups, electronic discussion lists, telemedicine, web-based education, flight simulation software and computer gaming, a sense of presence is vital for the success of the particular application.

It ought to be noted that the term "telepresence" has been used both interchangeably with and in opposition to the term presence. Jonathan Steuer, for example, adopts the latter use arguing that the point of departure between the two terms depends on the degree to which the subject experiences their environment as technologically mediated. As he explains, presence "refers to the experience of natural surroundings ... in which sensory input impinges directly upon the organs of sense."[6] In contrast, telepresence refers to "the experience of presence in an environment by means of a communication medium."[7] Steuer's model, however, has been criticised because it relies on a mistaken dichotomy between, on the one hand, "real," "natural" presence and on the other hand, "mediated" telepresence. This, argue Giuseppe Mantovani and Giuseppe

---

Lombard and Theresa Ditton, "At the Heart of It All: The Concept of Presence," *Journal of Computer-Mediated Communication* 3.2 (1997), http://www.ascusc.org/jcmc/vol3/issue2/lombard.html; William J. Mitchell, *"e-topia: 'Urban life, Jim—but not as we know it'"* (Cambridge, Mass.: MIT Press, 1999); Sheila C. Murphy, "Lurking and Looking: Webcams and the Construction of Cybervisuality," *Moving Images: from Edison to the Webcam*, eds. John Fullerton and Strid Söderbergh Widding (Sydney: Libbey, 2000) 173-180; Marie-Laure Ryan, "Immersion vs. Interactivity: Virtual Reality and Literary Theory," *SubStance* 28.2 (1999): 110-137; Thomas Sheridan, "Musings on Telepresence and Virtual Presence," *Presence: Teleoperators and Virtual Environments* 1.1 (1992): 120-125.

[6] The emphasis appears in the original. For the remainder of this paper I note only those instances where the emphasis has been added by me. It may be assumed, therefore, that if there is no notation, the emphasis appears in the original quotation.

[7] Jonathan Steuer, "Defining Virtual Reality: Dimensions Determining Presence," *Journal of Communication* 42.4 (1992): 75-6.

Riva, fails to acknowledge the mediated, culturally constructed nature of all communication environments. As they put it:

> presence is always mediated by both physical and conceptual tools that belong to a given culture: "physical" presence in an environment is in principle no more "real" or more true than telepresence or immersion in a simulated virtual environment.[8]

In addition to these critiques, a number of writers have attempted to historicise the socio-critical formulations of presence, telepresence and virtual presence but these phenomena have usually been confined to representations within electronic media.[9] The past several decades have also produced a substantial body of work that explores the ways that global communication networks reconfigure our experience of time and space. As a result of the rapid flow of data through digital information systems, distance appears to shrink and time seems to collapse. The speed up of communication and the concomitant perception of a collapsing time and space will often produce an intense, quasi-spiritual sense of presence: "through the computer, thought seems to come across like a flowing stream from mind to mind."[10] This sentence is instructive because it collocates "disembodiment," "presence," and an eclipse of the material vehicle of communication, conditions, that, as we shall see, are a defining formal property of the communication systems under

---

8 Giuseppe Mantovani and Giuseppe Riva, "'Real' Presence: How Different Ontologies Generate Different Criteria for Presence, Telepresence and Virtual Presence," *Presence: Teleoperators and Virtual Environments* 8.5 (1999): 547.

9 E.g. Richard Coyne, Technoromanticism: Digital Narrative, Holism, and the Romance of the Real (Cambridge, Mass.: MIT Press, 2001); Jeffrey Sconce, Haunted Media: Electronic Presence from Telegraphy to Television (Durham: Duke University Press, 2000); Vivian Sobchack, "The Scene of the Screen: Envisioning Cinematic and Electronic 'Presence,'" Materialities of Communication, eds. Hans Ulrich Gumbrecht and K. Ludwig Pfeiffer, trans. William Whobrey (Stanford: Stanford University Press, 1994) 83-106.

10 Michael Heim, "Humanistic Discussion and the Online Conference," *Philosophy Today 30* (Winter, 1986): 283.

investigation. However, current theorising about what David Harvey calls "time-space compression,"[11] generally limits itself to a history that begins with technological inventions such as the telegraph. What remains under-examined is the extent to which older technologies, such as the postal service, also foster the sense that the constraints of space and time can be overcome. In response, this paper traces the persistence of tropes of presence and intimacy though the texts and socio-technological representations of three sites of communication: letters, postcards and email.

Epistolary Presence
The construction of imaginary presence is a fundamental feature of letter writing. In Claudio Guillén's words:

> there is hardly an act in our daily experience, rooted in life itself, that is as likely as the writing of a letter to propel us toward inventiveness and interpretation ... the "I" who writes may not only be pretending to act upon a friend ... but acting also upon himself, upon his evolving mirror image.[12]

These epistolary inventions are both performance and interpretation. The letter writer performs a version of self and the recipient reads that performance. These interpretive acts help to produce the imagined bodies of epistolary communication. As Ruth Perry has observed, through the "solitary pleasures" of reading and writing, the lovers of epistolary relationships "summon up images of each other, without need for the visible presence of the other, and then react joyfully to their own creations."[13]

In face-to-face communication, questions of presence can seem unproblematic. Epistolary communication underlines the

---

[11] David Harvey, The Condition of Postmodernity: An Enquiry into the Origins of Cultural Change (Cambridge, Mass.: Blackwell, 1990).

[12] Claudio Guillén, "On the Edge of Literariness: The Writing of Letters," *Comparative Literature Studies* 31.1 (1994): 2.

[13] Ruth Perry, *Women, Letters, and the Novel* (New York: AMS, 1980) 101.

fact that, as Jacques Derrida has argued, presence depends on and is the effect of a complex set of assumptions and strategies.[14] As I shall argue, "presence" is dependent on (and in part created by) rhetorical strategies and effects such as intimacy, immediacy, spontaneity and disembodiment. At first sight, the last of these terms might appear not to belong to this list; yet in email and epistolary correspondence, presence often depends paradoxically on a type of disembodiment. In some instances this involves the eclipse of the material medium that supports and the temporal or physical obstacles that would otherwise thwart communication. As the author Elizabeth Barrett Browning (1806-1861) remarks to one of her closest epistolary friends: "thanks warmest & truest, my dearest Miss Mitford, for your delightful letter, which is certainly delightful, as it made me feel just as if I were sitting face to face to you, hearing you talk" (16 September, 1844, 9:136).[15] Disembodiment, as this quotation suggests, is in epistolary communication coincident with the emergence of a fantasy of bodily proximity or presence.

In a letter sent to Mary Russell Mitford (1787-1855), Barrett Browning provides insight into the ways in which the signifiers of presence operate within epistolary discourse. Barrett Browning writes:

> If I do not empty my heart out with a great splash on the paper, every time I have a letter from you, & speak my gladness & thankfulness, it is lest I shd. weary you of thanksgivings! (EBB, 24 March, 1842, 5: 269)

---

[14] Cf. Jacques Derrida, "Structure, Sign and Play in the Discourse of the Human Sciences," *Writing and Difference*, trans. A. Bass (London: Routledge, 1978), 278-293.

[15] All the letters referred to in the text are from *The Brownings' Correspondence*, eds. Philip Kelley and Ronald Hudson, 14 volumes (Kansas: Wedgestone Press, 1984). The in-text citations provide details of the date of letter, volume number and page number. For the purpose of the in-text citation, Elizabeth Barrett Browning is abbreviated to "EBB" and Mary Russell Mitford is abbreviated to "MRM."

Barrett Browning's claim that she writes letters by emptying her "heart out with a great splash on the paper" suggests authenticity, intimacy, immediacy and spontaneity. However, Barrett Browning's claims that her letters are written in blood that spurts from the author's heart also draws attention, in a somewhat macabre fashion, to the body. Within a discourse of disembodiment, there is a complex relation between the imagined body of epistolary discourse and the real "flesh and blood" corporeality of the epistolary actors. Since one is not physically co-present with one's interlocutor, references to the corporeal body play significant rhetorical and social functions in the production of meaning within letter writing practice. The physical absence of one's epistolary partner provides both the impetus and the "material" for a range of strategies, language uses and technological functions aimed at creating an imagined sense of presence. References to the physical body, to the scene of writing, to the place where the letter is received or to postal technology are often used by letter writers to convey and invoke a sense of immediacy, intimacy and presence:

> Mr Kenyon is here. I must end & see him—for the post will be fast upon his heels (EBB, 24 March, 1842, 5: 268);

> this tiresome post, going when I had so much more to say (EBB, 19 September, 1842, 6:83);

> You will never guess what I am doing—my beloved friend—or rather suffering!—oh—you will never guess. I am sitting ... rather lying for my picture. That sounds like vanity between two worlds, indeed!—only the explanation excuses me (EBB, 16 April, 1841, 5:36).

By referring to the "here and now" of corporeality—"you will never guess what I am doing ... lying for my picture"—these correspondents strive to collapse the time and distance that separate them. Depending on the skill and eloquence of the letter writer, the recipient can feel as if he/she is actually face-to-face with them. But, of course, a key point is contained in that small phrase "as if." Were the two writers present to one another, there would be no need to correspond. Yet for many letter writers of the nineteenth century, the face-to-face encounter is not necessarily superior to epistolary communication. Indeed, on some occasions, epistolary discourse may be the superior mode. Letters can provide one with the opportunity to express what was unsaid, or could not be said, during a physical meeting. After Mitford had visited her friend Barrett Browning in London, for example, the former wrote:

> My beloved friend how can I thank you enough! You came— you went away like a dream and as if it were a real dream, I never expressed or tried to express all the thankfulness & sense of your great goodness, which penetrated me through and through. You will let me thank you now, will you not?—and you will believe in the earnestness of the thoughts which revert to that day & go forward to you? (MRM, 18 November, 1843, 8:50)

For many correspondents, then, "absence" is creative; it opens a discursive space in which desires and subjectivities that might not otherwise be articulated can be explored.

Letters—like postcards and electronic mail—are conventionally understood as a technology that allows communication between bodies that are absent from each other. Epistolary communication is to that extent "disembodied." Yet the boundary between disembodiment and embodiment in epistolary practice is difficult to maintain strictly. Writing and reading letters are, of course, operations in which the body must play a role. As noted, the body of the absent correspondent can become "visible" in letter exchanges when, for example, the author refers to the epistolary scene of writing, its material supports and delivery systems or makes mention of the letter's temporality. These strategies aim for a sense of immediacy and presence by foregrounding the body of the writer. A related but not identical epistolary convention is one where the materiality of the letter is made to stand for the correspondent's body. Due to its physical proximity or contact with its author the letter can work metonymically; a function most obvious in amorous epistolary discourse where the letter is kissed, held, cried over or adored in place of the lover's body. In this way, the gap between letter writer and reader seems bridged. As Barrett Browning writes in a letter to Mitford, "I should like to be near you my beloved friend, to kiss both the dear hands twenty times which wrote & touched the paper of this most tender letter!" (30 March, 1842, 5:286).

Illustrations such as these may seem relatively unproblematic as signifiers of "embodiment," proof that the fleshly body of the epistolary author is "present" at the time of writing and therefore can guarantee authenticity of communication. But even in cases we may call unproblematic, the sign that stands for the body seems at times to eclipse its own materiality. Still more remarkably, at times the materiality of the body that writes, along with the signs it makes on the paper, are eclipsed for the reader by a strong sense of communion between minds or spirits.

Barrett Browning gives an eloquent illustration of this "eclipse" in a letter written shortly after Mitford had visited:

> My dearest friend's letter was like a shadow of her presence thrown back & brought to mind so strongly all the pleasure I had had in the "dear Sunshine" that the letter itself was for the moment annihilated ... not thought of! I thought of YOU too much. Oh, what a happy week for me! (EBB, 19 June, 1844, 9:23)

Barrett Browning is describing a transparency which many forms of communication have as an unachievable ideal: in the moment described, the material conditions of representation are effaced, "annihilate," "not thought of." Interestingly, then, this suggests that on occasion the media of epistolary systems may need to be forgotten in order to function efficiently, or conversely, that there are times when the materiality of a letter seems actually to get in the way of its ability to communicate. Arguably, this is a feature of representation in general; the desire to experience unmediated "reality" appears satisfied when the material conditions of representation (the pen, the screen, the keyboard) are eclipsed. The presence, intimacy and immediacy created between epistolary subjects relies upon a complex dynamic between, on the one hand, materiality, physical locatedness and embodiment and, on the other hand, references to the material conditions of epistolary communication and the corporeal body. In order to create a sense of presence and immediacy one may refer to the material conditions of the postal service or the corporeality of the letter writer. But if too much attention is drawn to the vehicle that is creating the sense of presence, then the construction and artifice of this "immediacy" becomes apparent; one sees the signifier not the signified. What, at first glance, may appear to be a reference to the materiality or "embodied" quality of letter writing actually might be operating at a different register since the letter's materiality turns into a sign for the presence of the absent correspondent: "Your letter, my dearest friend, is twenty times welcome—& stands for you, for that coveted presence, right worthily" (EBB, 21 November, 1843, 8: 53).

Paradoxically, then, references to the real, lived, situated, physical body of the epistolary exchange can produce a "fantasised body." That is, the letter form allows correspondents to enact an identity and even adopt a persona that may differ from their "real" or lived body and personae. This is not meant to imply there exists an authentic self from which the letter writer departs. Rather, this "imagined body" or virtual self is a productive effect of the epistolary exchange. As Lori Lebow notes, "letter writing involves the writing self as a joint venture undertaken by the writer and reader. Writer and reader construct identity from textual cues based on the received responses from the selected audience."[16] The

---

[16] Lori Lebow, "Woman of Letters: Narrative Episodes in the Letters of Emily Dickinson," *The Emily Dickinson Journal* 8.1 (1999): 75.

performance of presence in nineteenth century epistolary culture is enacted by a complex interplay between absent letter writers, face-to-face meetings and the material, epistolary system that renders problematic a strict dichotomy between embodiment and disembodiment.

Postcard Presence
Epistolary communication has been formally and aetiologically viewed as closely related to privacy, the "confidential inscription of private, inward, individual experience."[17] For Decker, the expectation of privacy and confidentiality is the "enabling condition" for the production of intimacy.[18] What happens, then, to Kittler's "discourse network" of the nineteenth century when these categories of affect are put in question by the 1865 invention of the postcard? Descriptions of the shift from a system dominated by the letter to one that employed letters and postcards are often couched in terms of apocalyptic loss and destruction: "Differing from a letter, a post card is a letter to the extent that nothing of it remains that is, or that holds. It destines the letter to its ruin."[19] Indeed, the postcard has provided critical practice with an eloquent trope for representing transformations to certain regimes of symbolic and material organisation.[20]

---

[17] Decker, *Epistolary Practices*, 79.

[18] Decker, *Epistolary Practices*, 5.

[19] Jacques Derrida, *The Post Card: From Socrates to Freud and Beyond*, trans. Alan Bass (Chicago: University of Chicago Press, 1987; 1980) 249. Eschatological and apocalyptic tropes are, of course, common narrative expressions for the interpretation of cyberculture and the movement of global capital. See, for example, Baudrillard, Jean. *The Revenge of the Crystal: Selected Writings on the Modern Object and its Destiny*, 1968-1983, trans. Paul Foss and Julian Pefanis (Sydney: Pluto Press, Power Institute of Fine Arts, University of Sydney, 1990) and Paul Virilio, *The Information Bomb*, trans. Chris Turner (London: Verso, 2000).

[20] See Mark Seltzer, "The Postal Unconscious," *The Henry James Review* 21.3 (2000): 197-206; Bernhard Siegert, *Relays: Literature as an Epoch of the Postal System*, trans. Kevin Repp (Stanford: Stanford University Press, 1997).

For correspondents of the late nineteenth-century, the postcard introduced a new system of postal writing in which traditional epistolary values and protocols were challenged and questions of class were raised. Fears were regularly expressed that postal clerks or servants would spend their time reading the postcards that passed through their hands. A newspaper of 1870 warned of the "absurdity of writing private information on an open piece of card-board, that might be read by half a dozen persons before it reached its destination."[21] Yet, those who have noted the threat to epistolary privacy posed by the postcard have invariably overlooked the point that in some sense, at least, the privacy of epistolary communication has often been at risk. During the mid nineteenth-century, for example, there was the distinct possibility that government officials, on the pretext of protecting national security, might open one's letters.[22] Even if one's letter arrived inviolate, one could not always assume that it would remain with its intended recipient. Quite often Barrett Browning, Mitford and their other friends would circulate letters without first securing the permission of their authors.

The disjunction between the imagined privacy of communication and the actual or possible dissemination, of this message to a wide audience, suggest that the latter must at least in part be occluded if epistolary communication based on the former is to continue. When intimacy or immediacy is the desired effect of a letter (not all letters strive for these qualities: business communication, for example, is informed by other characteristics), correspondents assume a level of privacy and act accordingly. It is worth noting, then, that privacy is a historically contingent and culturally determined term. Cultural theorists who posit the postcard's erosion of privacy, are fantasising about a level of epistolary privacy that, perhaps, has

---

[21] Richard Carline, Pictures in the Post: the Story of the Picture Postcard (London: Fraser, 1971) 55.

[22] Howard Robinson, *The British Post Office: A History* (New Jersey: Princeton University Press, 1948) 337-53.

never been available. This is not to deny that the postcard dramatically changed postal communication. Perhaps for the first time the postcard made visible the discursive practices of the general public. The texts of "the everyday," the products of "ordinary" writers, were now being circulated and read in a manner and on a scale that had not previously been possible. Nevertheless, this loss of actual (as opposed to imagined) "privacy" did not make impossible epistolary effects such as intimacy, immediacy and presence.

The correspondence between William and Elsie Fuller provides a rich archive for mapping the degree to which narratives of presence and intimacy play out in postcard communication. William Robert Fuller was born in 1899 in Richmond, a suburb of Melbourne. In 1915 he enlisted in the Australian Army, serving as Lance Corporal with the 21st Battalion and was awarded the Distinguished Conduct Medal in June 1918. He was repatriated to Australia on 20 October 1918 and died of Spanish influenza in July of 1919 aged twenty.[23] The earliest postcard in the collection is dated February 1916 and the last is August 1918. During this eighteen-month period, Fuller sent his sister, Elsie, about 140 cards.[24]

Aesthetic affect plays an important role in the production of presence and intimacy within the Fuller correspondence. The images carried by these postcards convey a range of emotions, desires and fears as well as fulfilling particular rhetorical functions. Fuller commonly uses the postcard to reproduce for his sister something he has seen or felt. The assumption seems to be that if both writer and reader look at the "same" sight, the

---

[23] Biographical and historical notes about the Fuller family are obtained from two sources: Papers of William Robert Fuller, Accession Number MS 9701, La Trobe Australian Manuscripts Collection, State Library of Victoria, Melbourne and Australian War Memorial database: http://www.awm.gov.au/.

[24] This calculation includes only the cards that bear messages. Fuller also sent Elsie cards without messages and counting these the full collection of postcards numbers about 170. Since William and Elsie share a last name, they will be referred to in the text by their first names.

latter will share the experience of the former: "at that building I have been on duty and where you see that person sitting I have also sat."[25]

The relation between picture and message is complex and takes a number of different forms. Sometimes, as with the above example, William appears to have seen the same monument, figure or streetscape that the card depicts. On other occasions, however, presence is produced despite the fact that William may not have seen the actual monument to which the postcard refers: "these are a few photos of what I have seen or intend to see, I have not seen the pyramids yet but I intend to see them. They are only a few miles out of Cairo. I will tell you about them."[26] In this case, a shared present is created by the fact that neither William nor Elsie have seen the pyramids. It is strengthened by, perhaps, their shared desire to see the pyramids and by the simulacrum of the pyramids that they have both seen on the postcard. In this case, the simulacrum helps to effect an intimacy one assumes is felt as natural and spontaneous.

A sense of intimacy, therefore, is not dependent on a close relation between image and text. One of the postcards sent to his sister, for example, carries on one side a picture of "the mosques of Sultan Hassan and Al Rifai" in Cairo. On the other side of the postcard, however, William describes a scene one would not expect to see on a commercially available postcard:

> While we were waiting for the train to go, at Suez, I saw a terrible sight, it was a young native boy about sixteen, he had legs about one inch thick and could not walk on them so had to walk on his hands with his knees doubled up under his chin. Just for all the world like a monkey poor chap. I gave him four piastres (one piastre worth 2½d) and he almost went mad. Some of our chaps got onto the river and just to pass the time

25 Robert William Fuller, "Papers," Accession Number MS 9701, *La Trobe Australian Manuscripts Collection*, State Library of Victoria, Melbourne, Australia: 27 May, 1916.
26 Fuller, "Papers," 13 March, 1916.

away they would push the natives into the water. It was very funny to see six of them in the water at once, but it did not hurt them for I could almost swear most of them never had a wash for months.[27]

While conveying the young boy's plight, William reveals something of his own "position" as a young Australian soldier. The language—a mix of emotional commentary and masculine bravado—tells much about the colonial discourses that help shape his views. This establishes an intimacy that is heightened by descriptions of difference and "foreignness." Although Elise does not view a visual representation of what William is able to see—the picture on the card is not the image, event or feeling that William wants to tell her about—a sense of intimacy is generated by the ideological position they share.

These instances provide the basis for thinking through the claims made by contemporary media theory that the postcard, as emblematic of a certain institutional and technological regime, brings to an end structures of intimacy, presence and affect. As noted above, a number of theorists focus on the letter as articulating a certain symbolic capital and cultural formation. The epistolary subject, so it is argued, is autonomous, has faith in authorial power, and believes that communication is the transparent exchange of thoughts from one consciousness to another. In short this is the Romantic subject re-worked by Postmodernism. Siegert, for example, argues that the combination of photography and the postcard had a significant impact upon contemporary regimes of representation and the belief in the originality of subjectivity. He writes:

> In addition to standard postage, standard format and standard text, there now was a standard picture, as well. With the advent of the picture postcard, visual memories departed from the human soul, only to await people thereafter on the routes of the World Postal Union. The picture postcard opened up the

27 Fuller, "Papers," 13 March, 1916.

territory of the World Postal Union as an immense space of forgetting, the object of which was the world itself ... Once memories circulated as picture postcards that could be sent any place on the globe ... travelling itself became unnecessary.[28]

Yet people continued to travel. However standardised early nineteenth-century correspondents felt their postcard images to be, they did not stop collecting and sending them. Siegert's argument about the relation between letters and postcards is based on a misreading of the cultural significance of "standardisation." It misses a key point about how dreams of presence, immediacy and intimacy endure in the postcard era rather than, as he seems to suggest, dissipate. The difficulty with Siegert's argument is that he opposes the formal, standardised, mass-produced format of the postcard to notions of intimacy, privacy, presence and individuality. The latter qualities, he argues, are tied to the epistolary era and are thus made problematic with the new media of the postcard. But why should standardisation rule out the subjective and individual realms? After all, commodity culture and mass production are shored up by the belief in the individual and the rhetoric of "choice."

Contrary to popular and academic belief, therefore, the postcard did not destroy postal intimacy. Refuting commonly-held views that the standardisation of postcard media threatened individuality because it removed the privacy in turn assumed to be necessary for intimacy, the Fuller correspondence demonstrates that postcard communication can in fact increase levels of individuality, presence, intimacy and affect. The postcards exchanged between Elsie and William illustrate the extent to which privacy is performed and imagined rather than existing as a real, empirical condition. Despite the fact that the Fullers's correspondence was available for the wartime censors to read, a fact of which the Fullers were

[28] Siegert, *Relays*, 161.

aware, these siblings found ways to construct their correspondence as private and intimate.

Conclusion

Seen through the lens of contemporary cultural theory, the relation between text and technology is too often conceived in dichotomous terms. Either technological materialities effect decisive, irreversible changes in the content of communication or the socio-cultural articulation under investigation transcends the particularities of the technological infrastructure and regimes of circulation. This tendency towards technological or textual determinism has been particularly acute in new media research which focuses either on the geo-political form of informational networks or the located practices of the ethnographer's text: form / content; global / local; theoretical / empirical; production / consumption. Rather than view these foci as strict binaries, however, I have attempted to map their symbiotic and dynamic relation. These dynamic relations underwrite the use by postcard correspondents, for example, of public communications systems to convey private emotions such as desire, fear and intimacy.

Recognising that fantasies of presence are embedded within material infrastructures and historical practice provides a critical framework within which to locate a theorisation of contemporary affective relations and "immersive aesthetics."[29] Postal poetics continue to exert institutional, symbolic and technological force on new media forms such as email[30] and mobile telephony.[31] As Chandler and Neumark remind us, in

---

[29] See Edwina Bartlem, "Reshaping Spectatorship: Immersive and Distributed Aesthetics," *Fibreculture Journal* 7 (2005): http://journal.fibreculture.org/issue7/issue7_bartlem.html

[30] See Esther Milne, "The Epistolary Body of Email: Presence, Disembodiment and the Sublime," *Southern Review*, 35.3 (2002): 80-93.

[31] See Larissa Hjorth, "Locating Mobility: Practices of co-presence and the persistence of the postal metaphor in SMS/ MMS mobile phone customisation in Melbourne," *Fibreculture Journal* 6 (2005): http://journal.fibreculture.org/issue6/issue6_hjorth.html.

order to assess the future of an effective and affective art practice one needs to acknowledge that the very idea of "the new" is, of course, very old. As they put it:

> in each era, the "new" plays a specific role, to carve out a territory as well as to provide the energy that throwing off the weight of tradition can require. However, pursuit of the "new" risks becoming a tradition itself, heavy and obligatory, if it refuses access to its precursors, the "new" of the recent past.[32]

In tracing epistolary intimacy and presence though geographically dispersed networks, this chapter has argued for a nuanced understanding of the postal conditions underpinning the relation between new and old media.

[32] Chandler and Neumark, *At a Distance*, 442.

Christian Bök

Unacknowledged Legislation

The Missing Referee

Oulipo (*Ouvroir de Littérature Potentielle*) is an exalted coterie of radical writers, who have dazzled the avant-garde for decades by experimenting with exaggerated, formalistic rules called *contraintes*. Oulipo has performed Herculean, if not Sisyphean, feats of poetic labour in order to demonstrate that, even when handicapped by the most unlikely postures of duress, language can still find the wherewithal to express an elegant thought. Older, mostly European, members of Oulipo (including, for example, such poets as Queneau and Roubaud)[1] have all perfected the methodical schematics for a kind of "structural" writing, which has gone on, in turn, to influence newer, mostly American, members of Ubuweb (including, for example, such poets as Goldsmith and Fitterman),[2] all of whom have perfected

---

[1] Oulipo has included, among its members, not only Raymond Queneau and Jacques Roubaud, but also François Le Lionnais, Noël Arnaud, Marcel Bénabou, Georges Perec, Italo Calvino, Harry Mathews, Jacques Jouet, Oskar Pastior, et al. Oulipo imposes rigorous criteria upon candidates for membership, restricting itself to a small cadre of invited writers who, once elected, enjoy permanent inclusion in this poetic clique.

[2] Ubuweb has included, among its members, not only Kenneth Goldsmith and Robert Fitterman, but also Christian Bök, Craig Dworkin, Brian Kim Stefans, Caroline Bergvall, Darren Wershler-Henry, et. al. Unlike Oulipo, however, Ubuweb rejects the exclusive protocols necessary for entry into an elite cabal, preferring instead to convene a small, but loose, union of poets, who provide the nucleus for a much larger, more public, listserv.

the procedural heuristics for a kind of "conceptual" writing. Ubuweb has often acknowledged its indebtedness to Oulipo— but not without betraying some misgivings that, even though such an *ouvroir* has imagined exciting theories of both mannerist constraint and aesthetic liberation, Oulipo has so far left inexplicit, if not unexplored, the political potential of such innovative literature, apparently preferring to constrain such potential, confining it primarily to a poetic, rather than a social, agenda.

Oulipo in fact never deigns to make explicit its political attitudes, even though the conceptual foundation of *contrainte* (with all its liberatory intentions) might lend itself easily to political agitation—and this lacuna in the artistic practice of the group seems even more odd, when we consider that many of the earliest members of Oulipo have participated in leftwing, militant activism, fighting for the Resistance during World War II, and some of these poets have even survived internment as political prisoners.[3] Oulipo at its inception almost resembled a cell of decommissioned revolutionists, yet the group has never published a political manifesto about literature (in the way that a writer like Breton—a wartime veteran—had done, for example, on behalf of Surrealism). Oulipo can, at best, offer only a few whimsical critiques of tyranny[4]—and even though

---

[3] Noël Arnaud, François Le Lionnais, and Jean Lescure all fought in the French Resistance, just as Italo Calvino fought in the Italian Resistance. Le Lionnais, moreover, survived political internment in a German labour camp, just as Oskar Pastior survived political internment in a Soviet labour camp. Noël Arnaud has even worked, as an editor, for a branch of the Situationist International (SI), just as Calvino worked, as a pundit, for a branch of the Italian Communists (PCI).

[4] Jacques Jouet is perhaps the only member of Oulipo, whose work seems most insistently politicized in tone, particularly in his novel-cycle *La République roman,* which includes, among an array of works, the social satire *Mountain* ®, a story about the evils of government corruption. Leland De La Durantaye remarks, however, that (like Queneau, whom Jouet has described as "apoliticienne"), "Jouet is ultimately less interested in denouncing, what he calls, the 'Irrépublique,'" or in installing "une nouvelle République réembastillée," so much as he is interested in uncovering, through the use of

---

Perec, a member of Oulipo, might recount a dystopic allegory about an Olympic kingdom (whose culture of blood sport calls to mind the field games of the *Hitlerjugend* and the death camps of the *Reichsführer*), Oulipo nevertheless ignores this pointed warning about the sociological correlations between athletic rivalry and militant fascism[5] in order to equate artistic freedom with the freedom of "marathoners" who excel at callisthenic enterprises.[6]

Oulipo and Unconscious Tyranny
Oulipo criticises the classical paradigm of inspiration by forsaking the utopian project of an antecedent Surrealism. Rather than rehearse the involuntary graphomania of Breton, for example, Oulipo repudiates the aleatory mystique of such unconscious artisanship in order to rediscover, at the behest of Le Lionnais, "techniques which can dismiss inspiration from [...] affectivity."[7] Oulipo rejects the metaphysical surrealism of

contrainte, "the literary freedoms [...] that a fictional republic offers." Durantaye, "The Republic of Jacques Jouet," *World Literature Today* 19 (Sep-Dec 2004): 52-55.

5 Georges Perec notes that, on the mythic island of W, where the rules of sport reign supreme: "The multiplicity of these Laws, their detail, and the great number and variety of the opportunities thus created, could lead one to believe that it really takes very little for an Athlete to become an Official" (since, as Perec seems to imply, the fascination with ludic rules can easily become an abomination of total power): "the same spirit moves them, the same combat thrills them, the same flame burns in them." *W, or The Memory of Childhood*, trans. David Bellos (Boston: David R. Godine, 1988) 153.

6 Roubaud writes that "Oulipo is anything but imperialist"—instead: "It [...] endeavours to rediscover another way in which to practice artistic freedom [...]: the freedom of difficulty mastered," and thus, "Like a marathon runner, the Oulipian [...] sometimes discovers [...] a 'second wind.'" Introduction to *Oulipo Compendium*, eds. Harry Mathews and Alastair Brotchie (London: Atlas Press, 1998) 41. Even Le Lionnais argues on behalf of Oulipo by citing an athletic metaphor: "People are a little too quick to sneer at acrobatics," since "Breaking a record in one of these extremely constraining structures can in itself serve to justify the work" "Second Manifesto," *Oulipo*, 30.

7 Le Lionnais, quoted by Jean Lescure, "Brief History of the Oulipo," *Oulipo: A Primer of Potential Literature*, ed. Warren F. Motte (Lincoln: University of Nebraska Press, 1986) 38. Le Lionnais admits that "work begins with an

inspired insights in order to embrace what Roubaud calls a "mathematical surrealism"[8]—a unique phylum of pataphysics, one that formulates methodical, if not scientific, procedures for the production of literature, thereby conceiving of difficult, potential problems that require a rigorous, imaginary solution. Oulipo imposes arbitrary, but axiomatic, dicta upon the writing process in order to evoke an unpredicted possibility from these experimental restrictions. Such laborious exercises reveal that, despite any instinct to the contrary, even the most delimited behaviour can nevertheless generate both artful liberty and poetic license. What Surrealism deems instinctive and inscrutable in its own automatic scription now arises, mechanically, not from the haphazard disavowal of rules on behalf of chance, but from the formulaic rehearsal of rules on behalf of choice.

Oulipo suggests that, even though Surrealism might subscribe to what Breton calls "a tenet of total revolt,"[9] in which every surreal project must align itself with the socialist overthrow of capitalism, the utopian project of such aleatory artistry nevertheless results in a condition, not of intentional freedom, but of unconscious tyranny: for example, Bénabou remarks that, to a member of Oulipo, like Queneau (a former Surrealist extradited by Breton), "inspiration which consists in blind obedience to every impulse is in reality a sort of slavery" because "the poet who writes that which comes into his head

---

inspiration … which must accommodate itself as well as possible to a series of constraints" (34).

[8] Jacques Roubaud, "Mathematics in the Method of Raymond Queneau," *Oulipo: A Primer of Potential Literature*, ed. Warren F. Motte. Lincoln: University of Nebraska Press, 1986. 80: Such math allegedly forsakes the will "to legislate for eternity."

[9] André Breton, "Second Manifesto of Surrealism," *Manifestoes of Surrealism*, trans. Richard Seaver and Helen R. Lane (Ann Arbor: University of Michigan Press, 1969) 125. Breton remarks elsewhere in his Second Manifesto that "Surrealism considers itself ineluctably linked […] to the movement of Marxist thought" (149).

[...] is the slave of other rules of which he is ignorant."[10] Random inspiration and chance composition do not in fact generate the extreme freedom desired by Breton, insofar as such tossing of dice and such drawing of lots can do little more than entrench our systematic ignorance about the unseen edicts that govern poetry. Oulipo appears to reframe the rhetoric of its own exercise within the *lingua franca* of a possible politics—one that might, in theory, expose the ideological foundations of discourse itself (perhaps by exaggerating the absurdist spectacle of these arbitrary protocols in literature, making grotesque their approved grammar, their censored content, their repeated message, etc.).

Oulipo argues that the aleatory caprices of inspiration can only imprison literati within the invisible labyrinth of a hackneyed discourse—but as Bénabou remarks, "the paradox of writing under constraint [is] that it possesses a double virtue of liberation,"[11] granting poets the power to make their own mazes, from which they might then find their own exits. When wilfully selected, constraints do not stifle, so much as excite ingenuity, giving a writer (like Bénabou) the chance to outwit these formal systems that might otherwise impose their covert control: "to the extent that constraint goes beyond rules which seem natural only to those people who have barely questioned language, it forces the system out of its routine functioning, thereby compelling it to reveal its hidden resources"—hence, "writing under constraint is superior to other forms insofar as it freely furnishes its own code,"[12] highlighting both the customs and the devices, which might otherwise serve to hobble poetry behind the scenes. Such *contraintes* reveal the degree to which, when forced to comply to a rule, we always prefer to be swayed

[10] Queneau, quoted by Marcel Bénabou, "Rule and Constraint," *Oulipo: A Primer of Potential Literature.* Ed. Warren F. Motte (Lincoln: University of Nebraska Press, 1986) 41.

[11] Bénabou, "Rule and Constraint," 43.

[12] Bénabou, "Rule and Constraint," 41. Note that, even if critics tolerate such forthright techniques, any "excess of [such] rules is perceived as shameful artifice."

by the obvious, rather than the unknown, master. We always prefer to follow, intentionally, rules created by us for ourselves, rather than to follow, unconsciously, rules created for us by strangers.

Oulipo argues that to fathom such rules emancipates us from them, since we gain mastery over their unseen potential, whereas to ignore such rules quarantines us in them, since we fall servile to their covert intention. Oulipo does not offer us a set of gimmicky formulae for ordering language into highly structured, but wholly unorthodox, genres of poetry (be they acrostics, lipograms, rhopalics, etc.), so much as Oulipo offers us an array of rules for exploring an array of rules. Even though the group may propose constraints for the formulation of literature, the group also imposes constraints upon the formulation of constraints themselves. Such *rules about rules* have, for example, included the following six axioms: first, the constraint must be extremely uncomplex to articulate;[13] second, the constraint must be extremely difficult to accomplish;[14] third, the constraint, if enacted, must mention its own existence;[15] fourth, the constraint, if enacted, must exhaust its own potential;[16] fifth, the constraint must avoid the use of any aleatory protocol;[17] sixth, the constraint must allow the use of

[13] Culled from diverse sources, these six axioms provide the foundation for a prescriptive constitution. In "Mathematics in the Method of Raymond Queneau," Roubaud first notes, for example, that a "good Oulipian constraint is a simple constraint" (86).

[14] In the "Second Manifesto," Le Lionnais notes that: "The efficacy of a structure […] depends primarily on the degree of [its] difficulty" (30).

[15] Roubaud also notes that, wherever possible, a "text written according to a constraint describes the constraint" ("Introduction," 42).

[16] In "Mathematics in the Method of Raymond Queneau," Roubaud notes in turn that, wherever possible, "the Oulipian text actualising a constraint [is] envisaged only on the condition that this text contain all the *possibilities* of the constraint" (95).

[17] Roubaud even notes that "Oulipian procedures are as remote as possible from […] any kind of literature whose strategic foundation is chance. ("Introduction," 41). (To me, this rule seems oddly prejudicial given that chance is an object of study in mathematics.)

one optional deviancy.[18] Such recursive doctrines almost seem to ratify a kind of pataphysical constitution—a playful statute that governs the anarchy of poetics by legislating our methodology for legislating the methodology itself.

Oulipo and the Pataphysicians

Ubuweb notes that, even though members of Oulipo might abstain from any social agenda, refusing to emulate the explicit, leftwing poetics of Breton, both Oulipo and Breton do in fact draw some of their radical impetus from a common source— pataphysics, "the science of imaginary solutions" imagined by Jarry.[19] Oulipo has in fact upheld a long-time, intimate alliance with the Collège de Pataphysique, a parodic academy of intellectuals, who propose absurd axioms and then use rigorous argument to explicate the logical outcome of these absurdities. Ubuweb recognises that, like mathematicians concerned only with the theoretic implications, rather than the pragmatic consequences, of a concept, the pataphysicians of Oulipo bracket reality in order to explore their own cognitive fantasies—and thus they have made themselves vulnerable to the kind of critique imagined by Vaneigem, who argues that, because pataphysicians subscribe to the dictum, *credo quia absurdum est* (in which every credo is equal, and no theory is too absurd for belief): "Pataphysics [...] leads us with many a twist and turn to the last graveyards."[20] He argues that, even though

---

18 Perec notes that, "when a system of constraints is established, there must also be anti[-]constraint within it"—inserted there as a minor error called a "clinamen." Quoted by Warren F. Motte, "Introduction" to *Oulipo: A Primer of Potential Literature*, 19-20.

19 Alfred Jarry, "Exploits and Opinions of Doctor Faustroll: A Neo-Scientific Novel," *Selected Works of Alfred Jarry*, eds. Roger Shattuck and Simon Watson Taylor, trans. Simon Watson Taylor (New York: Grove Press, 1965) 193.

20 Raoul Vaneigem, *The Revolution of Everyday Life*, trans. Donald Nicholson-Smith (London: Rebel Press/Left Hand Books, 1994) 126. Vaneigem argues that, in a world without value, each pataphysician makes a passive gesture toward nihilism: "he throws [...] dice to decide his 'cause,' and then becomes its devoted slave, for Art's sake" (178).

such nihilism can in fact nurture the inborn energy of rebellion, pataphysics nevertheless lends itself too easily to social apathy.

Ubuweb might admit that, while such charges of nihilistic conformity do apply to the attitudes of some pataphysicians— particularly members of the Collège (including, for example, Shattuck, who argues that: "Pataphysics preaches no rebellion […], no political reform")[21]—such misgivings do not take into account that, originally, Jarry lampoons every ideology in order to ignite an impish spirit of anti-bourgeois, anti-philistine disorder. When ideology imposes unreal reconciliations upon actual contradictions, such imaginary solutions are indeed forthrightly pataphysical, but they differ from the bizarre science of Jarry only insofar as ideology must disavow its own imaginariness. Such solutions must be final. They must forbid any deliberate suspension of disbelief. Even though the ruses of pataphysics may enable the rules of the ideological, such rules must oversee and control such ruses, for fear that these ruses might in turn expose the rules as provisional. We see that Oulipo, however, does not endow its own utilisation of pataphysics with much ideological consequence, despite the radical potential of such a parodic viewpoint; instead, Oulipo offers solutions to aesthetic, rather than political, problems, acting out a theory that limits any demand to propel such theory into action.

The Central Problem

Ubuweb admits that, with such an ample array of ludic rules, pataphysics has given Oulipo the grand power to write a noble canon; however, Ubuweb also argues that, although Oulipo sees fit to bandy about the loaded jargon of *freedom* and *slavery*

---

[21] Roger Shattuck, "What Is 'Pataphysics?" *The Innocent Eye: On Modern Literature and the Arts* (New York: Farrar, Strauss, and Giroux, 1984) 104. Shattuck notes that, because pataphysics is an alleged science of indifference, pataphysics cannot support any political viewpoint without endorsing them all: "the pataphysician suspends all values," and thus the "Pataphysics attempts no cures" (104).

in order to explain such principles of constraint, the political potential of these terms, their "legislativeness," if you like, goes unacknowledged, except insofar as they provide colourful metaphors for artistic triumph or creative setback—and when deployed to complain about the aleatory artistry of Surrealism, these two terms, *freedom* and *slavery*, almost risk taking on the Orwellian overtones of a fundamental equivalence. Oulipo may argue that surreal revolutions represent unaware enslavement to unknown constraints, but Oulipo does not account for the fact that, despite this problem, Surrealism nevertheless promotes forthrightly a radical mandate for social change, whereas Oulipo does not, despite its self-conscious, self-liberated algorithms for creativity. If *wilful ignorance* about such rules can result in covert obedience to their poetic dominance, yet still entail a social critique (as is the case for Surrealism)— how might *wilful obedience* to such rules result in a poetic critique, yet still entail a covert ignorance about their social potential?

Oulipo and the Conceptualists
Ubuweb has embellished the pataphysics of Oulipo by linking such procedural use of constraint to the principles of conceptual art (as seen, for example, in projects by such artists as Kosuth and LeWitt, who "dematerialise" their artwork, transforming its objecthood into a discursive experience—one subjugated to either a serialised heuristic or a permutable schematic). Just as Roubaud might suggest that literature operates according to a tautological series of mathetic "propositions,"[22] so also does Kosuth suggest that aesthetics operates according to a tautological series of analytic "propositions."[23] Both thinkers

[22] Roubaud writes that "language can be mathematized" ("Mathematics in the Method of Raymond Queneau," 82), and he notes among his eighteen propositions: "*Proposition 15:* Writing under […] constraint is […] equivalent [to] the drafting of a mathematical text, which may be formalized according to the axiomatic method" (89).

[23] Joseph Kosuth, "Art After Philosophy," *Art After Philosophy and After: Collected Writings, 1966-1990*, ed. Gabriele Guercio (Cambridge, Mass.: MIT Press, 1991)

equate these tautologies with the kind of "language-games" discussed by Wittgenstein,[24] who argues that, when playing such a game, "we look to the rule for instruction and *do something*, without appealing to anything else for guidance."[25] Both movements resort to logical systems in order to study the rules that govern a specific, artistic paradigm—and in doing so, both movements theorise that their creative practice culminates, not in the manufacture of a concrete object, so much as in a speculation about its abstract schema. The artfulness of a work now resides in the rationale for its experimental procedures, not in the outgrowth of any concomitant production.

Ubuweb goes on to accentuate these affinities between the idea of the "constraint" in poetic writing and the idea of the "conceptual" in visual artwork. Goldsmith, for example, discusses his own literary practice by rewriting the famous essay "Paragraphs on Conceptual Art" by LeWitt, substituting diction about "writing" for any mention of artwork (so that, if LeWitt writes: "the idea becomes a machine that makes the art"[26]—then Goldsmith writes: "the idea becomes a machine

20-21. Kosuth notes that: "what art has in common with […] mathematics is that it is a tautology"—i.e. "Works of art are analytic propositions," operating upon their own inner logic.

[24] Roubaud writes that "constraints provide the rules of a language game," and "this Great Game of Constraints" is, after Wittgenstein, "connected to a 'way of life'" ("Introduction," 40; 43). Similarly, Kosuth writes that "a process of cultural verification […] occurs in art when the *language-game(s)* of art accommodate an additional shift, and adjust to a new *rule*." Joseph Kosuth, "The Play of the Unsayable: A Preface and Ten Remarks on Art and Wittgenstein," *Art After Philosophy and After*, 247.

[25] Ludwig Wittgenstein, *Philosophical Investigations*, trans. G.E.M. Anscombe (Oxford: Basil Blackwell and Mott, 1974) 86e, 228. Wittgenstein asks a question worthy of Oulipo: "What is the difference between […] obeying a kind of inspiration and […] obeying a rule? For they are surely not the same. In the case of inspiration I *await* direction. I shall not be able to teach anyone else my 'technique'" (87e, 232).

[26] Sol LeWitt, "Paragraphs on Conceptual Art," *Conceptual Art: A Critical Anthology*, eds. Alexander Alberro and Blake Stimson (Cambridge, Mass.: MIT Press, 1999) 12. Like Oulipo, which spurns chance, LeWitt notes: "If the artist

that makes the text.")[27] Whereas Kosuth and LeWitt might exploit the rules of conceptual art in order to transmute the "concreteness" of *les objets des arts* into a textual experience of the artistic medium itself, Goldsmith borrows the rules of conceptual art in order to transmute the "abstractness" of *les textes des mots* into a somatic experience of the literary medium itself. Even Dworkin at Ubuweb has gone so far as to gather, online, an anthology that juxtaposes procedural writing by European writers and conceptual writing by American artists in order to showcase their parallel interest in what he calls "the direct presentation of language itself, with 'spontaneous overflow' supplanted by [a] logical process"[28]—a process whose ludic rules must explicate the tautology of their own autotelic coherence.

Ubuweb and Intentional Freedom

Ubuweb notes that, because the procedural work of the Europeans and the conceptual work of the Americans has portrayed language as a closed system of experimental speculations about constraint itself, the potentials of such constraint need not even be executed in mandatory practice, but only be proposed as possibilities: for example, Roubaud notes that, to Le Lionnais, the rule, once postulated, can go unfulfilled, since "the text that formulates the constraint" is "the only admissible text," and any "text deduced from a

---

wishes to explore his idea thoroughly, then […] chance [must] be eliminated from the making of the art" (13).

27 Kenneth Goldsmith, "Paragraphs on Conceptual Writing," *Open Letter: Kenneth Goldsmith and Conceptual Poetics* 12.7 (Fall 2005): 98. Like Oulipo and LeWitt, Goldsmith also notes (with irony): "If the author wishes to explore her idea thoroughly, then […] chance [must] be eliminated from the making of the text" (99).

28 Craig Dworkin writes that "conceptual writing […] is not […] writing in which the idea is more important than anything else"—instead, conceptual writing is a kind of "writing in which the idea cannot be separated from the writing itself: in which the instance of writing is inextricably intertwined with […] the material practice of *écriture*." Dworkin, "The Ubuweb Anthology of Conceptual Writing," http://www.ubu.com/concept.

188

constraint" is unrequired;[29] likewise, LeWitt notes that a rule, once prescribed, can go unperformed, since: "All ideas need not be made physical," given that: "Ideas alone can be works of art,"[30] and thus any work produced from the idea is gratuitous. Goldsmith jokes that, in the case of Oulipo, writing by its members may enjoy more enthusiastic appreciation if such writing goes uncreated, presented only in the form of a concept—of a "mapping," so to speak—since Goldsmith finds the proposed ideas of the group to be much more radical than the actuated texts by the group: "judging by the works that have been realised, they might be better left as ideas," since such "blandly conservative […] fiction […] seems to bury the very interesting procedures."[31]

Ubuweb admires Oulipo, but admits that, aside from a few athletic oddities, much of the poetic output by the group can look very procrustean, since the basic fulfilment of a given restriction can often seem to take precedence over every other formal issue (like euphonic expression or thematic profundity— among the many unadmitted, but no less subsidiary, constraints controlling the merits of poetry); hence, the results of these experiments often risk reiterating the execution of a rote task, one that might appear no more engaging than a fumbled sleight. Goldsmith adds to these concerns about Oulipo by saying that: "Even with complex systematic structures, […] the writers always tend to wrap their systems in conventional narratives,"[32] replaying, for example, the timeworn formulae of whodunits and novelettes, of fantasies and picaresques. Even though the wacky rules of Oulipo might imply a freedom from conventional storytelling, the content of such restricted literature often seems skewed towards

[29] Robaud, "Mathematics in the Method of Raymond Queneau," 91
[30] Sol LeWitt, "Sentences on Conceptual Art," *Conceptual Art*, 107. LeWitt notes that "all ideas are art if they are concerned with art" (107).
[31] Kenneth Goldsmith, "Interview (From *Read Me,* Issue 4)" conducted by Erik Belgum, http://wings.buffalo.edu/epc/authors/goldsmith/readme.html.
[32] Kenneth Goldsmith, "A Conversation with Kenneth Goldsmith" conducted by Marjorie Perloff, http://jacketmagazine.com/21/perl-gold-iv.html.

normality. In addition, the poetic tastes of the group can often seem quite banal, insofar as its members seem to enjoy dickering with the gearboxes of obsolete, literary genres (like the sestina or the rondeau), revivifying these antiquary styles, yet entrenching their canonical repute.

Ubuweb agrees with Oulipo that, unless we analyze our own authorial functions with mechanical detachment, we might find ourselves blindly obeying an instinct that, far from liberating us (as the Surrealists might aver), does nothing but entrap us even more subtly in the rote maze of our own poetic habits. Ubuweb notes, however, that just as Breton might claim to have freed himself from the ideology of such a constrained unconscious, all the while retrenching the capital economy of meaning (by using an aleatory protocol to express his spontaneity through the form of a coherent, rational sentence), so also does Oulipo claim to have freed itself from the ideology of such unconscious constraints, all the while retrenching this same capital economy of meaning—an economy that the principle of *contrainte* might have otherwise showcased and subverted. Ergo, Marxist writers from the L=A=N=G=U=A=G=E Group—writers, for example, like Andrews (who posits an "anti-systematic" writing)[33] or Bernstein (who posits an "anti-absorptive" writing)[34]—have admitted in conversation that they find Oulipo impressive in its formal technique, but inadequate in its social rationale, if only because Oulipo has yet to question the ideology of its own grammatical, referential bias.

---

[33] Bruce Andrews, "Constitution/ Writing, Politics, Language, The Body," *Paradise & Method: Poetics and Praxis* (Evanston: Northwestern University Press, 1992) 23. Andrews notes that, for his own anti-systematic, anti-capitalist writing, "politics rests on an explanation—a characterisation of the medium and [...] its constraints" (20).

[34] Charles Bernstein, "Artifice of Absorption," *A Poetics* (Cambridge: Harvard University Press, 1992) 22. Bernstein notes that, like Andrews, his own anti-absorptive, anti-capitalist writing, "makes obtrusive/the [...] ideological nature [...]/of language habits in which we are/ ordinarily so absorbed as to ignore/or repress" (35).

Ubuweb balks at the apolitical intentions of Oulipo, doing so not to impugn such an important legacy so much as to outline a, heretofore unexplored, potential within its aesthetic theory— a potential still available to younger writers, who might wish to mimic Oulipo in the hope of advancing the group's experimentation without repeating the group's accomplishments. Oulipo has already striven to implement computerised explorations of constraint (through ALAMO, for example),[35] but Ubuweb has in turn gone on to showcase the political potential of such devices, particularly in the general economy of the Web, where not only can literary software (like *The Apostrophe Engine*)[36] write poems without any human input—but even the concept for such a project can get distributed anonymously for free to anyone who might wish to exploit it or improve it. Ubuweb in fact sees much of its own poetic labour as an act of advocacy for the "copyleft movement,"[37] whose policies enshrine the file-swapping of data

---

[35] ALAMO (*Atelier de Littérature Assistée par la Mathématique et les Ordinateurs*) is an offshoot of Oulipo. Harry Mathews notes that ALAMO has written "litware" (*litteraciels*)—digital programs that computerize literary activity in three ways: first, through *combinatorial* systems (which permute and combine the components of a given lexicon); second, through *applicational* systems (which replace and install components of a given grammar); and third, through *implicational* systems (which analyze and produce original procedures for a given poetics). "ALAMO," *Oulipo Compendium*, 46.

[36] *The Apostrophe Engine* by Bill Kennedy and Darren Wershler-Henry is a piece of homespun, oracular software that can hijack Google in order to retrieve any online clause that begins with the words "You are…," thereby gathering and collating these retrievals into a series of "apostrophes," all of which address us in the voice of the second person. Anyone who writes online might become an inadvertent contributor to such a poem, and the poem might, in theory, expand without limits, linking together all of our disparate discourse, juxtaposing it through the infinite metonymy of a single, common utterance.

[37] Darren Wershler-Henry notes: "copyleft […] ensures that any piece of creative work […] can circulate freely—and can even be modified and extended— without being subsumed into […] private […] property"—so long as any supplementary modifications made to the original property continue to abide by this very same rule of unconstrained recirculation. Wershler-Henry, *Free as in Speech and Beer: Open Source, Peer-to-Peer and the Economics of the Online Revolution* (Toronto: Financial Times Prentice Hall, 2002) 23

and the open-sourcing of code. We see these values embodied, for example, in *The Tapeworm Foundry* by Wershler-Henry, who fulfils an apparently impossible constraint by giving away, without reserve, every marvellous idea that he has ever had for a potential book.[38]

The Missing Statute

Ubuweb has striven to interfuse the procedural writing of Europeans with the conceptual artwork of Americans, doing so in order to suggest the many ways in which their common notion of a proposed, but untested, constraint might nevertheless intersect in the kind of leftist project seen, online, in what Wershler-Henry has called the "commonspace"[39] of anonymous, automated collaboration—the overall *ouvroir* of the Web (whose output often resembles a kind of "gift," first installed for free, then later dispersed for free, with no user gaining exclusive ownership over the benefits from such exchange). Oulipo has in fact called itself an *ouvroir* in part to emphasise its status as a kind of "communal workroom," the meaning of which, in French, calls to mind the charitable enterprise of volunteers, who donate both their energy and their labour to a common motive. Ubuweb has striven to augment this vision of proletarian magnanimity, extending such a leftwing, economic overture into a metaphor for communal, artistic creation on the Web (consequently, a writer like Goldsmith goes so far as to make his entire oeuvre

---

[38] In *The Tapeworm Foundry, Andor the Dangerous Prevalence of Imagination* (Toronto: Anansi Press, 2000), Wershler-Henry dares us to enact each of his ideas: "andor steal it from a writer who is not as talented as you are because your audience is going to think that your victim is actually the one who has stolen the idea" (37), "andor come up with a more interesting list than this one" (39), "andor don't and then see if I give a fuck" ([15]). Read it online at http://www.ubu.com/ubu/wershler_tapeworm.html.

[39] Mark Surman and Darren Wershler-Henry define "commonspace" as "the collective, many-to-many world [...] online"—a networked community, non-hierarchical and non-prescriptive, its emergent features evolving into "the epitome of [...] connected diversity." *Commonspace: Beyond Virtual Community* (Toronto: Financial Times, 2001) 6.

available digitally, for free, so that websurfers everywhere can readily access it and quickly recopy it, thus exploiting it for their own creative purposes).[40]

Oulipo may exaggerate its formalism, but rather than propel its "stricture" into an extremism that might exhaust the potential of all "structure" (including even grammar and meaning), the literary politics of the group differs from the norm more in degree than in specie, accentuating these laws rather than interrogating them. Oulipo does not stress enough that, in literature (if not in all ideologies), *contrainte* entrenches a given habit by making it repeatedly imperative. Goldsmith has suggested in conversation that Oulipo invests so heavily in artful labour that the group never considers writing according to some of the most difficult, but otherwise forbidden, constraints—like being "uncreative" or being "unengaging" (two of his own, apparently impossible, poetic values, in which one must write by restricting oneself exclusively to the repetition of both the already said and the totally dull, doing so in a way that still creates surprise and engages interest).[41] If Oulipo fails on rare days to impress us, perhaps it does so because it ignores a subsidiary constraint that might have otherwise augmented its merits—and if Oulipo appears apolitical, perhaps it is so because it has yet to include in its pataphysical constitution a missing statute, one requiring that every constraint acknowledge its political potential.

---

40 Kenneth Goldsmith has posted his output at http://epc.buffalo.edu/authors/goldsmith/.

41 In "Uncreativity as a Creative Practice," Goldsmith notes: "to be as uncreative in the process as possible [is] one of the hardest constraints [that] an artist can muster." http://epc.buffalo.edu/authors/goldsmith/uncreativity.html. Likewise, in "Being Boring," Goldsmith notes: "I love the idea of doing something [...] exciting in the most boring way possible." http://epc.buffalo.edu/authors/goldsmith/goldsmith_boring.html.

Louis Armand

Avant-Garde Machines, Experimental Systems

It is not surprising, given the historical genealogy of avant-garde practice, that mechanisation and machine metaphors should figure so largely in the literary and plastic arts of the last century-and-a-half. More than a mere technological symptom, mechanisation has come to signal a *condition* at the very core of cultural experience and cultural production; indeed, it has come to frame a condition not only of contemporary culture but of discursive structures generally. For this reason, the concept of "the machine" is less an historically-determined one, than one that has been temporalised in terms of a "crisis" in those broadly rationalist doctrines underwriting the Enlightenment discourse of the human sciences. Notwithstanding a certain technological metaphysics that has from time to time taken hold in western thought, this machinic conception draws our attention to the radical *materiality* of sign operations and hence to a general structural situation upon which such things as consciousness, representation and meaning are ultimately predicated.

1

The "modern" conception of the machine issues from the Industrial Revolution—itself a term for a disparate and uncoordinated tendency towards mass mechanisation, prefigured by the Renaissance, but only realised in practice from the eighteenth century onwards—and this conception is thus also tied to the emergence of a particular type of scientific discourse, one in which the speculative or theoretical disposition is increasingly linked to experimental and technological verification (or what Karl Popper has called "falsifiability" as the criterion of empirical statements in science).[1] This trend is particularly evident, for example, in the genealogy of ideas and practices linking the early time-and-motion studies of Étienne Jules Marey, Frederick Taylor, and Lillian and Frank Gilbreth, to the advent of mechanised production and Ford's automated assembly-line. It is a genealogy that draws together the self-regulating free market ideology of Adam Smith and the regulated efficiencies and division of labour that characterise Taylorism, thus giving rise to the various "contradictorily coherent" mechanisms and structural "crises" of the contemporary global economy. However, mechanisation acquires a global significance in another sense during the latter stages of the Industrial Revolution—in that it is in terms of *discursive* structures, recursion and complex relations of environmental causality, that ideas of mechanisation come to predominate in the work of key nineteenth century thinkers like Charles Darwin, Karl Marx, and C.S. Pierce. (In the twentieth century, this increasingly global, discursive view has been most widely represented in the work of Norbert Wiener, Buckminster Fuller, Marshall McLuhan and more recently Bernard Stiegler.)

Initially, industrial-era machines were regarded as entirely predictive—as mindless prostheses of the human will-to-progress—their operations determined according to a strict set of protocols. Yet already in the 1830s Charles Babbage—in his study *On the Economy of Machinery and Manufacture*—had recognised ways in which programmable mechanical

---

[1] Karl Popper, "Science, Pseudo-Science, and Falsifiability," *Conjectures and Refutations* (London: Routledge & Kegan Paul, 1978 [1962]) 33-39.

procedures might give rise to recursive structures capable of what, in cybernetics, is called auto-poiesis. That is to say, of self-programming, learning machines, or so-called "artificial intelligence." This in turn called into question such received philosophical pieties as the nature-technics dichotomy, or the separation of mind from matter, and consequently exposed a need to accommodate effects of unpredictability in mechanical and computing systems, and indeed in the understanding of all *dynamic* systems, thus transforming a dominant concept of the nineteenth century—systematicity—from one of totalisation to one of radical indeterminacy.

This move away from positivism and the idea of the machine as a prosthesis of the human idea, towards a conception of a general mechanistics *underwriting* material, discursive systems—from machine metaphor to semiotic mechanism—likewise implies a transformation of what is meant by terms like mechanism, mechanistics and machine, as no longer signalling a type of industrial-era "contraption," but rather—as Peirce suggests—any binary relation mediated by a third element.[2] Or in other words, what we might call a *programmē*, as the underwriting condition for any concept of agency, operation, or event-state of semiosis. (Importantly, this transformation has also come to effect the way in which we conceive language and sign systems generally, such that today we can speak of phenomena of semiosis as arising in *any* dynamic system whatsoever—in a state that would formerly have been bracketed-off from the realm of signifiability as a state of base materiality or "mindless mechanistics.")

At the same time, the discursive aspect of mechanisation—and of technology *per se*—begins to reveal itself as being other than the locus of a continuous historical progress, and instead as an "agent" of discontinuity and *anachronism*. In its orientation towards a certain futurity vested in the

---

[2] Charles Sanders Peirce, "Logic as Semiotic: The Theory of Signs," *Philosophical Writings*, ed. Justus Buchler (New York: Dover, 1955) 99-100.

technological object,[3] semio-mechanisation articulates a perpetual movement of supercession; a breach in the "teleological hypothesis"[4] of historical discourse that henceforth describes a repetition automatism, as Freud says, wherein the historical relation is constantly refigured as one of ambivalence.[5] This ambivalence is firstly experienced as a disjointedness in the "time of production," as a figuring of the present as *anachrony*: the constant deferral of the to-come which mirrors the deferral of gratification and the alienation-effect of commodification, as described by Marx. Moreover, this movement of deferral is perpetuated as a *condition*, not as a departure from the norm or as a perversion of a teleological (ends-means) system of production-consumption. With the advent of industrial "modernity," historical periodisation thus cedes to a machinic periodicity; just as in Nietzsche the history concept cedes to a mode of eternal recurrence.

This counter-historical movement can be regarded as one of the defining characteristics of what has been called the *avant-garde*, whose claim to being somehow *before its time* ties it, in often unanticipated ways, to an inherent "anachronism" of political-economy and the experimental sciences. Moreover, this movement accomplishes itself in a two-fold way, since its orientation towards the unrealised and the "unpresentable" at the limits of received knowledge is always accompanied by a dependency upon previous forms of representation and conceptualisation in order to formulate, precisely, an idea of what the limits of knowledge in fact are, and what the "unpresentable" might be.[6] John Dewey argues this in his 1958

---

3 Which, like the machine, is not a *thing as such* but rather a "figure" or "trope" (in this case of the always *to come*, the ideally unrealised end of production).

4 Samuel Beckett, *Proust* (New York: Grove Press, 1931) 71.

5 Cf. Sigmund Freud, *Beyond the Pleasure Principle*, trans. C.J.M. Hubback (London: The Hogarth Press, 1922).

6 This two-fold movement can otherwise be characterised as a recursion, or what cyberneticists describe as a feedback loop. The sense of the preposition *avant* is thus always qualified by the necessary conservatism of the verb *garder*, to keep: it remains conditional, tentative, an attempt at defining limits—so that the term

book *Experience and Nature,* linking the anachronism of conceptual dependency to the constructivism of "deviating from a norm."

"In the history of man," Dewey writes, "the individual characteristics of mind were regarded as deviations from the normal, and as dangers against which society had to protect itself. Hence the long rule of custom, the rigid conservatism, and the still existing regime of conformity and intellectual standardisation." As a consequence, the development of modern science—or of modernity *per se*—began only when "there was recognised in certain technical fields a power to utilise variations as the starting points of new observations, hypotheses and experiments. The growth of the experimental as distinct from the dogmatic habit of mind is due to the increased ability to utilise variations for constructive ends instead of suppressing them."[7]

Henri Lefebvre has attempted to locate the ambivalence of this two-fold status of anachrony and unpresentability—and of the experimental and the constructive—in terms of what he calls the *antithesis* of "modernism" and "modernity," as contrary aspects of the so-called avant-garde moment. According to Lefebvre, *modernism* designates "the consciousness which successive ages, periods and generations had of themselves; thus modernism consists of phenomena of consciousness, of triumphalist images and projections of self." While *modernity,* is understood as "the beginnings of a reflective process, a more-or-less advanced attempt at critique and autocritique, a bid for knowledge. We contact it in a series of texts and documents which bear the mark of their era and yet go beyond the provocation of fashion and the stimulation of novelty. Modernity differs from modernism just as a concept which is being formulated in society differs from social

"avant-garde" always involves a notion of insufficiency and the task of defining the very totality whose limits it would test. As William Blake wrote, in "The Marriage of Heaven and Hell: *"Enough, or too much!"*
[7] John Dewey, *Experience and Nature* (New York: Dover, 1958) xiv.

phenomena themselves, just as a thought differs from actual events."[8]

In a more or less similar gesture, Jean-François Lyotard, locates modernity in terms of a certain discursive ambivalence that he defines as a *post-effect* in advance of the fact, as it were. For Lyotard, it is the "unpresentable" ambivalence of the relation of thought and event—as the normative object of an institutional exclusion (the limits of knowledge, the thinkable or "historical consciousness")—which defines a fundamental aspect of what he consequently refers to as the *postmodern*. In Lyotard's view:

> A postmodern artist or writer is in the position of a philosopher: the text he writes, the work he produces are not in principle governed by pre-established rules, and they cannot be judged according to a determining judgement, by applying familiar categories to the text or to the work. Those rules and categories are what the work of art itself is looking for. The artist and writer, then, are working without rules in order to formulate the rules of what *will have been done*. Hence the fact that the work and text have the character of an *event*; hence also, they always come too late for their author, or, what amounts to the same thing, their being put into work, their realisation (*mise en œuvre*) always begins too soon. *Post modern* would have to be understood according to the paradox of the future (*post*) anterior (*modo*).[9]

It is in this paradox (of future-anteriority) that the condition of "the machine" resides—that is to say, as a *mode of enactment* contiguous with the "unpresentable"—and according to which it describes a systematicity which is at once recursive and "experimental." We are concerned here, in other words, with a notion of mechanism linked to a certain performativity; to the

8 Henri Lefebvre, *Introduction to Modernity*, trans. John Moore (London: Verso, 1995) 1-2.
9 Jean-François Lyotard, *The Postmodern Condition: A Report on Knowledge*, trans. Geoff Bennington and Brian Massumi (Manchester: Manchester University Press, 1991) 81.

performance of operations, above all *sign-operations,* and the recursive nature of the relation between such performances and what is called a "programme." That is to say, we are concerned with a logic of representation and of representability, insofar as the experimental points beyond itself to a mode of understanding that is "without model."

Hence, for Lyotard, the postmodern "would be that which, in the modern, puts forward the unpresentable in presentation itself; that which denies itself the solace of good forms, the consensus of taste which would make it possible to share collectively the nostalgia for the unattainable; that which searches for new presentations, not in order to enjoy them but in order to impart a stronger sense of the unpresentable."[10] In this way, "a work can only become modern if it is first post modern. Postmodernism thus understood is not modernism at its end but in the nascent state, and this state is constant."[11] This is what Lefebvre describes, vis-à-vis the reifications and mechanical ambivalence of such a *constant* "nascent state," as the "idea of cyclical regularity of change, and of change as a norm."[12]

2

In a lecture delivered in Turin in November 1967, entitled "Cybernetics and Ghosts," Italo Calvino argued that it is primarily through stochastic and recursive processes of *anticipation, rupture* and *reintegration,* that previously unapparent forms are arrived at and consequently acquire a normative status; that new combinations of elements are obtained, as Calvino says, "through the combinatorial

---

[10] Lyotard, *The Postmodern Condition,* 81.
[11] Lyotard, *The Postmodern Condition,* 79.
[12] Lefebvre, *Introduction to Modernity,* 168. The problem that arises here is not which of Lyotard's or Lefebvre's terminologies are most appropriate to the circumstances, but whether or not their arguments offer some sort of means of accounting for the apparent impasse in the status of avant-gardism and its paradigm of the machine.

mechanism itself, independently of any search for meaning or effect on any other level." In place of a continuous linear progression, the "future-anteriority" of experimentation functions by discontinuity, readjustment, and contingency within what are nevertheless definable as "procedural constraints" or *structural norms*—whether or not these are recognised, as Lyotard says, in the form of "pre-established rules," or methods of prediction and production, or are only recognised and recognisable *after the fact*. Once normalised, however, such contingencies then become "charged," according to Calvino, "with an unexpected meaning or unforeseen effects which the conscious mind would not have arrived at *deliberately*: an unconscious meaning in fact, or at least the premonition of an unconscious meaning."[13] Such outcomes define what Dewey termed the "constructive ends" of experimentation, whose contingencies nevertheless define a *limit-effect of ambivalence* in the discourse of knowledge, for example, and in which the ego—as Jacques Lacan says—is accorded the status of something like a mechanism, rather than that of an inaugurating intentionality or "will."

In relating the experimental to the experiential aspect of "consciousness"—or the "imaginary function of the ego" as the outward manifestation of *unconscious agency*—Lacan identifies in the "paradoxical expression *thinking machine*" the co-implication of structural contingency and structural necessity in defining so-called *acts* of language. "The paradox of consciousness," Lacan argues, is that "it both has to be there, and not be there."[14] This paradox reappears elsewhere, in a more insistent form, in the discourse surrounding the question of modernity in philosophy and the arts, above all with regard

13 Italo Calvino, "Cybernetics and Ghosts," *The Literature Machine*, trans. Patrick Creagh (London: Secker and Warburg, 1987) 21-2.
14 Jacques Lacan, "From the *Entwurf* to the *Traumdeutung*," *The Seminar of Jacques Lacan. Book II: The Ego in Freud's Theory and in the Technique of Psychoanalysis 1954-1955*, trans. S. Tomaselli (London: Cambridge University Press, 1988) 117-120.

to the status of language in its relation to the "real." Still in February 1955, Lacan was able to write: "The big question for the human sciences now is—what is language?"[15]

Confronted with an increasing number of ellipses in the predictions of scientific method (under the fading constellation of Cartesianism), and with the consequent problem of the status of language in conditioning and constituting the experience of the knowable, more and more writers in the late nineteenth and early twentieth century had already began to ask about the *definitional* character of reality, and the emerging supposition that "behind" the idea of the real there is only discourse. As Samuel Beckett remarked in his 1931 study of Proust: "the transcendental apperception that can capture the Model, the Idea, the Thing in itself," failed to materialise under scrutiny.[16] Taken beyond the literary and philosophical domains, this problem likewise invested the physical sciences, which discovered a need to account, among other things, for its disturbances of the object of scientific observation. Niels Bohr and Werner Heisenberg's principle of indeterminacy is the well-known consequence of this development. But as the ambivalence of language and the increasingly recognised materiality of discourse came to effect scientific method and experimentation (with its initial dependency upon *models of the real*), more broadly semiotic questions also began to arise. What, for example, is it that we mean when we speak of reality? And, indeed, what does it mean when we speak of *language*? or the *reality* of language? In other words, confronted with the incompatability of consciousness, as defined by Lacan, and the observer paradoxes of quantum mechanics, how could the so-called object of language itself be anything but "experimental," unpresentable or otherwise indeterminate?

While language thus appeared, on one level, to assume an increasingly abstract or "theoretical" aspect, on another level its radical materiality necessarily came more into focus. These two

---

[15] Lacan, "From the *Entwurf* to the *Traumdeutung*," 119.
[16] Beckett, *Proust*, 69.

characteristics—abstraction and materiality—emerge at this point as defining a state of *complementary*: the first linked to the speculativity of signification (vis-à-vis Saussurean semiology), the second to its inherently "procedural" function (vis-à-vis Lévi-Strauss's structural anthropology and Claude Shannon's mathematical theories of communication). It is in this sense, for example, that language reveals itself as a "system" of mechanical (event-state) transformations, iterations and reversions; as a type of machine, in other words, made not of an enumeration of symbols, but of a topology of symbolic relations or "sign operations." Moreover, in place of any deterministic ego, agency or deus ex machina, the term "operation" here—through its allusion to something like an *operator*—comes to designate instead what we might call an algorithm or "rule," which *automatically* (and arbitrarily) co-ordinates a given function with some other function: for example, metaphor, metonymy, or any analogous translational, "totemic," or "coding-decoding" process. This implies what we might call a mechanism of generalised equivalence across contiguity—not only with regard to tropic or "rule-orientated" operations, but to the status of any assumed relation *between*, say, signification and materiality.

What we mean by "rule," in this context, has a purely definitional character. Its operative principle is that of ambivalence as such—and of ambivalence as a "causal agent" of signification. It thus also marks a transition in thinking about language, from deterministic laws to probabilistic ones, or from an epistemological or paradigmatic status of meaning to a contingent, definitional and above all *complementary* status. It is not—in effect—a matter of mediating *between* states or changes of state (i.e. *between* signification and materiality), but of constituting an event-state of complementarity: for example, in speaking about the materiality *of* signification—wherein neither of these terms may be said to assume an autonomous, discrete or objective status. Consequently, this "rule"—arbitrating, as it were, between two modalities of causation, or what Peirce elsewhere terms "the law of mind"[17]—represents a fundamental "equivalence across contiguity"; a resistance and a transference; or what Gaston Bachelard refers to both as an "epistemological obstacle" and as an "epistemological rupture." In doing so it reveals a fundamental contradiction in the logic and structure of so-called "laws" of reason, even when they are accommodated to what Bachelard refers to as "the notion of epistemological discontinuity in scientific progress."[18] This interpolation of the arbitrary within the totalising movement of reason *as* law—being, on a fundamental level, the very *articulation* of law[19]—does not represent a perversion or deviation, but rather a logical or structural inherence: for example, between the *letter* of the law ("lex") and the truth-status of its logos, *the word* itself ("lexis"); what we might in fact call a *perturbation at the origin* of any signifying system.

Such a perturbation, as Lacan points out, is necessarily sublimated in the operations of the law of reason in the guise— for example—of justice, whose arbitrations represent a kind of parenthesis in which the referent of the law (such as the transcendence of "the good") passes beyond reach and must be approached by way of a certain detour. By detour we would also mean, by metaphor or metonymy; in other words, by way of a "rule" of discourse or *discursus*. To illustrate this formulation, Lacan makes reference to a passage from *The Story of Justine*, by the Marquis de Sade. "Tyrants," Sade writes,

> are never born out of anarchy. One only ever sees them rise up in the shadow of laws; they derive their authority from laws. The reign of law is, therefore, evil; it is inferior to anarchy. The greatest proof of this position is the obligation of any government to plunge back into anarchy whenever it wants to

---

[17] Peirce, "The Law of Mind," *Philosophical Writings*, 339ff.

[18] Gaston Bachelard, *Le Matérialisme rationnel* (Paris: Presses Universitaires de France, 1953); cited in Georges Canguilhem, *A Vital Rationalist: Selected Writings*, ed, François Delaporte, trans. Arthur Goldhammer (New York: Zone, 1994) 32.

[19] Whether it be defined as the *a priori* as such, the *given* of meaning, the *acts* of signification (i.e. as formally determined and *mimetic*).

remake its constitution. In order to abrogate its ancient laws, it is obliged to establish a revolutionary regime in which there are no laws. Under this regime new laws are eventually born, but the second is less pure than the first since it derives from it, since the first good, anarchy, had to occur, if one wanted to achieve the second good, the State's constitution.[20]

In Sade, the dream of rationalism is worked out *in extremis*, its mechanistic universe articulating an inescapable logic that is at the same time recursive, deranged, and self-fulfilling. On the one hand a radical critique of Kantian "categorical imperative," on the other an apparatus of narrative discursus and "degeneracy" in which the lineaments of literary and philosophical modernity are clearly visible in the complementarity and contrariety of *rule* and *law*—or otherwise discursive "anarchy" and the "tyranny" of forms—by which the ambivalence of any system of values is ultimately constituted. Much of nineteenth- and twentieth-century literary modernism can be seen as a critical extension—if also "rectification"—of Sade's anti-rationalist project, mediated, for example, by certain facets of Marxism and Darwinism, according to which re-evolution, or epistemological rupture, retains a *positivistic* or *homoeostatic* function.

Sade's extremism finds itself seconded to a project of aesthetic and epistemological reform—such as the ultimately reformative ambitions of Surrealism—in which the revolution of values and of consciousness is linked to a project of social reconstruction: anarchy sublimated in a "new" constitutionalism, a "new" epistemology, a "new" system of judgement. Indeed, if—as Georges Canguilhem has argued— "epistemology provides a principle on which judgement can be based,"[21] it is nevertheless upon the "crisis" of epistemological rupture that judgement itself can here be seen to be *founded*, as

---

20 Cited in Jacques Lacan, "The Function of the Good," *The Seminar of Jacques Lacan. Book VII: The Ethics of Psychoanalysis*, trans. Dennis Porter (New York: Norton, 1992) 221.

21 Canguilhem, *A Vital Rationalist*, 43.

the regulating mechanism of the otherwise arbitrary convulsions of *the law*. Sade, writing at the height of the French Revolution, identifies law as the very *inversion* of justice, whose subsequent discourse however only serves to mask the revolutionary character of the epistemological break in terms of "correction" or "reconstruction."

Within the framework of rationalism, crisis does not represent the unthinkable or the unpresentable, but rather an alibi—a *justification*. And this in turn points to the difficulty in conceiving an avant-garde *method* which would lead to anything other than a positivistic reintegration. Jonathan Swift, in 1726, was already attentive to such implications in his satirical treatment of scientific positivism in the "Academy of Lagado" section of *Gulliver's Travels*. Among other things, Swift's critique focuses upon the idea of an experimental random-text machine, "for improving speculative knowledge by practical and mechanical operations."[22] The mostly nonsensical formulations produced by Swift's machine assume an oracular function—reducing the labour of thought to a "merely" mechanical procedure—while providing the substance of poetic, philosophical and juridical treatises, anthologised by an otherwise mindless priesthood of *technicians* (predecessors of Karel Čapek's "universal robots"). A type of semiotic "anarchy" thus becomes the rule upon which universal laws are founded, interpreted and enacted. However, the satirical aspect of Swift's machine resides not in its suggestion that such an idea is foolish as such, or that a positivistic science which sublimates "true" knowledge to technological production is necessarily foolish, but rather that science itself and the arbitrariness of law, and of language (Marinetti's *parole in libertà*), in fact imply and require it. In Swift's analogy, moreover, there is a recognition of the fundamentally satirical character of any epistemological, semantic or legalistic code that attempts to exhaust the arbitrarily descriptive possibilities

---

[22] Jonathan Swift, *Gulliver's Travels* (London: Wordsworth Edition, 1992) III.iv.195.

of so-called truth statements. This is because all such codes—as discourse—are effectively excessive, devolving upon an "excess at the origin" which cannot be remediated by means of any "law" since it itself is the underwriting condition of the law, of its limits and of its norms of judgement.

3

Swift's and Sade's rejection of a purely procedural rationalism has often been seen as prefiguring twentieth-century avant-gardist critiques of Enlightenment reason—like those of Marcel Duchamp, Francis Picabia and Jean Tinguely, whose satirical, counter-functional "machines" affect something of a rebuke to the ideologues of late nineteenth- and early twentieth-century industrial "progress." But in prefiguring the avant-garde, Swift and Sade also necessarily prefigure the sinister "triumph" of a rationalism embodied in the systematic disorders of industrialised warfare and the Nazi extermination camps. Irrationalism, Swift and Sade tell us, is not a deviation from the rule, but the very foundation of the rule itself and of its "reason."

Framed at either end of its history by Auschwitz and the Place de la Concorde, the avant-garde has always run the risk— in the revolutionary mode identified by Peter Bürger with the "historical avant-garde"[23]—of becoming little more than an aestheticised form of political conscience or socio-cultural *symptom*. It is not so much a question of whether or not, as Theodor Adorno argued, poetry after Auschwitz could still be possible (or merely "barbaric").[24] Rather it is a question of the "burden of history" as a type of reactionary classicism, or negative tradition, and of the rule of platitude in defining a certain historical *imminence*. This has always been the struggle

---

[23] Peter Bürger, *Theory of the Avant-Garde*, trans. Michael Shaw (Minneapolis: University of Minnesota Press, 1984).

[24] Theodor Adorno, *Prisms*, trans. Samuel and Shierry Weber (Cambridge, Mass.: MIT Press, 1967) 34.

of experimentalism, situated between historical agency and historical object. Such is likewise the case not only with the historicisation of "the avant-garde" but, also, what we might call the classicising of modernity. It implies a classicism that perpetuates itself merely by a rote form of "equilibrium": an *identification* of what is knowable with what is known, and according to which experimentation is cognate with *method*.

In his lecture on "Cybernetics and Ghosts," Calvino broaches the subject of classicism and method in terms, like Sade's, of an intervention in the historical transmission of social-aesthetic norms which also delineates the very possibility of norms.[25] This intervention, associated by Calvino with a type of avant-gardism, functions as a mechanism of difference that re-sets the classical mechanics of aesthetic stasis, allowing for a renewal of the classical idea as one of movement and re-invention. Accordingly, Calvino proposes an almost Swiftian scenario in which literature would become "a machine that will produce avant-garde work to free its circuits when they are choked by too long a production of classicism."[26]

The question is, however, does such a "freeing of the circuits," as Calvino says, amount to anything more, ultimately, than a form of historical reversioning—since classicism here implies not simply a type of conservation, but also a periodic totalisation; a closed cycle that is at the same time expansive, inflationary, accumulative; of *both* entropy *and* discursus; teleology *and* recursion? "Is this," Calvino asks, "the triumph of the *ir*rational? Or is it the refusal to believe that the irrational exists, that anything in the world can be considered extraneous to the *reason of things*, even if something eludes the reasons

---

[25] It is precisely such an idea of stultifying and overly "rationalised" classicism that we encounter, for example, in Pier Paulo Passolini's film *Salò*, in which Sade's *120 Days of Sodom* is transposed into a critique of the last days of Fascist Italy—the infamous Repubblica di Salò (last refuge and death-place, incidentally, of Fillipo Marinetti, founder of Italian Futurism and one of the leading figures in the avant-garde cult of the machine).

[26] Calvino, "Cybernetics and Ghosts," 13.

determined by our historical condition, and also eludes limited and defensive so-called rationalism?"[27]

Calvino attempts to confront this problem by way of Sartre's question "What is literature?" For Calvino, the difficulty of situating "literature" in the context of industrial modernity derives from the ultimate ambivalence of the terms "rational" and "irrational," and their status with regards to the *controlled unpredictability* of experimental method with its own ambivalent relation to the underwriting condition of "absolute chance," as Peirce says. Where "rational" and "irrational" remain definitional (and probabilistic), experimentality obtains at the level of the possible, and in this sense the term "literature"—as *writing*—designates an experimental condition of language itself. That is to say, a condition of absolute *unconditionality*, as defining the very chance of language *as language*; its underwriting iterability and technē of inscription. Calvino writes:

> Did we say that literature is entirely involved with language, is merely the permutation of a restricted number of elements and functions? But is the tension in literature not continually striving to escape from this finite number? Does it not continually attempt to say something it cannot say, something that it does not know, and that no one could ever know? A thing cannot be known when the words and concepts used to say it and think it have not yet been used in that position, not yet arranged in that order, with that meaning ... The struggle of literature is in fact a struggle to escape from the confines of language; it stretches out from the utmost limits of what can be said; what stirs literature is the call and attraction of what is not in the dictionary.[28]

As in Sade, the formal and thematic rigidities, the compulsive repetition and enactment, the staging of a narrative and its mechanical "performance," all point to a conception of

27 Calvino, "Cybernetics and Ghosts," 20.
28 Calvino, "Cybernetics and Ghosts," 18.

literature as operating under the sign of a programmatic ambivalence—in which the concept of "the machine" no longer remains straightforwardly linked to instrumentalism, but rather to its *détournement.*

A certain détournement of instrumentality can likewise be found in the "genetic distributions of language" in Mallarmé, in the encyclopaedic schematisations of Joyce's *Ulysses* and *Finnegans Wake*, in the entropic spirals of Beckett's minimalism, in the "minute vivisections" operated by Natalie Sarraute and Christine Brooke-Rose, or in the quasi-automated textual apparatuses of Georges Perec's *La vie mode d'emploi* and the counter-causal mechanistics of Pynchon's *Gravity's Rainbow, V,* and *The Crying of Lot 49.* Alain Robbe-Grillet, principle architect of the Nouveau Roman, has himself described the legacy of Sade as practically reducing narrativity to a "vast nomenclature of perversions, comparable to the botanical classifications of Linnaeus or to Mendelejev's periodic table of elements."[29] This description is itself reminiscent of comments made about Robbe-Grillet's own texts, such as *La Maison de Rendez-vous,* notable for its "accrued frequency of themes of deprivation: drugs, fascination with crime, unnatural love, casual Sadism, necrophilia, cannibalism, etc."[30] Themes of crisis, perversion, anarchy and anachronism, also proliferate in Joyce, Beckett, and elsewhere in the body of "modernist" literature, yet this would hardly be noteworthy in and of itself if it did not involve a certain testing of the limits of presentability, as it were. Just as we might say that terms like *indecency* are nothing if not definitional—culturally and historically contingent—so too we may speculate that other aspects of the unpresentable may also be "reducible" to a set of cultural or ideological procedures.

[29] Alain Robbe-Grillet, "L'ordre et son double" (1965), *Le Voyageur* (Paris: Christian Bourgois, 2001) 86.

[30] Robbe-Grillet, "Un écrivain non réconcilié," *Le Voyageur*, 100.

4

Arguably, one of the challenges posed by modernity has been the relinquishing of a moral viewpoint or *judgementalism*. That is to say, the relinquishing of any "ethics" that is ideologically founded. The question remains whether or not this challenge—exemplified in Sade's critique of legalistic reason as the tyranny of an entirely abstracted "mind"—will itself inevitably be reduced to something like a "standard deviation" within the circuit of the cultural system? (It is noteworthy, in any case, that where the mere mention of Sade's name was once scandalous in itself, it now barely raises eyebrows). This in turn raises the question of the effective virulence of any "avant-garde"—since the operations of recursion that underwrite its various ruptures and discontinuities also serve as mechanisms of reintegration and homoeostasis. That is to say, as *engines of entropy*. We might pose this question otherwise, as whether or not the epistemological rupture brought about by modernity is not simply the necessary condition of an epistemological reconstruction and renewal? If, in other words, the ideology of what we might call "modernism" (as a continuation of the Enlightenment project) is not simply a dialectical reification of what is made to amount to a mere systemic perturbation or rote form of experimentation—what Bachelard terms "obsolete science."

With the liberatory phase of so-called postmodernism having passed—and with the status of avant-gardism and the possibility of criticism (of judgement) once again in dispute—the question arises as to the relation of experimentality to a future that, however unpresentable and enigmatic it may appear, has become overburdened by a type of *neo*-classicism. A classicism, that is, of both a speculative and material "revolution" of sense and of the senses—of the epistemological and the experiential, the cultural and the political, and so on. In other words, we are confronted with a question not merely of *viability*, but of a pervasive limit-effect of what Lefebvre terms "change as a norm." Under such procedural conditions—in which procedure itself veers between permissibility and possibility—the Duchampian critique of post-industrial rationalism and its stylisation in the form of avant-gardist method, or in the *commodification* and *consumption* of the "avant-garde," points to a situation of historical recursion that possesses no immediately recognisable axes of critical differentiation.

Yet when François Lyotard wrote of James Joyce that his writing "allows the unpresentable to become perceptible in his writing itself, in the signifier," he was signalling a change not in the aesthetics of revolution or historical consciousness, but in the very logic of signifying agency, and with regard to all of its possible social registers. "The whole range of available narrative and even stylistic operations is put into play without concern for the unity of the whole," Lyotard argues. Consequently: "The grammar and vocabulary of literary language are no longer accepted as given; rather they appear as academic forms, as rituals originating in piety (as Nietzsche said) which prevent the unpresentable from being put forward."[31] The question remains, of course, as to whose idea of the unpresentable we are speaking of here—if not that which is underwritten by the very resistance *of the presentable itself.* For it is indeed, here, a question of the mimetic status of presentability and of the assumption, in discourse, of something like an object. Even if this object is taken to be "discourse itself."

In any case, we need to ask ourselves about the significance of the relation of these various conceptions of agency and the mechanics of signifiability that underwrites them. If this question, as Lyotard suggests, is one that is linked to a particular experience of language as technē, then what can the work of writers like Swift, Sade or Joyce tell us about the general semiotic character of the mechanisms of presentability

---

[31] Lyotard, *The Postmodern Condition*, 80-1.

themselves? What do they tell us, in other words, of what we might call "grammars of emergence"? Is the "unpresentability," as Lyotard contends, of such structural grammars or sign operations, a mere symptom or instead a condition of language? Or rather, is it by means of a certain symptomatology bound to the conditional that we may speak of the unpresentable at all, as something that may become "perceptible" in writing itself, in the signifier? As Roger Shattuck has argued: "An avant-garde gains its special status from its adversary relation to the main body of the culture to which it is reacting," even if this culture is one that attaches especial significance, precisely, to avant-gardism.[32]

Contemporary preoccupations with hypertext, hypermedia, the recursive "collage-effect" of the World Wide Web, point again to an idea of language as both heterogeneous and yet procedurally constrained—one which is neither deviational nor positivistic, but rather an event-driven "state of affairs." Suggestive of a general condition of semiosis, this idea of language extends the literary medium to the very limits of "concretion," particularisation, and phenomenality— describing, as Andruid Kerne says, an interface with a "re-processed experiential archive," that is "in flux and yet bound to its material objects."[33] For cyber-ecologists like Kerne, "Interfaces are the multidimensional border zones through which the interdependent relationships of people, activities, codes, components, and systems are constituted."[34] Such an interface-effect is already signalled in the genealogy of procedural poetics extending from Mallarmé, Gertrude Stein and John Cage, to the OuLiPo, L=A=N=G=U=A=G=E poetry, and the advent of the "new" digital media—spawning, among other things, such Swiftian "textual machines" as Mark

32 Roger Shattuck, *The Innocent Eye: On Modern Literature and the Arts* (New York: Farrar, Strauss, and Giroux, 1984) 74.
33 Andruid Kerne, "CollageMachine: An Interactive Agent of Web Recombination," *Leonardo* 33.5 (2000): 347-350.
34 Louis Armand, "Interface Ecologies," *Solicitations* (Prague: Litteraria, 2005) 124.

America's *Grammatron*, Douglas Davis's *The World's First Collaborative Sentence* and Kerne's own *CollageMachine*.

These "machines," which integrate recursive and chance procedures in the production of multi-dimensional textual interfaces in "real time," describe a type of Joycean *tetragrammaton*—or word-of-words. Like Babbage's "Analytic Machine"—a mechanical device capable (at least in theory) of "weaving algebraic patterns"—these interfaces are not so much produced as performed, in the sense that they are themselves *mechanisms* within a larger recursive structure of "interactions" and "interference." And if such effects may be said to be effects of semiosis, or indeed "phenomena" implying something like an agency (if not a consciousness), then the question remains as to whether or not this is by consequence of a mechanisation *applied* to some prior state of affairs, or by consequence of a mechanical *inherence* constitutive of any form of signifying materiality, or indeed of any *system* as such.

Laurent Milesi

From *Logos* to *Muthos*: the Philosophy of Pound's and Olson's Mythopoetics

The essence of modernity may be said to lie in a moment of cultural and historical crisis which, at the level of expression, took the form of a rupture of the traditionally more comfortable position of the subject with regard to language. In their respective ways, the trauma and aftermaths of the first World War, the ambient scientific discoveries and the advent of new disciplines or ways of thinking (such as the rise of phenomenology and modern linguistics, the concurrent emergence in several areas of a more fluid apprehension of time, etc.), all contributed to a radical change in the subject's perception of itself and of its place in the world. This fluid ideological climate also entailed a renewed awareness of the linguistic medium as such and of its impact on cognitive operations, and new forms, methods and idioms capable of translating more adequately the current view of an isomorphic relationship between language and the processes of the real were searched for. Thus, according to T. S. Eliot in *"Ulysses*: Order and Myth,"* the conventional "narrative method" gave way to the "mythical method" in Joyce's *Ulysses*, a "scientific discovery" which Eliot praised for its ability to map an order onto the chaos of the contemporary world.[1] In a similar spirit, Pound was striving towards his own "method of science" or "ideogrammic method,"[2] which took a more decisive shape during his editing of Ernest Fenollosa's *The Chinese Written Character as a Medium for Poetry*, in which the ideogram is presented—or rather presents itself—as a kind of visual synecdoche, "a vivid shorthand picture of the operations of nature."[3] The essay investigates how the transcription of the root perception of natural processes at work in the configuration of the ideogram defined as a field of verbal action can profitably become the nuclear unit of, and provide a new grammar for, modern poetic practices. In keeping with Fenollosa's views, the methodological superposition of myth onto contemporary reality and the compacting of the latter with other ages within the Poundian ideogram—what Robert Duncan identified as "the mythopoeic weavings of Pound's *Cantos* in which 'all ages are contemporaneous'"[4]—were held to be *scientific*, rather than *logical*, attempts to grope for a new language, which implied a radical redefinition of language itself and the link between poetic voice, history and ancient lore, and nature. In Laszlo Géfin's words: "The isomorphic-cumulative ideogram is almost invariably tied to myth, and through myth to fundamental processes of nature."[5]

Modernist writers like Joyce rediscovered the "poetic wisdom" or "poetic metaphysics" of Vico and the cyclical laws of his ideal eternal history, which the ambient Crocean and,

---

[1] Eliot's history-making review appeared originally in *The Dial* LXXV.5 (November 1923): 480-83. Eliot's slick distinction, which seems to leave out the question of the poem's own narrative, is ironically undercut by the fact that, for the Greeks, the myth carried with it notions of "plot" and "narrative" as it was embedded in a socio-cultural practice of story telling. For an attempt to solve Eliot's perplexing opposition, see Michael H. Levenson, *A Genealogy of Modernism: A Study of English Literary Doctrine 1908-1922*, (Cambridge: Cambridge University Press, 1984) 197 ff.

[2] Ezra Pound, *ABC of Reading* (London: Faber, 1951) 26.

[3] Pound, *ABC of Reading*, 12.

[4] Pound, ABC of Reading, 6.

[5] Laszlo Géfin, *Ideogram: Modern American Poetry* (Milton Keynes: Open University Press, 1982) 39-40.

more generally, neo-Hegelian aesthetics had helped to bring into fashion, but also early Greek thinkers, with their conception of cyclical time and their view of reality as a continuous flux. Both Viconian and pre-Socratic philosophies carried with them a renegotiation of the relation between language, history and myth or story telling, and Heidegger's later long-standing efforts to retrace the forgotten origins of the underpinning concepts of metaphysics to their more concrete, interactive configurations will provide an epistemological counterpoint against which the full redeployment of the more primitive equation between *muthos* and *logos* similarly undertaken in the sphere of poetics by Pound's postmodernist epigones can be appreciated. It is within this perspective of a convergence of ideas and methods in the arts and other disciplines and, more specifically, in the cross-light of the manifold implications which the early Greek logos had in philosophy and arts that I would like to situate my rereading of some of the practices and key concepts of (post)modern poetics and map out points of intersection between the uncovering by contemporary philosophy of the foundations of the original "myth" and Pound's (and subsequently Olson's) mythopoetics or, in the felicitous coinage of Jed Rasula, "muthologistical grounding."[6]

---

[6] Another starting point can be found in the following remark by Michael Davidson: "'Logos,' for someone like Charles Olson, does not mean prior reason or authorising signification but 'what is said,' regardless of any appeal to its truth-value. His desire to antedate modern associations for words like 'myth,' 'history,' and 'truth' in Indo-European roots reflect his attempt to recover a kind of physical, material basis at the heart of all speech acts." Davidson, "Archeologist of Morning: Charles Olson, Edward Dorn, and Historical Method," *ELH* 47 (1980): 199. The present essay would like to test the validity of Davidson's statement for Pound's poetics and extend to modernist poetry the convergence between postmodern literary procedures and Heideggerian phenomenological inquiry into language in the wake of Rabaté's methodology and rationale for bringing together Pound and Heidegger (see Jean-Michel Rabaté, *Language, Sexuality and Ideology in Ezra Pound's Cantos* [London: Macmillan, 1986] 2) rather than the ideological focus of, *inter alia*, Bové's *Destructive Poetics* (see Paul A. Bové, *Destructive Poetics:*

1. Logos in early Greek philosophy

Martin Heidegger's patient exegeses of pre-Socratic fragments, collected in *Early Greek Thinking*, infuse his linguistic inquiry into the essence of "Being" in *An Introduction to Metaphysics*. Of particular relevance for this essay is the reading of Heraclitus's Fragment B 50 on "Logos," but also of "The Anaximander Fragment," which originally appeared in 1954 and 1950 respectively; there the German thinker, in his usual procedure, tries "to reach what wants to come to language."[7] Subsequently reduced to *Ratio*, hence our reason or "logic," by the philosophical schools, and to *Verbum* by theologians, *Logos* originally also conveyed the more essential meaning of "to say, utter" (that which is said was therefore the *legomenon*) and was even more primitively identified with "to gather." "Λέγειν properly means the laying-down and laying-before which gathers itself and others,"[8] hence: "Λέγειν [...] can be nothing other than the essence of unification, which assembles everything in the totality of simple presencing.[9] This disclosure of what is present in its presencing is what the Greeks called *alētheia*, which we misguidedly turned into our metaphysical "truth," and in attempting to uncover or recover "true" speech in its diversity, Heidegger's own philosophical parsing is equally "aletheic" insofar its etymological procedure aims to shed light on the linguistic kernel of authenticity (*etumon*) concealed in a word. Heidegger's true speech, as opposed to the idle talk which he denounced in *Being and Time*, has its poetic counterpart in Olson's opposition between the cheap use of "words, words, words / all

Heidegger and Modern American Poetry [New York: Columbia University Press, 1980] 217-81 on the *Maximus* poems) or of the Winter 1976 issue of *Boundary 2*.

7   Martin Heidegger, "The Anaximander Fragment," *Early Greek Thinking*, trans. David Farrell Krell and Frank A. Capuzzi (San Francisco: Harper and Row, 1984) 25.

8   Heidegger, "Logos," *Early Greek Thinking*, 60.

9   Heidegger, "Logos," 70.

over everything"[10] and his root words such as "tansy" in "Letter 3" (*Maximus*, 13 [I.9]). It also recalls Giambattista Vico's *veriloquium* which, towards the beginning of the section aptly titled "Poetic Logic" in his *New Science* (§ 401),[11] he equated with "myth" or *vera narratio*, in a "mythopoetic" gesture which, via Joyce's transmission, might have had an indirect impact on Ezra Pound himself. Although it would seem at first sight that the German philosopher is moving away from "rational thought," such an overstepping of the limitations of traditional logic was precisely for him a "radical" and more rigorous way of thinking—as was the Poundian-Fenollosian rejection of logic in favour of science—which hoped to approach the essence of language in the light of Being,[12] conceived of as a state of flickering unconcealment,[13] and retrieve the originary relationship between being, *logos*, and *physis*, the latter not merely as "nature" but also as being-in-nature (*IM* 123). Thus, for Heraclitus, insofar as "the *logos* is this togetherness in the essent" (*IM* 127 [Fragment 2]) and "The word ὁ Λόγος names that which gathers all present beings into presencing,"[14] it became the guiding word "so as to think in this word the Being of beings."[15] Whence it follows for Heraclitus that, in the exercise of philo*sophy*, "wisdom consists in saying the truth and acting in accordance with nature,"[16] a principle of

---

[10] Charles Olson, *The Maximus Poems*, ed. George F. Butterick (Berkeley: University of California Press, 1983) 17 [I.13]. Subsequent references to *The Maximus Poems* will be in-text.

[11] Giambattista Vico, The New Science of Giambattista Vico. Unabridged Translation of the Third Edition (1744) with the Addition of "Practic of the New Science," eds. Thomas Goddard Bergin and Max Harold Fisch (Ithaca: Cornell University Press, 1984) 127.

[12] Martin Heidegger, *An Introduction to Metaphysics*, trans. Ralph Manheim (New Haven: Yale University Press, 1959) 122 [hereafter *IM* with page reference].

[13] See e.g. "The Anaximander Fragment," 26, and "Logos," 70.

[14] Heidegger, "Logos," 76.

[15] Heidegger, "Logos," 78. Or, to repeat the succinct formula used by David Farrell Krell in his introduction to *Early Greek Thinking*, logos is "the unique gathering of beings which language is" (8).

[16] Heidegger, "Logos," 71 [Fragment B 112].

thinking and living which nourished the emphasis placed on myth by several American postmodernist poets.

This renewed experience of the originary essence of true language, in its intimate association with being and nature, that informs Heidegger's writing finds an artistic parallel in the development, from Pound onward, of an increasingly processual poetry, which ritually enacts the processes of the real in the agonistics of its form.

2. Logos as muthos in early Greek poetics

What there was of saying and uttering that was gathered in the original essence of the philosophical logos also had a function within Greek art, and in its complex relationship with acting or doing (*dromenon*, hence "drama"; *poiēin*), the logos underwent similar mutations, severing in particular its primitive equation with *muthos*. The radical element of "gathering" and "togetherness" which lay under the early Greek logos also implied that the latter referred to a joint production by which teller and audience were gathered in a ritual dia-logic exchange of speaking and hearing. A *logos* was not, therefore, the free expression of a single mind but the slowly matured fruit of a process which might occupy generations of story tellers and their audiences. The success of its telling was not how "truthful" (i.e. what we now mean by this) it was but lay in the teller's ability to critically select those constant features blending the historical and the natural which, in the migration from *polis* to *polis*, would keep present or bring into presence the togetherness of the culture and secure the solidarity of the community.[17] Thus, *logopaeia* was the art of narrating an event whose power did not reside in the truth content of the tale, and, as one of Charles Olson's major sources

[17] Under the tendency of pan-Hellenism, poetry evolved towards the concept of *alētheia*, as distinct from *muthos*, since the latter, as it either reinforced the truth-values of a given community or was held to be false (*pseudos*) by another, came to stand for the mutability of its itinerant practices and thus compelled the poet to select the least common denominator. George A. Kennedy, ed. *The Cambridge History of Literary Criticism*, vol. 1: *Classical Criticism* (Cambridge: Cambridge University Press, 1989) 29-30.

on the ancient Greek logos reminds us, the Greek meaning of *mythology* was not what we imply nowadays when we use and abuse the word.[18]

Comparable to the centrality of "Sage Heracleitus"—to borrow Pound's own tribute in *Hugh Selwyn Mauberley*[19]—and more generally of the pre-Socratics, for the beginnings of Greek philosophy was the crucial place held by Herodotus the *Muthologos*, as Aristotle dubbed him, for whomever wanted to master the logopoeic style, with its emphasis on form rather than material.[20] We know both Olson's esteem for Herodotus's conception of "history" as narration[21] and his individual process of '*istorin*, which Thomson glosses as "finding out for oneself" and which he writes had already been used by philosophers,[22] and his scorn for Thucydides's wish to destroy the mythic element in history envisaged as a mere collection of *true* facts. Less well-known, however, is Pound's passing judgment in "How To Read" to the same effect that "Herodotus wrote history that is literature. Thucydides was a journalist. (It is a modern folly to suppose that vulgarity and cheapness have the merit of novelty; they have always existed, and are of no interest in themselves.)"[23] This opposition, which had already been "systematised" by Pindar, between a "true," i.e. factually provable, logos and a false *muthos*, adorned with cunning *fiction* which is meant to deceive—with the *legend* (from *legein*) or "unconscious fiction in the field of history"[24] in-between—forms the backbone of "Letter 23" of Olson's *Maximus* poems

---

18 J.A.K. Thomson, *The Art of the Logos* (London: Allen and Unwin, 1935) 17.
19 Ezra Pound, *Selected Poems* (London: Faber, 1975).
20 Thomson, *The Art of the Logos*, 14.
21 This now accepted redefinition of history as narration had already been ventured by Vico in his *New Science*, paradoxically in order to lay a secure foundation for history: "history cannot be more certain than when he who creates the things also narrates them," § 349 (104).
22 Thomson, *The Art of the Logos*, 237n13.
23 *Literary Essays of Ezra Pound*, ed. and intro. T. S. Eliot (London: Faber, 1954) 30.
24 Thomson, *The Art of the Logos*, 18; 21.

and is further developed in his essay "It Was. But It Ain't."[25] As a corollary, whereas Herodotus, from a keener sense of commonality, wrote with a popular audience in mind, Pindar, anathematised by Olson but also by Pound in *Mauberley* for his "big rhetorical drum"[26] showed a more proprietorial interest in the sacred stories or *hieroi logoi*.[27] Leading to a selfishly individual truth disconnected from communal practices and beliefs, Pindar's view runs counter to Pound's conviction, voiced as early as *The Spirit of Romance*, that the ancient myth is the articulation between a personal vision and the expression of communal life, and this in spite of the obfuscation of the *Cantos*'s original vocation as the personal record of communal myths: "Greek myth arose when someone having passed through delightful psychic experience tried to communicate it to others and found it necessary to screen himself from persecution."[28] Thus, for Pound, myth would seem to be both what cannot be articulated—if only because it is itself a method of articulation—and yet must be told, as Pound's emphasis on *Sagetrieb* or "urge to say" (German *Sage* also means "legend")

---

[25] Charles Olson, *Human Universe and Other Essays*, ed. Donald Allen (New York: Grove Press, 1967) 141-43 [hereafter *HU*]. See George F. Butterick, *A Guide to "The Maximus Poems" of Charles Olson* (Berkeley: University of California Press, 1980) 145-47, for the passages from Thomson that helped shape Olson's argument, and Sherman Paul, *Olson's Push: Origin, Black Mountain and Recent American Poetry* (Baton Rouge: Louisiana State University Press, 1978) 105-06, for a brief articulation of this context with "Letter 23." Olson's choice of poetry versus the traditional notion of history may recall Roland Barthes's contemporaneous observation that the critic can choose between history and poetry, although the latter's distinction should be revised in the view of this more "archaic" conception of myth that our paper tries to recover, as not merely something obscuring reality. Thus the gap between the mythic and the historical which Pound's ideogrammic method, aided by his mythic consciousness (thus redefined), seals, according to R.G. Carpanini's paper on "Roland Barthes and Pound's Uses of Mythology" (read at the 15th Ezra Pound International Conference on "Nature and Myth in Ezra Pound," held at Rapallo 13-16 July 1993), would not be so wide in the first place.

[26] Ezra Pound, *The Selected Letters of Ezra Pound 1907-1941*, ed. D.D. Paige (London: Faber, 1982) 91.

[27] Thomson, *The Art of the Logos*, 86.

[28] Ezra Pound, *The Spirit of Romance* (London: Peter Owen, 1952) 92.

implies (see later). And although, as Michael André Bernstein has shown, Pound's mythopoetic imagination does not successfully interact with the more explicitly historical and didactic narrative of the *Cantos*,[29] Pound's celebrated aphorism that "an epic is a poem including history" cannot be envisaged outside this legacy of a complex set of relations tying narration, history, nature and myth or legend.

3. *Logon poiein: (post)modernist mythopoetics*

We have seen that *legein* and *poiēin* were "opposed" but as two complementary activities, usually attuned to each other "in accordance with nature" in order to express the myth. If logopoeia came to designate, as it were, an artistic "speech act" which could be directly reflective of nature, the *muthos* or thing spoken, uttered or "acted" by the mouth, had its antithesis or rather correspondence in the thing done or en-acted, the *ergon* or

---

[29] Michael André Bernstein rightly relates Pound's usual impatience with the interpretative schemas proposed by orthodox historians to his attempt to fill in the gaps of history by relying on the metamorphic presentation of mythological thinking, and locates the clash between historical causality and mythical insight in the dimension of time. (Similarly, in his "Spatial Form in Modern Literature" (1945), Joseph Frank had identified a shift from "the objective historical imagination" to "the mythical imagination for which historical time does not exist" with the advent of modernism [quoted in William V. Spanos, "Breaking the Circle: Hermeneutics as Dis-closure," *Boundary 2* V.2 (Winter 1977): 441].) However, in his otherwise correct diagnosis, the disjunctive temporalities of the mythical and historical forces at work in the *Cantos*, and consequently their lack of synthesis, is correlated to a failure in fusing Logos and Mythos which, setting aside the unclear associations of their passing mentions (Bernstein, *The Tale of the Tribe: Ezra Pound and the Modern Verse Epic* [Princeton: Princeton University Press, 1980] 117; 126), seems to rest on a traditional divide whose relevance for the emerging modernist poetics this paper precisely wants to challenge. Metamorphic presentation will also be the linguistic mode of operation for Olson's *Maximus* poems, which Dibakar Barua attempts to formulate by using Derrida's account of Levi-Strauss's analysis of the discourse of myth to the effect that mythological discourse must itself be mythomorphic: unlike the epistemic discourse of abstraction which divorces intellectual processes from the workings of nature, the mythomorphic mode aims to inform and enact its content (Barua, "One and Many: The Paradox of 'Methodology' in Charles Olson's *Maximus*," *Massachusetts Studies in English* 9.1 [1983]: 14).

work. As Jane Ellen Harrison puts it in her influential study of the social origins of Greek religion, which we know Charles Olson consulted and held a copy of:

> The primary meaning of myth in religion is just the same as in early literature; it is the spoken correlative of the active rite, the thing done; it is τὸ λεγόμενον as contrasted with or rather as related to τὸ δρώμενον.[30]

Harrison further notes that the first *muthos* was possibly the interjectional utterance *mu*, and no doubt Olson's awareness of the strong mythical power in the Greek radical for "mouth"[31] lies behind his repeated judgment of the dissonance or "mu-sick" of western civilisation (e.g. *Maximus*, 7 [I.3]). However, in its double capacity as a verb expressing marked situations in ritual or the everyday life of the group, the Greek *muo* could mean both 1° *I say, or see, in a special way,* and 2° *I have my mouth, or eyes, closed,*[32] to which the ancient "mysteries," which, like the myths, Pound saw as an essential element of the community's life and well-being, must also be traced.[33] Its dual dimension of utterance and inarticulateness neatly aligns with Vico's double Latin and

[30] Jane Ellen Harrison, *Prolegomena to the Study of Greek Religion*, 3rd ed. (Cambridge: Cambridge University Press, 1922) 330.

[31] Cf. Charles Olson, *Muthologos: The Collected Lectures and Interviews*, ed. George F. Butterick (Bolinas, CA: Four Seasons, 1978 [vol. I] and 1979 [vol. II]) II.38 [hereafter *M*].

[32] Kennedy, *The Cambridge History of Literary Criticism*, I.3.

[33] In a short section on Eleusinian mysteries in her *Prolegomena to the Study of Greek Religion*, Harrison notes that the *mystes*, or one initiated into the mysteries, it is supposed, "is the person vowed to secrecy who has not seen and will not speak of the things revealed" (153). Pound might have known about this other influential study of Harrison's, which had reached its second edition by 1908. His predilection for the Eleusinian mysteries in particular has been documented by Leon Surette. Cf. also the opening of Duncan's crucial essay on "The Truth and Life of Myth" which bears on the (in)articulability of the myth seen above: "Myth is the story told of what cannot be told, as mystery is the scene revealed of what cannot be revealed, and the mystic gnosis the thing known that cannot be known" (1). See also Herbert Schneidau, *Ezra Pound: The Image and the Real* (Baton Rouge: Louisiana State University Press, 1969)137.

Greek lineage for "fable" and "myth," as when he writes in his section on "Poetic Logic" that:

> "Logic" comes form *logos*, whose first and proper meaning was *fabula*, fable, carried over into Italian as *favella*, speech. In Greek the fable was also called *mythos*, myth, whence comes the Latin *mutus*, mute. For speech was born in mute times as mental [or sign] language, which Strabo in a golden passage says existed before vocal or articulate [language]; whence *logos* means both word and idea. [§ 401][34]

Possibly linked by folk-etymology, which Thomson reminds us was a common source of *logoi*,[35] the semantic oscillations of the radical for "myth" are reminiscent of Heidegger's observation that "Λόγος is *in itself and at the same time* a revealing and a concealing" ("Logos," 71), in the spirit of the Greek *alētheia* which also found its way into the Jewish tradition of the Divine Word being at once revealed and hidden (*Shem ha-meforash*). The articulation of visual and verbal processes is also worth bearing in mind for Pound's reading and use of myth. Rabaté has shown how, in Pound's and Heidegger's recourse to Greek and Germanic roots, the saying in poetry is always a showing, both working together to disclose the mythic "truth," and how the poet's *Sagetrieb* which "suggests a collective process of myth-making" was equally phanopoeic (*sagen, zeigen*).[36]

The choice of the last adjective was motivated by the fact that the visual technique is emphasised in one of Pound's earliest accounts of his project of the *Cantos*, in a 1917 letter to Joyce: "I have begun an endless poem, of no known category. Phanopoeia or something or other, all about everything."[37]

34 Vico, *The New Science*, 127.
35 Thomson, *The Art of the Logos*, 55.
36 Rabaté, *Language, Sexuality and Ideology in Ezra Pound's Cantos*, 7-8, 276-77.
37 *Pound/Joyce: The Letters of Ezra Pound to James Joyce, with Pound's Essays on Joyce*, ed. and with Commentary by Forrest Read (London: Faber, 1965) 102. Pound's emphasis on the visual in the original, provisional title of the *Cantos*, not merely for the ideogrammic method of composition but also for the structure and themes of his epic, is no doubt already motivated by the desire to recreate a

More significantly, it points up the possibility of uncovering the phenomenological orientation of some of the best-known founding propositions of Ezra Pound's poetics as well as that of rereading them in the prismatic light of the above reflections on the centrality of the original "mythic" *logos* for poetry, narration (art), history, and nature.[38] In "How To Read," Pound identifies "three kinds of poetry," the second and third of which, phanopoeia and logopoeia, are especially relevant for understanding the poetic techniques of his own mythic method. Phanopoeia, "which is a casting of images upon the *visual imagination*," is a process of visualisation which posits a relation between the objective physical *eidon* and its subjective imagin(in)g as a poetic *idea*.[39] The more "tricky and undependable mode" of logopoeia, memorably defined as "the

vision of paradise which would eventually "lead back to splendour" (Canto CXVI).

[38] Although we cannot confront here the implications of Spanos's procedure with, for instance, the growing redeployment of space versus time in montage poetry and projective verse, the following observation, dictated by his project of reinstating the temporal-existential reading of literary texts, provides an interesting epistemological framework for our more specific inquiry: "What needs to be thematized [...], especially in the context of the question of the relation between Heidegger's thought and the Western literary tradition and its hermeneutics, is that *this reification of existence is a spatialisation of time or, as the etymology of 'metaphysics' clearly suggests, constitutes a coerced metamorphosis of temporality into image or picture, i.e., an aesthetic structure the model or prototype of which is the plastic or architectonic— visual—arts*" (Spanos, "Breaking the Circle," 431). His reading of modernist texts and poetics, however, seems to ignore their preoccupation with the possibilities of poetic language as showing (itself), i.e. as, precisely, phenomeno-logical, and Pound's invective against pedants "obscuring the texts with philology, / hiding them under their persons" (Canto XIV)—which must not be confused with the drift of (post)modernist American poetry towards the revitalisation of language by taking words at their "true" etymological root—arguably rests on a visionary's faith in the "apophantic" nature of the text showing itself in its pure clarity (cf. Michael Davidson, "'From the Latin *Speculum:*' The Modern Poet as Philologist," *Contemporary Literature* XXVIII.2 [1987]: 187-205). This study is therefore, at one level, another way of approaching what Spanos identifies as the ontological priority of the visual in literature; see also my "'Suspended in time, between pole[s] and tropic:' Eliot's *Four Quartets*."

[39] Pound, *Literary Essays*, 25; my emphasis. Cf. also *ABC of Reading*, 52.

dance of the intellect among words" (which Olson will echo, in a truncated form, in his "Projective Verse" essay; see *HU* 55), is a process of verbalisation which rests implicitly on the relation of poetic language to the physical body and, adds Pound, which "holds the aesthetic content which is peculiarly the domain of verbal manifestation, and cannot possibly be contained in plastic or in music."[40] The marked preoccupation with the relationship between the verbal and the visual found its expression in the recurrent concept of "energy," which acquired an increasing importance in Pound's poetics throughout the 1910s. Jean Hagstrum usefully differentiates between two related types of "putting into action or work" (*ergon*): *enargeia*, which "implies the achievement in verbal discourse of a natural quality or of a pictorial quality that is highly natural," and *energeia* which "refers to the actualisation of potency, the realisation of capacity or capability, the achievement in art and rhetoric of the dynamic and purposive life of nature."[41] This discrimination, Wendy Steiner argues, collapsed with modern writers, who "exchanged the notion of *enargeia* for *energeia* in determining how art could be like reality";[42] or to put it differently, she locates a shift from the traditional vivid description to a more "essentialist" enactment of natural processes. Here again, one should bear in mind and gather all the latent "mythical" (i.e. verbal as much as visual) implications of "energy" in trying to understand the philosophical foundation of the (post)modernist kinetic

---

[40] Pound, *Literary Essays*, 25. Kennedy notes that, in Archaic and Classical Greece, visualisation is "connected with the analogy between literature and the arts, but also with the developing interest in epistemology from the fourth century BC onward" (*The Cambridge History of Literary Criticism*, xiii), and as it has been suggested before, this renewed emphasis on the visual may be seen to go hand in hand with the rise and impact of phenomenological procedures. That analogy has been documented in Wendy Steiner's excellent study *The Colours of Rhetoric: Problems in the Relation between Modern Literature and Painting* (Chicago: University of Chicago Press, 1982), to which we shall presently refer.

[41] Quoted in Steiner, *The Colours of Rhetoric*, 10.

[42] Steiner, *The Colours of Rhetoric*, 10-11.

aesthetics (from Greek τα αισθητά: things perceptible, as opposed to τα νοητά: things thinkable, immaterial) and the conception of poetry as enactment, namely Olson's subsequent view of the poem, via Pound and especially Williams, as a field of verbal action. The following selection from Pound and Olson, via Fenollosa's emphasis on truth as a (natural) transferential process, will highlight the convergence between the gradual foregrounding of the concept of "energy" (or related keywords) and the increasing emphasis on the kinetic dimension of the Image or the ideogrammic form in (post)modernist poetics:[43]

1. Pound

Let us imagine that words are [...] charged with a force-like electricity, or, rather, radiating a force from their apexes [...]. When this conjunction occurs let us say their force is not added one's to the other's, but multiplied the one's by the other's; thus three or four words in exact juxtaposition are capable of radiating this energy at a very high potentiality[44]

I pointed out that energy creates pattern. [...] I would say further that emotional force gives the image. By this I do not

[43] See Ian F.A. Bell, *Critic as Scientist: The Modernist Poetics of Ezra Pound* (London: Methuen, 1981) 27-42, for a stimulating account of the (largely unacknowledged) contribution of Hudson Maxim's *The Science of Poetry and the Philosophy of Language* (1910) to Pound's aesthetics from "The Wisdom of Poetry" (1912) onward (*Selected Prose 1909-1965*. ed. and intro. William Cookson [London: Faber, 1973] 329-32), in particular its advocacy of the energising powers of poetry but also its presentation of a Fenollosian conception of poetry as action-based and verb-centered. Ian Bell's overall perspective of inquiry is to show how science provided Pound with a vocabulary capable of bringing into focus the poet's efforts to define a system of poetics and the modernist critic's procedure. Richard Godden is right to state that "'Phantastikon,' 'image,' 'ideogram,' and 'vortex' are Poundian synonyms for energy which are easier to draw than to describe verbally" ("Icons, Etymologies, Origins and Monkey Puzzles in the Languages of Upward and Fenollosa," *Ezra Pound: Tactics for Reading*, ed. Ian F. A. Bell [London: Vision P; Totowa, NJ: Barnes and Noble, 1982] 222. "Nature is both source and destination to mythic models of language" [229]).

[44] "I Gather the Limbs of Osiris" (1915), *Selected Prose*, 34.

mean that it gives an 'explanatory metaphor'; though it might be hard to draw an exact borderline between the two. We have left false metaphor, ornamental metaphor[45] to the rhetorician.

[...]

In either case the Image is more than an idea. It is a vortex or cluster of fused ideas and is endowed with energy.

[...]

Energy, or emotion, expresses itself in form. Energy, whose primary manifestation is in pure form, i.e., form as distinct from likeness or association can only be expressed in painting or sculpture. [...] Energy expressing itself in pure sound, i.e., sound as distinct from articulate speech, can only be expressed in music. When an energy or emotion 'presents an image,' this may find adequate expression in words.[46]

VORTEX IS ENERGY![47]

The man who doesn't now *want* to learn ideogram is a man half-awake. No one in Europe is in position to say whether Japan or China contains, at the moment of writing, the greater cultural energy.[48]

2. Fenollosa

The transferences of force from agent to object, which constitute natural phenomena[49]

---

[45] Some of the implications, discernible here, of Pound's distrust of the static decorative metaphor and his redeployment of the trope into a kinetic, interpretive, natural process—in short, an image (cf. Pound's note to the Fenollosa essay, p. 27)—are examined in my "Montage moderniste et re-montage postmoderne. De Pound à Olson," *Montages / Collages*: Actes du second colloque du CICADA 5, 6, 7 décembre 1991, textes réunis par Bertrand Rougé (Pau: Publications de l'Université de Pau, 1993): pp. 123-38.

[46] "*Affirmations*—As for Imagisme" (1915), *Selected Prose*, pp. 344, 345, 346.

[47] *Gaudier-Brzeska* (1916), p. 22 [hereafter *GB*]. Gaudier's "Vortex" (pp. 20-24) uses energy several times; see also quotation from p. 92 given *infra*.

[48] "For a New Paideuma," *Selected Prose*, p. 255 (orig.: 1938).

[49] Ernest Fenollosa, *The Chinese Written Character as a Medium for Poetry*, Foreword and Notes by Ezra Pound (London: Stanley Nott, 1936) 11.

all truth is the *transference of power*[50]

3. Olson

A poem is energy transferred from where the poet got it [...], by way of the poem itself to, all the way to, the reader. [...] Then the poem itself must, at all points, be a high energy-construct and, at all points, an energy-discharge. So: how is the poet to accomplish same energy, how is he, what is the process by which a poet gets in, at all points energy at least the equivalent of the energy which propelled him in the first place, yet an energy which is peculiar to verse alone and which will be, obviously, also different from the energy which the reader, because he is a third term, will take away?
("Projective Verse" (1950), *HU* 52)

the *process* of the thing, how the principle can be made so to shape the energies that the form is accomplished (*HU* 52)

the EXCEPTIONAL man, the "hero," loses his description as "genius" —his "birth" is mere instrumentation for application to the energy he did not create—and becomes, instead, IMAGE of possibilities implicit in the energy, given the METHODOLOGY of its use by men from the man who is capable precisely of this, and only this kind of intent and attention.[51]

To which we could add Gary Snyder's view of the poem's growth "from an energy-mind-field-dance"[52] and his rewriting of Pound's vortex-as-energy as "sharpening the utterance down to a point where a very precise, very swift message is generated, an energy is transmitted." Thus, the ideogram teaches "to hew back to the lines of force by which an Anglo-American word has its power," says Olson in his essay "Against Wisdom as Such" (*HU* 68), where the word "wisdom" is itself parsed along an

50 Fenollosa, *The Chinese Written Character*, 16.
51 "The Gate and the Center" (1951), *HU* 22 (and *passim*).
52 Stephen Berg and Robert Mezey, eds. *Naked Poetry* (Indianapolis: Bobbs-Merrill, 1969) 357.

etymological line of force as, precisely, a "way of being or acting," i.e. of being-in-nature, in the physical world.

We may now return to the link, briefly mentioned above in connection with phanopoeia, between the outside stimulus of the physical *eidon* and its subjective expression as a poetic IDEA in the light of the following statements from "Vorticism" (1914) and "*Affirmations*—As for Imagisme" (1915):

> The image is not an idea. It is a radiant node or cluster; it is what I can, and must perforce, call a VORTEX, from which, and through which, and into which, ideas are constantly rushing.[53]

> the Image is more than an idea. It is a vortex or cluster of fused ideas and is endowed with energy. If it does not fulfil these specifications, it is not what mean by an Image.[54]

Pound's insistence lays not so much on the disconnection between image and idea, which would somehow disqualify a critical articulation between the concrete, visual plane and a more philosophical process of mental abstraction, as, precisely, on the *ideo*grammic nature of the Image as a kinetic aggregate of "visual ideas."

A "putting into work" or en-ergy as a transferential or meta-phorical process is thus at work in the Poundian Image, and it is on its behalf that he will vigorously denounce "Amygist" practices.[55] It is also defined in Pound's famous explanation of the process underlying the imagist haiku "In A Station of the Metro" as an attempt "to record the precise instant when a thing outward and objective transforms itself, or

---

53 Ezra Pound, *Gaudier-Brzeska: A Memoir* (New York: New Directions, 1970) 92 [hereafter *GB*].

54 Pound, *Selected Prose*, 345.

55 "The defect of earlier imagist propaganda was not in misstatement but in incomplete statement. The diluters took the handiest and easiest meaning, and thought only of the STATIONARY image. If you can't think of imagism or phanopoeia as including the moving image, you will have to make a really needless division of fixed image and praxis or action" (*A B C of Reading*, p. 52).

darts into a thing inward and subjective" (*GB* 89). This statement is grounded on the traditional (though late) Greek philosophical opposition between being / object(ive) and thinking (*noein*) / subject(ive), which crystallised once the *eidon* or image had become *idea*lised,[56] a dichotomy which Olson will deem somewhat casually to be supererogatory when, in the course of the "Projective Verse" essay, he ventures the label "objectism" (*HU* 59). Let us recall that for the Greeks, being was not only tied to logos and physis but also *harmonia* (cf. *HU* 4, *infra*), *alētheia* ("truth"), *phainesthai* ("to show oneself"),[57] and that the One (*Ev*: Parmenides) was expressed in early Greek language and thought by various forms of presencing, such as *energeia* (Aristotle), *idea* (Plato), *Logos* (Heraclitus), etc. ("The Anaximander Fragment," p. 56.[58] But *ov* (being) was also coextensive with τὸ καλόν (the beautiful)—or in Heidegger's words: "art is disclosure of the being of the essent" (*IM* 132)— since presence was conceived as pure radiance or the beauty of pure *phainesthai*, and by a complex and circuitous process of borrowing and definition, Pound's conception of the beautiful can be shown to tie in with nature and his taxonomy of the major ingredients in the art of poetry.[59]

---

56 Cf. Heidegger, *IM*180: "The word *idea* means that which is seen in the visible." In "The Anaximander Fragment," Heidegger retraces the entropic translation of the Greek *energeia* into *actualitas*, then *Wirklichkeit* or reality, and finally objectivity (56).

57 *IM* 133. Edward Hussey notes (p. 56) that the features of Hearclitus' style suggest that he wishes to use language to "show how [each thing] is," and likewise, Heidegger has connected the "Being-true" of the logos to its apophantic manifestation (Hussey, "Epistemology and Meaning in Heraclitus," *Language and Logos: Studies in Ancient Greek Philosophy Presented to G.E.L. Owen*, eds. Malcolm Schofield and Martha Craven Nussbaum [Cambridge: Cambridge University Press, 1982] 56). See also e.g. Heidegger, *Being and Time*, trans. John Macquarrie and Edward Robinson (Oxford: Basil Blackwell, 1962) 56).

58 Cf. also Maurice Blanchot, *L'Écriture du désastre* (Paris: Gallimard, 1980) 158 (explained as the ways in which being gives itself while withdrawing itself).

59 In the poem "In Durance," Pound alludes to Coleridge's essay "On the Principles of Genial Criticism" where the English poet states that "the Greeks called a beautiful object καλόν quasi καλοῦν, i.e. *calling on* the soul, which receives instantly, and welcomes it as something connatural," and expresses his approval in *The Spirit of Romance* by referring to "Coleridge's most magical definition of

In spite of what would seem to be an indiscriminate undifferentiation or amalgamation in the name of this gathering that the logos once stood for, critical principles of selection or decision and hierarchy were respected. For, as Heidegger also tells us, what the Greeks meant by *to kalon* was restraint (*IM* 131), as against a loose "aesthetic" construct to designate what relaxes, gives pleasure and keeps idle, on a par with the idle talk which he castigates in *Being and Time*. Pound's conception of the discipline of free verse and the rigorous economy of his imagist tenets are similarly infused with, among other things, this pre-classical Greek sense of the artistic and the beautiful, as is the later proclamation of an often reiterated belief in "τὸ καλόν / order" (canto XCVIII) or "KALON as beauty or order."[60] And to the empty and imprecise "words, words, words," Olson will similarly oppose the rigorous aesthetics of a precise technical language and restrained, flawless gestures (as in "Tyrian Businesses" in the *Maximus* poems), just as the Greeks matched the mythical processes of visualisation and verbalisation to the "happening" or *dromenon,* geared to the doings of everyday life in the community. Olson called himself a researcher in myth, a professional mythologist (*M* I.61), a label which we saw had been applied to Herodotus himself. Olson parsed "mythology" as "what is said of what is said,"[61] thereby displaying an awareness of the original equation between "muthos" and "logos" (cf. *M* II.37-38). His "Causal Mythology"

beauty" (p. 156). Ruthven conjectures (pp. 11, 154) that Coleridge's categories of poetry in the same essay may have shaped Pound's own tripartite division between melopoeia, phanopoeia (which replaced "imagism," under which the first two principles of the original imagist manifesto had become fused) and logopoeia.

60   Ezra Pound, *Guide to Kulchur* (London: Peter Owen, 1966) [hereafter *GK*] 316; see also *Jefferson and/or Mussolini,* 128. For a detailed evolution of Pound's aesthetics of the beautiful, see John Espey, "The Inheritance of Tò K óv," *New Approaches to Ezra Pound: A Co-ordinated Investigation of Pound's Poetry and Ideas,* ed. and intro. Eva Hesse (London: Faber, 1969).

61   Charles Olson, *The Special View of History,* ed. and intro. Ann Charters (Berkeley: Oyez, 1970) 57.

(*M* I.63-96) meant "the kosmos inside a human being"[62] and was a "hard science" (*M* I.46) which enabled man to experience the earth as familiar (*M* I.70),[63] thus implicitly bridging the gap between *muthos=logos* and *phusis* in an intimate relationship or "inner inherence."[64] This feature of inherence is bound up with the "coherence" of his favourite primitive cultures (Sumerians, Aztecs and, from early 1960s onwards, the culture of Pleistocene Man) which, Olson argues, our "logical," i.e. demythologised civilisations, have lost the sense of,[65] and this in turn recalls the spirit of Pound's mixed admission towards the end of the *Cantos* that "it coheres all right / even if my notes do not cohere" (Canto CXVI).

Olson's mythological program thus trips up conventional logic and history in a double way. As he himself suggests in *Additional Prose* (40), it is at once *pre*-historical, since it is an archaeology "from Homer back, not forward," before the intrusion of history as a mechanical record of demythologised, truth-grounding facts, and *post-historic*, in line with contemporary rediscoveries of the individualised narrative hermeneutics of '*istorin*. And insofar as it exhumes comparably originary conceptions of a full and living speech and myth prior to our western discursive "logic,"[66] Olsonian mythopoetics is

---

[62] *Special View of History*, 53 (see also the Outline, page 61). One is reminded here of the necessity, in Heraclitus' maxims, to study one's own self in order to interpret the cosmos, i.e. the attempt to ground cognitive processes in the physical world; see e.g. Hussey, "Epistemology and Meaning in Heraclitus," 41.

[63] Thus, Bernstein's comment that "Olson's ideal historical poem would, in effect, demythologize history itself so that it might again become what is most familiar: the expression of our own activity in the world" (p. 235) seems to rest on a view of the relation between history and mythology which must be seriously challenged in the light of Olson's hope to renew an older historiographic tradition represented by Herodotus, which Bernstein himself recalls on p. 240.

[64] Charles Boer, *Charles Olson in Connecticut* (Chicago: Swallow Press, 1975) 59.

[65] See e.g. "A Syllabary for a Dancer," "The Gate and the Center" (*HU* 17-23), and "Letter 3" (*Maximus*, 15 [I.11]).

[66] "Logos, or discourse, for example, has, in that time, so worked its abstractions into our concept and use of language that language's other function, speech, seems so in need of restoration that several of us got back to hieroglyphs or to ideograms to right the balance" (*HU* 3-4).

pre-logical, as well as admittedly *post*-logical,[67] which we may also choose to interpret as Olson's wish to take further Pound's inchoate, implicit attempt at re-mythologising the logos in his conception of *logopoeia*. It is therefore fitting that the growing search in Pound, then in Olson, for a principle of mythic inherence and coherence, in the pure spirit of the original logos which gathered the one and the many,[68] and in which one may also register the influence of Whitehead's holistic philosophy of processes as constant rhythmic alternations between the two poles, should increasingly summon dance, "the act of the gods, of creation, the primal mythic work,"[69] as the major organising trope in / of writing. We saw earlier that Olson had appropriated Pound's definition of logopoeia, syncopating it to "dance of the intellect," in his seminal essay on Projective Verse poetics. There, Olson propounded a rhythmics regulated on breath which would reintegrate poetic metre, song, music and dance according to the paradigm of ancient Greek drama and the originally unique art of the Muses or *mousikē*,[70] and one of the main aims of the new poetics was to restore the relation between (poetic) language, the physical body and the universe. The trope may also describe the organisation of the discrete components of the ideogram; as Martin Pops noted,[71] the agile projective writer is a glyph-enacting dancer and competent writing "obeys the figures of the present dance" (*Maximus*, 5 [I.1]). Unlike the centrifugal enunciative strategies that underwrite the *Cantos*, the tropic figure of Maximus, a mythic

---

[67] "The harmony of the universe, and I include man, is not logical, or better, is post-logical; as is the order of any created thing" (*HU*, p. 4).

[68] Cf. the epigraph to the *Maximus* poems, "All my life I've heard one makes many," and the strong Heraclitean flavour of "Maximus, to himself" (pp. 56-57 [I.52-53]).

[69] Paul, *Olson's Push*, 87.

[70] That is to say, "a drill in performance upon musical instruments, in singing and elocution, in memorisation of poetry, and in deportment and manners." Eric A. Havelock, "The Linguistic Task of the Presocratics; Part One: Human Science in Search of an Abstract Vocabulary," *Language and Thought in Early Greek Philosophy*, ed. Kevin Robb (La Salle: The Hegeler Institute, 1983) 8.

[71] Martin L. Pops, *Home Remedies* (Amherst: University of Massachusetts Press, 1984) 50-1.

collective grounded in the locale of the fishing community at Gloucester who oscillates between one and the many, provides a resting point for the mythic explorations of Olson's own epic. In this attempt, implicit in Pound, more fully articulated with Olson and Duncan, to redeploy the ancient mythic essence of language and restore its link with (being-in-)nature, using for the purpose the combined resources of philo-logy or etymo-logy, archaeo-logy,[72] and ancient philo-sophy or "wisdom," the dance emerged as the gathering trope which, if the choreo-graphy was performed ("projected") adequately, would hold the key to a holistic vision (Pound's vision of an earthly paradise or "splendour") expressed in a total art form.[73]

Despite its at times unstable, simplistic, contradictory assumptions, Pound's scientific "poetic logic"—his restoration of the logos to its polytrophic roots and its re-mythologisation in a natural pantheon, his handling of visual and verbal processes—may be said to have intuited in its own way the recovery of ancient thought structures which contemporary philosophy was likewise soon going to be drawn to and which Olson will adopt in his "causal mythology." It is, arguably, not going too much against the anti-philosophical currents in Pound's "system" or overexploiting its inner tensions to claim eventually that both pre-Socratic thinking and Confucianism— the first one, however, more ambiguously than some critical articulations of the common "ideology" underlying Pound's modernism and postmodern poetics are prepared to acknowledge[74]—shared a prominent role in his wish to

[72] Cf. Olson's summary of the real ingredients of his "literal study of mythology" in *M* I.76.

[73] See my "From Tropic Song and 'Rhythmus' Onwards: Whitman and the (Post)modern Dance," *Utopia in the Present Tense: Walt Whitman and the Language of the New World*, International Conference on Walt Whitman, University of Macerata, 29-30 October, 1992, ed. Marina Camboni (Rome: Il Calamo, 1994) 213-34.

[74] See Géfin, *Ideogram*, 36. Cf. for e.g. Pound's contrastive dismissal of Heraclitus' vacuous thinking as opposed to Confucius' positive "ideas into action" at the end of "The New Learning: Part One" (*GK* 34). However, in his reading of Artistotle's

construct an "Ideogram of philosophers" (*GK*, p. 348) and paideuma on mytho/cosmo-logical, as opposed to logical, methods (cf. "The History of Philosophy Is...?," *GK*, pp. 97-98). In "Kulchur: Part One" (*GK*, p. 128), which kicks off with a Confucian exemplum, Pound's praise of the intuitive,[75] yet wholly truthful "mythological exposition" and of the balanced, rigorous honesty of myth which "knows where to stop," is made to combine with his advocacy of a concrete, vitalistic, perhaps Heraclitean apprehension of phenomena into such an ideogram, in which poetry and philosophy join in an "aletheic" process (the same passage implicitly registers a distrust of philosophy which rejects poetry or which reads like "inferior poesy" [p. 127]). In trying to exhume such a philosophical platform in Pound's and Olson's mythopoetics, the intention has been not so much to perfect and refine for poetry a "philosophy of art," like the one Hulme adumbrated in *Speculations*, as to open further the possibility for a philosophical reading of (post)modern poetics inseparably from a poetic approach to philosophy, an "archaic" dialogue of the times when the western divides between philosophy / truth on the one hand and poetry / myth (i.e. untruth) on the other were not so deeply entrenched.[76] Such a two-way traffic would then go beyond the limitations and watertight compartmentalisation in Yeats's statement to Olivia Shakespeare, following a passage

---

Nicomachean Ethics, Pound sees "daemon," "almost an ideogram," as a lead down onto the pre-Socratic paideuma, into folk-lore (*GK* 307).

[75] Levenson rightly detects a convergence between the "image" of modernist literary theory and Bergson's philosophy of intuition (*A Genealogy of Modernism*, 45-46); see also *GB* 91. See Henri Bergson's own *Introduction to Metaphysics* (London: Macmillan), which T. E. Hulme himself had translated in 1913, for the French philosopher's conception of a fluid, kinetic, mental activity "capable of following reality in all its sinuosities and of adopting the very movement of the inward life of things" (59).

[76] Cf. Havelock, "The Linguistic Task of the Presocratics," 80: "Philosophy proper arose as a commentary upon and correction of the cosmic imagery of Homer and the cosmic architecture of Hesiod's *Theogony*," i.e. modernist emphasis on Homer goes back to traditions onto which the roots of early western philosophy grafted itself.

in which he defines his achievement in *A Vision* as "picturing a state as 'phenomenal' as that from birth to death," that "I have constructed a myth, but then one can believe in a myth—one only assents to philosophy";[77] it would thus truly inaugurates a (post)modernist dialogue between poetry and philosophy.

[77] William Butler Yeats, *The Letters of W. B. Yeats,* ed. Allan Wade (London: Rupert Hart-Davis, 1954) 781.

Keston Sutherland

Ethica Nullius

1. *Medium te mundi posui*: I have placed you at the centre of the world. This is the utterance of God to man central to the syncretistic cosmogony of Pico della Mirandola, *De Hominis Dignitate*.[1] This specific divine low-down is echoed throughout Jeremy Prynne's *The White Stones*: not just man but his language too, and also the only possible human reckoning of that language (known in the history of Biblical exegesis as *hermenutica profana*), originate from where and what man is, namely, "the / mere & lovely centre, of the earth."[2] Man is the

1   G. Pico della Mirandola, *De Hominis Dignitate, Heptaplus, De Ente Et Uno*, ed. Eugenio Garin (Firenze: Vallecchi Editore, 1942) 106; *On the Dignity of Man*, trans. Charles Glenn Wallis (Indianapolis: Bobbs-Merrill, 1965) 5.
2   J.H. Prynne, "Whose Dust Did You Say," *Poems* (Fremantle: Fremantle Arts Centre Press, and Highgreen: Bloodaxe, 2005) 102. For a discussion of *hermeneutica profana*, the interpretation of texts of non-divine origin, see Peter Szondi, *Introduction to Literary Hermeneutics*, trans. Martha Woodmansee (Cambridge: Cambridge University Press, 1995). Augustine gives a good description of the experience of the contrary type of exposition, *hermeneutica sacra*, which is possible only with inspired texts, when he says of the Bible that: "We submit our intellect to it, and hold it for certain that even language closed to our comprehension is right and true." *Confessions*, trans. Henry Chadwick (Oxford: Oxford University Press, 1991) 293. Certain commentators on Prynne would have us believe either that this cognitive genuflection before the sacred is what his work demands from us, and that our excited performance of it is the proof of his work's literary-historical monumentality, or, alternatively, that his work makes this demand (a) with contempt, (b) without meaning, or (c) without having "earned" the right to make it. For a now distantly pre-emptive

centre and he is also the end: he is the last addition to the creation, delivered, writes Pico, *in extrema fetura*, "the final parturition." He is both the extremity of the world's inauguration and the centre of its perennation as beauty, light and greatness; he is *mundi copulam*, "the bond tying the world together" both at the single crowning moment of the cosmogony and forever thereafter, throughout "time" which is the life of the world.[3] The centrality and the finality of man, together with his binding of the world into a whole, make up what Pico called his dignity.[4] For Pico's influential nineteenth century English admirer, Walter Pater, this "theory" of dignity was "founded on a misconception:" the earth *is* not the centre of the universe and man *is* not its bond or vinculum (still, "the theory had its use," Pater offers).[5] Prynne however develops out of Pico not merely the humanist sentiment or religious antinomianism eulogised by Pater, but something altogether less intelligible to the Victorian connoisseur, something we might call the *ethics* of syncretistic cosmogony.[6]

satire on these various forms of narcissistic homily and the significance they claim to apprehend in the act of "getting it right," see the 1971 poem "A New Tax on the Counter-Earth," *Poems*, 172-3.

[3] *De Hominis Dignitate*, 104; 102. *On the Dignity of Man*, 4; 3. Prynne alludes to this image in saying that death (or "biologic collapse") is "like untying a knot" ("A Gold Ring Called Reluctance," *Poems*, 21).

[4] In its positioning of man as the *particular* cause of and authority for the dialectical relation of part to whole, Pico's concept of the dignity of man resembles what Hegel (particularly in the *Logic*) called the dignity of thinking. On Prynne's engagement with Hegel, see the excellent essay by Kevin Nolan, "Capital Calves: Undertaking an Overview," *Jacket* 24 (2003) http://jacketmagazine.com/24/nolan.html

[5] Walter Pater, *The Renaissance: Studies in Art and Poetry*, ed. Donald L. Hill (Berkeley: University of California Press, 1980) 30-1.

[6] "Syncretistic" because Pico combined Platonic philosophical and Christian theological elements in his account of the creation of the world. For a rival account that resists (chiefly by appealing to scriptural and patristic authority to refute Plato's theory of ideal forms) the intellectual seductions of what Pater called "antinomian" syncretistic thinking, compare St. Thomas Aquinas, *Cosmogony, Summa Theologiæ*, vol. X [Ia. 65-74] (London: Blackfriars, 1967).

What I mean by this phrase is first of all that there is a kind, or at least a dimension, of ethical thinking proper exclusively to syncretistic cosmogony of the kind expounded in *De Hominis Dignitate* (and expounded also in Charles Olson's *The Maximus Poems*, which Prynne described as "a lingual and temporal syncretism, poised to make a new order").[7] In other words, there is a kind or dimension of ethical thinking whose necessary inaugural idea is that man is at the centre of the created world, which might equally well be the Gloucester coastline in Massachusetts, or "Ierusalem," or any place at all where we might "walk, even quite jauntily, over the grass";[8] and furthermore that he is at the centre of the world by reason of a supreme prerogative (or by reason of what twentieth century phenomenology would more simplistically call radical immanence).[9] Prynne believed in the late 1960s that this central position of man in the created world cannot ever be abrogated by psychic or spiritual injury, by dissent, or by any form whatsoever of rational or irrational discountenance.[10] In *The White Stones*, being at the centre means being in "the world

7 J.H. Prynne, "Charles Olson, Maximus Poems IV, V, VI," *The Park* 4/5 (Summer 1969): 64-66. Reprinted in *Io* 16 (Winter 1972-73): 89-92.

8 "The Holy City," *Poems*, 43.

9 The phrase "radical immanence" is a generic one in phenomenology, but I borrow it here from Michel Henry, *Philosophy and Phenomenology of the Body*, trans. Girard Etzkorn (The Hague: Martinus Nijhoff, 1975) 54-55: "subjectivity in its radical immanence, identical to life." For a synopsis of this rival account of the impossibility of radical alienation, see ibid.: "We are in possession of our movements, we are never absent from them at any time while we perform them, we are constantly informed concerning them, with a knowledge whose originality and exceptional characteristic we have already shown, because we are one with these movements ..." I have offered some thoughts on Henry's concept of immanence and its usefulness for thinking about poetry in three previous articles: "Nervous Breakdowns in Chris Emery's *The Cutting Room*," *Quid* 5 (2000); "Prosody and Reconciliation," *The Gig* 16 (2004); and "What is Called John Wilkinson?" *The Gig* 17 (2004).

10 For example, the rhetoric which re-characterizes subjectivity as "decentred" would on this view be a form of rational discountenance that may express polemical, but may *not* express veridical, variance with the prerogative that positions subjectivity at the centre of the world.

without length," that is, being at the centre without the possibility of evacuating it by *longing* for somewhere or anywhere else more complete. This is a world in which the specific desire for transcendence that we might call "longing," rather than being the evidence of our homelessness or alienation, or of our ineradicable dependence on the perspectives of eschatology, is really "the turn to a virtue, of extent / without length."[11] The extent of longing and desire is both our own extent and the extent of the world around us, and we are at the centre of the world around us by a supreme prerogative. The ethical content of prosody and versification in *The White Stones* is specific to this idea, whose *literalness* Prynne seeks to make commensurable with the rhythmic shifts, the cognitive and lexical sonority, and the forms of expectancy and estrangement voiced by the silences and words of poetic language. Turning in verse means turning at the centre, toward the material and knowable world whose bond we are. That line break, "extent / without length," voices an intercession on behalf of desire re-known as "the turn to a virtue," against the idea that the end of the line is a site projected for impatient expectancy or eschatological premonition.[12] It is an ethical line break in that it aims not merely to mimic its own argument, but rather to effectuate it in sensibility, and then also reflexively to explicate that effectuation as a way of soliciting the critical judgment of a reader. It aims to do all this by means of a particular motion and suspension of sense. The line break is a moment of expectancy calculated to resolve itself into an almost catechistic balance of corrective thought over against misthought. It activates the completely tacit intimation that while the *sentence* is displaced by enjambment, and then

---

11 "From End to End," *Poems*, 62. I mean by distinguishing Prynne's concept of "longing" from the familiar concepts "homelessness" and "alienation" to emphasise that his criticism of the rhetoric and psychology of transcendence is truly neither Heideggerian nor Marxist, as is sometimes assumed. Rather, it is specific to the possibilities for thinking inaugurated by syncretistic cosmogony.

12 Cf. "The place / rises, as a point of change" ("How It's Done," *Poems*, 44).

displaced still further by the inset typographical position of the end of its final clause ("without length"), *we* are not, and cannot be, displaced from our central authority for the unity of poetic and cosmogenic understanding by this or any other shift in language, however abrupt. This is what Prynne in 1967 called "most radical image of calm which is to be found, now."[13]

> Desire is the turn to a virtue, of extent
> without length.

For so long as Prynne understood ethics in the light of cosmogenic human centrality, the burden of his poetry was to describe and argue for a way of knowing "where / we are."[14] That is, of knowing not simply that we are at the centre of the world, and therefore *mundi copulam* in the humanist, Wordsworthian or Hegelian sense, but of knowing also the quality of the *posui*, the prerogative expressed in our being *placed* there. We can know this quality of place, of being placed, through the commensuration of it activated in the qualities of physical and intellectual perception as they are re-inaugurated by poetic language. The primary ethical burden of that language is to make in *sound* and in convictive expression "the most radical image of calm," which meant, for Prynne, to confront and to disavow not only the desire for transcendence, but also the technical rhetorics of transcendence cultivated by philosophy, as well as the interference of its vernacular and its million pop songs with everyday consciousness.[15]

> So that I will state quite clearly & without question, I decline the offer of assistance with superlative vision. In my own figure and shared by the stately non-involvement of people in the

13 Prynne, "About Warning an Invited Audience," *The English Intelligencer* (1967) n.p. *TEI* was not a journal but a set of mimeographed pages circulated privately amongst contributors. It can be consulted in the Cambridge University Library.
14 "Airport Poem: Ethics of Survival," *Poems*, 38.
15 Prynne, "About Warning an Invited Audience." Cf. "The Holy City," *Poems*, 43: "There's no mystic moment involved: just / that we are…"

street there is a difficult motion which in my wildest dreams I would not allow to be improved.

It is an essential argument of Prynne's early poetry that the progress of enlightenment comfortably invoked by Pater does not and cannot expose this ethics to be a misconception; rather, the misconceptions of enlightenment itself flow from its compulsory occlusion of the ethics of syncretistic cosmogony.

From *Kitchen Poems* onwards, Prynne's poetry is an interpretation of the physical place of man and of his capacity for coordinating and creating his presence within that place through language. In the interpretation of that capacity offered by *Kitchen Poems* and *The White Stones*, ethical thinking about specific political or social circumstances tends to be resolved into ontological thinking whose predominance over the particularity of ethics is secured by Heideggerian privilege: ontology is a more inaugural order of thought, nearer to "where we are." As Prynne writes in "A Gold Ring Called Reluctance," what we can and what we should mean by "we" is first of all "a clear question about place" (*Poems*, 21); and man "more or less in his place"[16] is who he most *is*: *mundi copulam*. This predominance of ontological thinking over ethical thinking is first (and perhaps most violently) admonished in *Brass*. From this point on in his poetic thinking, Prynne is intensely refractory to the ideology that would make "being" absolutely superordinate to ethics; and the pressure of contradiction engendered by that irreversible resistance is more and more concentrated in *language*, which in consequence becomes almost invariably more recalcitrant to interpretation with each of his successive books. The intensification of that recalcitrance, arguably still unabated in Prynne's latest book, *Blue Slides At Rest*, is not a process of merely hermetic or factious "linguistic innovation"; it is the testimony of language to the increasing and violent disparity between ethics and ontology. With each new book, the two kinds of thinking are made to suffer

---

16 "The Common Gain, Reverted," *Poems*, 89.

increasingly what Gillian Rose would call "diremption": they are split off from each other, torn apart.[17]

Where and *who* we are have become positions altogether different in *NOT-YOU* from those patiently exalted in the cosmogony of *The White Stones*. The coordinates are by this point dominated by the ethics of a cosmogony infinitely more intricate and dialectical. It is a cosmogony in which man cannot choose but persist as "the final parturition," but in which he does so only through the "deep discount" of understanding this final parturition to be, equally, the final *anguish* (in which each of us in our separate histories will now forever "terminate" alone).[18] *Extrema fetura* is "now" *extrema angustia*: our perennial birth, and the cosmogony or perennial birth of the world, is the extremity of its and our narrowness and restriction, the infinitely straitened extent of subjectivity not "without" length but excoriated from it. Man is "now" the *negative* mundi copulam: still indeed the "bond," but now (in a characteristically violent pun) "the bond of care annulled;"[19] and he is "central" not *as* "the turn to a virtue," but only *to* some indifferent one of its schemes:

> He was calm itself and
> central to a scheme of virtue, not absent nor
> wincing

("Landing Area" (1974) *Poems*, 224)

---

17 Readers of contemporary avant-garde British poetry will be familiar with the phrase "linguistic innovation," which is a sort of anxious colonial equivalent of the American phrase "language poetry."

18 The citation in my parenthesis echoes the conclusion to Prynne, "Es Stand Auch Geschrieben: Jean Bollack And Paul Celan." http://www.cccp-online.org/archive/cccp12/page_49.html: Where we now are is "the ordinary world in which not quite innocent people (we, and they, and us) dwell unpoetically upon the earth and terminate in anguish there." This is also the "real world" of *Word Order*, *Poems* 360, "towards / which we travel in purity and in truth ..."

19 "Listening to All," *Poems*, 349.

Notice what five years have done to Prynne's idea of enjambment: the indifference of that momentarily terminal "and" and "nor," the dissimulation of effortless disregard for what I early called prosodic effectuation in sensibility that is staged in the positioning of the word "central" as a mere overspill; and notice the effect of five years on the tonality of the expressions Prynne uses now merely to hint at the idea of self-sameness (or the opposite of transcendence): "he was calm itself," that is, the object of colloquial plauditry in tight proximity to cliché. Central not *as* but *to*: here in miniature or in grotesque is the satire against ontology. It is tightly characteristic of Prynne's later poetry that even the satire against his former thinking should be diminutive, restricted to and by the mimicry of casual utterance, as though merely overheard. The satire itself is a corruption inflicted compulsorily on poetic language by the diremption of ethics and ontology. As this brief analysis of a fragment of a poem from 1974 suggests, the satire is not at all contained in language at the level of argument or propositional content, but is pervasively corruptive, shining dark in the whole traduced flow of prosody and versification and in the whole connivance of the poetic lexicon. The terminal restriction of *extrema angustia* is as wide as language, and as wide as heaven and earth.

To be both the final parturition and the final anguish is to be finally contradictory. Our centrality to the world is the contradiction tying it together; and the destiny of human existence is "now" more tightly than ever before negative: we cannot be displaced from our central authority for the irreducible contradictoriness of poetic understanding.[20] This

---

[20] A similar idea finds more salubriously dialectical expression in Whitman, "Song of Myself": "Whoever degrades another degrades me, / And whatever is done or said returns at last to me. // Through the afflatus surging and surging, through me the current and index." Degradation is here mitigated and even valorised by reference to an ethics altogether different from Prynne's. Whitman is indifferently underneath and overhead and off to the side: unbounded fraternalism makes all degradation vicarious, such that the "self" who is its terminus and index can neither have final authority for degradation (his own or

type of contradiction is still cosmogenic, still the sinking grounds of our responsibility to deliver "a lingual and temporal syncretism, poised to make a new order."[21] This responsibility is still ethical and still cannot be obviated, no matter how deeply Pico's or Prynne's beautiful conception of man as "a soul set in order and purified" is routinely and successively discounted.[22]

One aspect of this contradiction in the language of Prynne's late poetry can be seen in the way he hints at descriptions of self-awareness using the vocabulary of spatial co-ordination. *NOT-YOU* in particular is dominated by this vocabulary: *under, ahead, inside, not far in front, end-up, over, next to each mouth, beneath, on, in, rises, turning, falling, bolted to the floor* (*Poems*, 383-9). These are always ethical words and phrases, though not (as we might expect) because they simply connote the misdirection of moral instinct away from its intended aim. That misdirection was already the target of critical sermonising in *The White Stones*:

> All the quick motions
> as we nip upstairs, turn
> to steps we take: leading
> > to the moral exits
> which we see enjoined. Some idea of
> > completeness; protection
> is wretched and what we pay for.

("For This, For This" *Poems*, 72-3)

the world's), nor experience immanance in authorititative centrality as anguish (because there is simply nowhere different from the centre into which the self can legitimately even imagine itself to be displaceable). This more or less explains the most ethically significant difference between Whitman's surging versification and and the astrictive versification of Prynne's later poetry.

[21] "Just a treat sod Heine you notice | the base going down ..." *Poems*, 314. The poem includes a good example of Prynne's violent satire against enjambment: "pent up / and boil over." Glance next at the next page (315): "the whole / falling short ..."

[22] *De Hominis Dignitate*, 114. *On the Dignity of Man*, 9.

Marching off to the moral exit is here nothing but the desire for transcendence muffled into sanctimony. The semi-colon after "Some idea of / completeness" stages a punishment routine against that attitude, and against what Prynne rounds on and castigates as its deep insouciance; what follows is "wretched and what we pay for," the protection of what in *Brass* is incredibly referred to as "the millennial landscape" with its "stream of evening sun" and "grass crown."[23] Negativity in these lines from "For This, For This" is pastoral and therefore dutiful, and its means of compulsion are overtly metrical. The verse turn is everywhere self-admonishing, everywhere an act or specimen of pastoral deterrence. Metre is the means of a deterrent negativity; but language itself is not yet by any ethical prescription negative, or "undisimprisonable" from the anguish and restriction of negativity. And this is partly because in *The White Stones* the misdirection of moral instinct is almost simply a matter of *failure*: it is what happens when we con ourselves out of our own rectitude, despite our unalterable centrality to the world. Ethics can in this way be sustained as a crucial but subordinate dimension of ontology: whether or not we are right in what we do depends finally on whether we know who we are by right.

The vocabulary of spatial coordination in *NOT-YOU* has very little to do with rectitude in this sense: there is in any case, the poem declares, hardly anything of it left. The ethical dimension of that vocabulary consists more radically in the problem that these words are the prepositional and deictic limits of a language constrained to express the identity of parturition and anguish, which is our central "self difference;"[24] but that they cannot do this without at the same time procuring in *overtone* a whole moralism of evasion and rectitude whose familiar finery of distinctions converges always on *self sameness* as the grounds of its valour. What the poem declares is hardly left to be thought thus reappears intractably in how we cannot

---

[23] "A New Tax on the Counter-Earth," *Poems*, 172-3.
[24] "Attending Her Aggregate, Detour," *Her Weasels Wild Returning, Poems*, 413.

help but *overhear* the language of its declaration. Language is in this way, under the duress of this radical stricture, almost irrevocably not true. This is more than simply a question definable by rhetorical accounts of ambiguity or of "slippage."[25] It is a contradiction which Prynne's later poetry tells us is not capable of being accommodated or sublated by those rhetorics, for the reason that this poetry is still, and is inescapably, bonded to the ethics of cosmogony. There is a specific upshot. If the language of our most extreme parturition and anguish is almost irrevocably not true, then so also is the world for which that language is the undisplacably central authority. This problem is intractable even by satire, as Prynne shows in the specimen of a satire against it near the beginning of *NOT-YOU*:

Got a pervasive overtone in decision,
to reach back, maybe harmless in flight
of the amount, be ready, see through what

it says to be done.

(*Poems*, 386)

What is maybe harmless in flight? For one thing, capital. For another, a missile. The poem begins chattily: "Got a ..." might more familiarly lead to *good deal on those fences* or *tanks*, or to *problem with that?* Into "pervasive overtone" there is secretly packed the English "sieve over," later echoed in the "sift over" of *Her Weasels Wild Returning*,[26] both of which point through

---

[25] Neither is it enough to say even-handedly that "Language, which in its communicative aspect participates in the clarity of conceptual logic, also participates in the mimesis of the nonidentical." "Introduction" by Shierry Weber Nicholson and Jeremy J. Shapiro to Adorno, *Hegel: Three Studies* (Cambridge, Mass.: MIT Press, 1993) xxix. This equitable view of language is nowhere near enough since "mimesis of the nonidentical" is unavoidably an identification. In other words, language which participates in the mimesis of the nonidentical nevertheless involves a definitive testimony of self-sameness. The imitation of aconceptuality by art is always comprehensively conceptual.

[26] "Will either sermon / sift over, down with his line…" *Poems*, 410.

overtone to a military aviation mission (the US military, for example, recently "sieved" white phosphorus, known to those in the game as "shake and bake," over the civilian population of Fallujah). Also secreted in echo is the Latin *sive eo*: *if by that, or if by that, or else by that,* the decontextualised fragment of an extended correlative expression which would typically be forked: either do, or don't. In decision there is indecision, compounded by the comma and its decisive activation of a line break; "to reach back" follows after without the syntax it needs behind it to reach for, and without any specified object that might be reached, but leads after another comma to a casual speculation concerning the harmfulness of a "flight" which has no grammatical subject (the names are protected); flight twists into "flight of the amount," hinting at a tax fugitive, but hinting too that the next comma is not a pause in syntax but a repressive violation of it: in flight of the amount *of what*? What has been clipped off or hidden? The violation spreads backward: is "maybe harmless in flight," apparently a coherent clause or part of one, in fact two fragments of clauses jammed together with their rift concealed? *Maybe harmless* could be one fragment, and then, from elsewhere and in another voice entirely, *in flight*; that would allow *in flight of the amount* to be the *middle* of some otherwise deleted sentence: "the pilots are ignorant while in flight of the amount of damage their weapons cause." *Maybe harmless* pre-empts this speculative recovery of deleted syntax, getting there first in order to cast doubt on what it would say; but in any case the predicament of the language is transformed by the abrupt metrical *overbearance* of the third line after its first comma: "of the amount, *be ready, see through what*." Why suddenly these five stresses uninterrupted by weakness, these pep-talk imperatives? The second imperative makes it across the stanzaic division and is resolved: "see through what // it says to be done." For a moment it feels as though the echoes are shut down: *it says to be done* is stilted, monosyllabic, yielding no quick connotation; but could there not be an *is* missing after that *says*, or is it that the passive voice of "to do" cannot yield to the verb *says* that describes colloquially some indicated but unidentified instruction? If the instruction is *it*, what it *says* is silent; or rather, is a text voiced and sounded in your head or by your mouth: *it says here I should do this.* Whatever it says to be done is however to be seen through, or *was* at least, before the stanzaic division interrupted the sentence and made its coherence doubtful. To see through something: most obviously to perceive the falsity of its appearance and the true meaning which that appearance conceals. But also, physically to perceive an object through something which is an aperture or viewing device or window: the window here would be *what it says to be done*. And then the third possibility, to see by means of something: rather than to see through (or by) *looking*, to see instead through (or by) *what it says to be done*, so that the phrase and what it denotes is a kind of "looking" in itself. Syntax in this way sanctions the coercive adaptation of an interpretive phrase into a metonym for a window, or for my eyes, or for a military viewfinder; and the interpretive phrase in question is moralism depleted by catachresis, its "is" missing.[27] Again there is a negative invocation of ontology in the deletion of the verb *to be*; but the invocation is no longer properly satirical, since it is now too extremely diminutive and too deeply or bathetically sub-argumentative even for the diminishing returns of satire.

In Prynne's later work, the procurance of moralism in overtone is evidence of a radical aberration of human authority. The language we are beneath is language *pro cura*, its echoes become an irrebuttable surrogate both for care and for cure.

> The cure is won across twice, in glitter
> patches so cheap they thrill each bidder,
> staring ahead to the empty room where
>
> brightness is born and tagged; to beat

---

[27] The disallowed echo of Lenin's "What Is To Be Done?" is nearly overt: with the verb *to be* wiped out, *it says* is the replacement sanctioned by grammar. *Wo Ich war, soll Es werden.*

the windows of the dying year's fast
turn to a faction cut-back. Ever so

smiling at this sudden real candour,
what to shun of this set cure's topmost
retort: remember me: and give now over.

(*NOT-YOU, Poems*, 390)

"The ears," wrote Augustine, "are certainly not otherwise
accessible to good sounds than to bad ones."[28] From the author
of *NOT-YOU* might come the retort: true, *but they are not the
same ears.* If our authority is aberrated by the moralism
procured for us in irrefusible overtone, then so also is whatever
world we bind together even as contradiction: the ethical
imperative of poetry is not then to get on with sublating this
aberrated contradiction, but somehow to show it and to sing it
fully unaberrated. Insofar however as language is our
procurator, its parturition and anguish are just nowhere near
extreme enough. That is, not justly so extreme as *we* are. You,
and the light of thought which cosmogony says you are—
whether Pico's *naturalis philosophae lumine*, Merleau-Ponty's
existential *fulguration*, or Prynne's "light in de- / light"[29]—are
tagged (on the ear) *not-you* as soon as you are born, and then
forever again in candid and empty anticipation of the next birth
and the next, the whole perennial cosmogony traduced by
anticipated occupation of the transcendental empty womb
ahead. The problem cannot be solved in Prynne's poetry by
choosing ascetically *what to shun* of this procurated cure, "set"
like a thrillingly cheap menu we each nonetheless define

---

[28] *De Musica, The Fathers of the Church.* vol.4, *Writings of Saint Augustine*, vol.2.,
trans. Robert Catesby Taliaferro (New York: Fathers of the Church, 1947) 327.

[29] *De Hominis Dignitate*, 114; *On the Dignity of Man* 9. Cf. Maurice Merleau-Ponty,
Sense and Non-Sense, trans. Hubert L. Dreyfus and Patricia Allen Dreyfus
(Evanston: Northwestern UP, 1964) 152; and Prynne, "The Numbers," *Poems*,
10. Compare also Henry, *Philosophy and Phenomenology of the Body*, 44: "the being
of each individual is the light of the world, and more profoundly, it is, as
original truth, the light of this light."

ourselves by bidding for. In other words, the overtone cannot simply be purged or pulled down to our own level: its unreachable theatre of implications is *"terra nullius* overhead,"[30] that is, the sky tagged in *Her Weasels Wild Returning* as military airspace free for imperial seizure in accordance with the provisions of Roman law. *Terra nullius* is no-man's land, *terra nullius* overhead is the sky which law declares is owned by no-one. The imperial claim to it comes from two places: from the US Air Force, first of all (it is the sky over Iraq, raided by the Wild Weasels);[31] and *secondly* from you at the centre of the

---

[30] *Poems*, 416.

[31] In June 1965, North Vietnamese ground forces first began to use SA-2 Guideline surface-to-air missiles (SAMs), guided by ground operators using a radar system code named "Fansong" by NATO and fired at invading US Air Force bombers. These advanced systems were supplied by the USSR. They were to prove critical in the air war, since they effectively disabled American pilots from flying at the middle height which was necessary to avoid conventional flak but low enough to maintain the visibility of ground targets. For "one short period" the missiles had a 100% strike rate.

The Pentagon required a weapon which could eliminate these SAM installations, which at first were impossible to locate until their missile had been fired. The Pentagon contracted Applied Technology, a small electronics company from Palo Alto, California, to develop their new radio frequency receiver/direction finder into a component that would enable USAF bombers to identify the position of the Soviet radar emitters. At the same time, manufacturers working under contract to the USAF developed the AGM-45 Shrike Missile, which could home in on the emitters, allowing the "SAM hunter" the "safety of a few miles stand-off range." The first plane to carry both new components was the F-100F; later the F-4G became standard. This technological makeover was high priority and therefore exceptionally rapid: the first F-100F "kill" —that is, destruction of a Vietnamese SAM installation—came on 22 December 1965. The F-100F would lead a team of heavier F-105 "Thuds" over the target area, identifying the SAM position to their pilots and enabling them to deliver their ordnance before a missile had been fired.

This mission had the code name "Wild Weasel."

The mission needed a name, and originally it was going to be "Wild Ferret," but that name had been used in Korea. So instead, the code name selected was "Wild Weasel," a reference to the little creature with sharp teeth who brazenly goes into the burrows of much larger, more powerful enemies and kills them. The weasel is a rather cute little guy, fearless and energetic, and he gets the job done. See Hans Halberstadt, *The Wild Weasels: History of US Air*

253

world who are its bond and interpreter, placed beneath it "to love its beauty, and to wonder at its greatness."[32] The pervasive overtone streaks to us from that double yet self-same sky, violated beyond all poetic repair or any other reach of idealist fantasy; and *who we are*, with ontology dirempted by that violence from our ethics, is still and always must still be the whole thing, the total violation reborn endlessly in *extrema angustia*.

The most constant motive of Prynne's late work is to discover in language an ethics radically incommensurable with procurated, echoic subjectivity; it wants *ethica nullius*, the ethics of no-one whose centrality is radically superintended by the moralism of overtone. It seeks to discover this ethics not as a completed whole, not by scanning for the outline of a system or the materials of a potential system, but in always unpredictable poetic increments bitterly won across the *terra nullius* of self-sameness and aberrated contradiction. In this it is fundamentally different from his early work, since the push into an ethics incommensurable with procurated subjectivity is directly competitive with the movement of the whole person into knowledge that had provided the ontological schedule of *The White Stones*. The de-authentication of language is no longer proof of our failure to know who we are by right. Rather, it is now by knowing who we are *as inalienable wrong* that we can truly know the imperative to countermand linguistic de-

Force SAM Killers, 1965 to Today (Osceola: Motorbooks International Mil-Tech Series 1992) 17.

The mission code name was adopted as the name of the pilot teams. The Wild Weasels were, in each team, a pilot (or "stick") and an Electronic Warfare Officer (or EWO; or "bear"). They were equipped, during the conflict over Vietnam, first with an F-100F; then with an F-105F "Thunderchief" (or "Thud"—the first plane able to launch the AGM-45 Shrike) in 1966, followed by the improved F-105G in 1968, then by the F-4C Phantom in 1969. The last of these improved aircraft was improved yet again, to become the F-4G, 48 of which returned to action among the 1,376 military planes of various types used by the US in the Gulf War of 1990-91. See *Military Lessons of the Gulf War*, ed. Bruce W. Watson (Novato: Presidio Press 1991) 236.

[32] *De Hominis Dignitate*, 104; *On the Dignity of Man*, 4.

authentication, which is the de-authentication of *mundi contradictio* also, by the only radical means still possible, namely by reaching forever and as if forever terminally for an ethics incommensurable with life.

Lisa Jarnot

San Francisco's Burning

> this is the breed of the poet—...not just that we are bad
> tempered, but we are really trained to move with tremendous
> feeling on the least hints— and how to manage our human lives
> needs a tremendous keel.
>> —Robert Duncan, 8 December, 1978

> Duncan behaved badly.
>> —Jacqueline Cantwell, *Poetry Flash*

Robert Duncan was at home in San Francisco in time to vote in
the November elections, during the course of which the Briggs
initiative, Proposition 6, was defeated in California. The
proposition, backed by a number of conservative and
fundamentalist organisations, would have made it legal to
remove gay school teachers from their jobs. Duncan and Jess
saw a production of the opera *Fidelio* on the evening of 11
November with Hilde and David Burton, and Duncan spent
time with Jess in the midst of the year's busy tour schedule. He
completed his poem "In Waking" on the 14th of the month,
returning again to the particular ambivalent emotions he
associated with his marriage to Jess, and reflecting upon the
trajectory of their relationship. There was also grim news to be
faced in the larger San Francisco community that autumn. On
the 18th of the month, the Jonestown Massacre took place in
Guyana. 914 followers of the Reverend Jim Jones, many of them

former San Franciscans, died in a mass suicide. United States Congressman Leo Ryan, who had visited Jonestown on a fact-finding mission, was also shot and killed. On 27 November, another tragedy befell the city. Mayor George Moscone and city supervisor Harvey Milk were assassinated in City Hall by Dan White, a disgruntled district supervisor who had recently resigned. Two days later a memorial service was held for Milk and Moscone in San Francisco's City Hall. Over ten thousand people filed past the closed caskets of the murdered men. Milk, born in 1930, and a long-time resident of the Castro district, had been San Francisco's first openly gay public official and had played a crucial role in local and national struggles for gay rights.[1] White's motives were initially unclear, although his interactions with Milk had been terse and during his tenure on the board of supervisors he had vocally disagreed with Milk's views, espousing a more conservative and at times homophobic agenda. When White was tried during the following year, his lawyers claimed that he had been depressed at the time of the murders, partly because of his excessive consumption of junk food. As a result of what was later labelled the "Twinkie Defence," White received a sentence of six years in prison. In the wake of the verdict, San Francisco's gay community was mobilised in violent protests during which police cars were burned and the windows of City Hall were broken.

In the midst of the community's grief that fall, life continued, poets gathered to go about their business, and another battle raged in the arena of San Francisco poetry. As David Bromige remembered:

> in 1978 things were getting so interesting … I left Sonoma County and found a place in San Francisco just so that I could

---

[1] Duncan seems to have been silent about these events, although his students (particularly Aaron Shurin and others) attended the Dan White trial, which took place in 1979. White was eventually released from Soledad prison on 6 January, 1984 after serving a five-year sentence. He committed suicide on 21 October, 1985.

be around for all the fun ... 80 Langton Street had been started up, so the talks were happening there and the panels, and there was a great reading series at the Grand Piano on Haight Street.[2]

One order of business that Winter took the form of a programme called "An Evening with Louis Zukofsky for a Showing of the Out-takes." The event began at 8:30 p.m. on 8 December at the San Francisco Art Institute on Chestnut Street and admission was three dollars. A film of outtakes of Zukofsky's 1965 National Educational Television interviews were shown, and Robert Duncan and Barrett Watten shared the stage to talk about Zukofsky who had died in May at the age of 75. Ron Silliman later recalled an important aspect of the event's planning:

> Putting Robert and Barrett together on the same bill discussing Louis Zukofsky was at one level a symbolic event, identifying a way in which the New American poetics and this new poetry grew out of similar concerns and sympathies. Putting Robert on stage *first* was also symbolic, and it really gave the evening an Oedipal air.[3]

After a short introduction by organiser Tom Mandel, a younger writer then the director of the San Francisco Poetry Centre,

[2] David Bromige, personal interview, 6 May 1998. Barrett Watten started the reading series at the Grand Piano. As he said, "I started it in September '76 and Ron [Silliman] and Tom Mandel took over in January '77. About Fall '78 Rae Armantrout and Ted Pearson were the curators, and Steve Benson and Carla [Harryman] ended it ... it went through 1979. Also, as Ron Silliman recalled, "In 1978, langpo was still fairly new to the broader community of poets—to those of us doing it, it was anywhere between 4 & 8 years old. The term language poetry had yet to be assigned to the group, in fact—that didn't come about until '79. Tom Mandel becoming the head of the S[an] F[rancisco] Poetry Centre that fall was a huge deal in terms of recognising this new writing & everyone in the poetry scene in SF recognized it as such (consider, for example, that Charles [Bernstein] and Bruce [Andrews] did not start the mag[azine] L=A=N=G=U=A=G=E until that year)" (email to the author, 21 March 2006).

[3] Ron Silliman to the author, 21 March 2006.

Duncan discussed the film and gave a basic biographical background of Zukofsky for those in the audience who were unfamiliar with his work. He opened the evening on an enthusiastic talking jag, locating his own early encounters with Zukofsky and weaving together several threads of subject matter in Zukofsky's work, from communist politics to immigrant attitudes to the influences of Henry James, Henry Adams, and the Modernists. As David Bromige remembered, Duncan was in high form: "Duncan was playing the part to the hilt of 'The Poet'. He had his ... Spanish hat on with the low crown and the broad brim. He had his cape on, and he was just swanning about there on stage."[4]

The film program followed Duncan's introductory talk, after which Barrett Watten gave a presentation on Zukofsky's poetry. The thirty-year-old Watten admitted with some deference to his co-presenter that he had been reading Zukofsky's work for ten years as opposed to Duncan's forty. Watten then utilised an overhead projector to show the audience selections of Zukofsky's "A" as it appeared on the page, and he began into his own meticulous evaluation of the poet's work and its intersections with the political world.[5] At various points during his presentation he was interrupted by audience members' comments and questions, with Duncan and poet Larry Eigner acting as the most frequent interjectors. Watten also competed with noise from a punk rock concert in a neighbouring venue, and at one point in his talk an audience member shouted at him to speak more directly into his microphone. For an audience that had just listened to elder poet Duncan speak and had

4 Ron Silliman to the author, 21 March 2006.
5 This paper originally included excerpts of Barrett Watten's 8 December, 1978 talk as well as Watten's later evaluations of the event. Watten has not yet granted the author permission to quote from these materials, but two recordings of the Zukofsky event are available to the public: one is housed at The Poetry Center at San Francisco State University, and Duncan's copy of the recording is housed in the Robert Duncan archives at the State University of New York at Buffalo.

watched a film about Louis Zukofsky, Watten's detailed lecture began to feel laboured. Too, Watten stirred Duncan's ire early in his presentation when expounding on Zukofsky's statement "the words are my life". Watten mused to the audience, "I always thought that this was an incredibly difficult thing for me to understand—you know, how are the words your life? Your words are one thing. Your life is another."[6]

As Watten plodded along with his analysis of Zukofsky's texts, the audience's interjections became more frequent and Duncan leapt to the stage in an attempted to close out the evening, after which Watten asked that he be allowed to finish his presentation. Duncan complied, though Watten, seemingly dazed by the assault, soon after ceded the stage to the elder poet who launched into an impromptu reading of Zukofsky's final collection of poems *80 Flowers*. Duncan, clearly agitated by the evening's events, pointed out his disagreement with Watten's readings of Zukofsky, bringing forward an idea that was integral to his view of the world and its poets: "it is human life that imprints itself everywhere." Touching upon his own generation's indebtedness to Freud for his studies of language and the unconscious, Duncan was intent upon reinforcing a less constructivist reading of Zukofsky than Watten had presented.[7] As he finished his somewhat barbed closing statements, a brief open discussion followed, and while there may have been tension building in the room, most of the questions revolved around technical issues in Zukofsky's work rather than in an assessment of what had just transpired between Duncan and Watten.

But in the weeks and even years to follow, it was clear that the event set off bad feelings throughout the San Francisco

---

[6] Zukofsky Event recording, Poetry and Rare Books Collection, State University of New York at Buffalo.

[7] Duncan's lecture "Warp and Woof", presented at the Naropa Institute during the summer of 1976, touched upon a number of similar issues.

poetry scene, particularly between Duncan and younger members of the community, as well as between Duncan's future New College students and the San Francisco writers affiliated with what would be come to known in the following year as the "Language" movement. As Ron Silliman recalled, "After the disaster at the Art Institute ... I tended to steer further away from Robert—I'd been appalled at his behaviour and viciousness toward Barrett, who'd been my roommate and was/is my oldest friend, dating back to high school days."[8] Bay Area poet Stephen Rodefer's assessment of the event in a letter to the editor of *Poetry Flash* some years later arrived at a lighter perspective regarding the controversy:

> I would like to say that Robert Duncan's literally taking over the podium from Barry Watten that night was both arrogant and annoying to those in the crowd (many) listening to the connections being proposed by BW, but it was possibly necessary to keep the evening from getting boring ... In that sense Robert Duncan was, it seemed later, saving the evening from the kind of over-long and potentially tedious analysis Barry Watten was not so much proposing as already relentlessly enacting—one which had forceful intelligence but little scale and Duncan simply saw the need to return the evening to Zukofsky and his measure.[9]

[8] Ron Silliman to the author, 11 September 1998. It was David Levi Strauss's mention of the event in an article published in *Poetry Flash* six years later that re-ignited the controversy. Strauss's piece, "On Duncan & Zukofsky On Film" in the June 1984 issue of Poetry Flash, set off a flurry of angry letter-writing among San Francisco poets. Silliman also related another aspect of the Language Wars, in a 21 March 2006 email to the author: "There were other langpo-identified poets with whom Robert had far greater sympathies than he did Watten. Palmer, Melnick, myself. Even *after* this event, for example, Robert deliberately put me and Richard Baker-roshi, the head of the SF Zen Centre, together that led to Bob Perelman and I starting the reading series at the Tassajara Bakery in late '79 (this was the successor to the Grand Piano). That could not have happened without Robert's intervention."

[9] *Poetry Flash*, August 1984.

David Bromige, for whom Duncan had been a mentor since the two met in Vancouver in 1961, found himself in the aftermath of the event drawn into a closer alliance with the younger poets of Berkeley who came to contribute to the Language writing movement. Bromige recalled that:

> Robert presented it as people getting ahold of the stick at the wrong end. I remember him saying to me "you can never make an art out of a medium" ... I was always surprised when Robert came up with something like that over and over again because his mind was quite various, but it had these rigidities ... the first time I heard him say that it was about Brakhage's work, when Brakhage was cutting up film or destroying a frame ... Brakhage is trying to make you aware that your eyes are watching something and that light is the chief medium of that, but that film is the intermediary there. And Robert claimed that that was not enough for an art ... so of course Language writing, which is making an art out of a medium, could not be an art, since it can't be done. And I was disappointed, because Robert was capable of going into some things with great depth in a very involved way, and it seemed like he just had a way of stopping short here ... and I found him very wanting in sympathy that way. And this was someone who twenty years before had been very encouraging to us about his own generation's innovations.[10]

While Bromige and others were surprised that Duncan never came forward to explain or to apologise for his actions, Duncan seemed to quickly move on to focus on other aspects of his life as a writer. He made no reference to the San Francisco Art Institute event in his notebooks, although he did speak of it briefly in the course of an interview conducted by Eloyde Tovey during the following week:

> I dominate the scene I'm in. This meeting on Zukofsky last Friday, for example. Oy vey! There was a young poet who was

10 David Bromige, personal interview, 6 May 1998.

going to speak on … there's a circle that studies Zukofsky, the way in which they read Zukofsky. Well, after about twenty minutes of this young guy's address—it's so stupid in my mind and still seems so appallingly stupid—I started charging in and dominated unforgivably just blasted so he couldn't get to the end of what he was doing. And I realise I often dominate the situation because I don't want to hear stupidities. I'm really very unwilling to hear some tedious discussions. Of course, it means that often I'm not allowing for something that's not going to be stupid too.[11]

---

[11] Eloyde Tovey, interview with Robert Duncan, "Conversations with Robert Duncan, December 1978," University of California, Berkeley.

Robert Sheppard

A Carafe, a Blue Guitar, Beyonding Art: Krzysztof Ziarek and the Avant-Garde

1. Not Paris

I'm not good with big abstractions, unless they are my own: the mushy ideas of my poetics, malleable enough to push around into any situation, to get a poem going, permit an expression. But the argument against the avant-garde, as I understand it, runs something like this. Under modernism the avant-garde flourished, negating the autonomy of art as established during the "bourgeois" period of Aestheticism, and also negating Kantian notions of "disinterestedness" established before it, but in an ultimately self-defeating way, sowing the seeds of its own assimilation, even while it attempted to destroy the concept of Art in the name of an utopian desire to dismantle the division between art and life, in order to transform the latter.

Under postmodernism, the concept of the avant-garde, strictly speaking, becomes inoperative, since any "advanced" style is only a style and is available to all, on the level playing field, for purposes of pastiche and parody. The shock of the new is "consumed," in several senses. Under modernism, for example, the manifesto—that doctrinaire fixing of particularities—was exemplary. Under postmodernity, manifestoes become parodic, or personal, like O'Hara's "Personism," self-consciously defensive, already assimilated into the now-pluralistic definitions of a safely re-enthroned Art.

This is what critics seem to have been taking for some years from Peter Bürger's *Theory of the Avant-Garde*. My first paragraph is a summary of that book, my second, my account of hostile derivations from that theory—hostile, that is, to the kinds of art, particularly poetry, that I value.[1]

Sometimes these valued poets themselves muse upon the avant-garde moment. In Lee Harwood's uncollected poem, 'to/for Tristan Tzara (Rosenstock) a letter/message/report,' he remarks

let's set this in time & space
march 65 London
not Paris not Zurich not New York
not 1916 or 17 or 30 or 55
let us be concrete[2]

Harwood's spacetime coordinates locate the avant-garde in the past, respectively in Paris and Zurich Dada, 1930s Parisian Surrealism, and at the advent of the New York School (of poets, modelling themselves, however parodically, on the New York painters they were among), the 'last avant-garde' as the title of a book calls them. (Nineteen fifty five was also the year Ginsberg first publicly declaimed *Howl* on the West Coast.) Ten years later Harwood is found praising Tzara but sinking into the "drug induced visions" of the London counter-culture. But is not 1965 precisely a seminal pivot in the building of another avant-garde, the British Poetry Revival at the heart of which I place Harwood (and do so in my book *The Poetry of Saying*)?[3]

---

[1] The evocation of postmodernism should remind us of the negative derivations that such critics take from Fredric Jameson's various theses on the subject, which, bearing in mind his demands for a new cognitive mapping are not as single-mindedly antipathetic to postmodernism or the avant-garde, as some make out.

[2] Lee Harwood, *title illegible* (London: Writers Forum, 1965) n.pag.

[3] *The Poetry of Saying: British Poetry and its Discontents 1950-2000* (Liverpool: University of Liverpool Press, 2005), contains most of what I want to say about these avant-gardes. My chapter, "The British Poetry Revival 1960-1978," offers a history of this work, and a similar serialised work "The History of the Other"

Harwood's poem is a flawed acknowledgement of the concrete conditions of that moment (without seeing it as a moment), but showing a debt to a previous avant-garde, a paradoxical heritage. He even youthfully attacks the institution which will one day accommodate him ("L iterature A rt have nothing to/do with this"), even as he quotes Tzara:

> you said "the individual only affirms
> himself in the struggle, by the struggle ..."
>
> & these words have a skin & eyes & ears
> they're not just abstractions[4]

They struggle precisely, do not appear as abstractions at avant-garde moments, even while the participant may not recognise the historical particularities as such. Nostalgia for the black and white avant-garde classic haunts the mimeographed psychedelia of the British poetic underground.

2. The Obstacle of the Avant-Garde

Libbie Rifkin's *Career Moves: Olson, Creeley, Zukofsky, Berrigan, and the American Avant-Garde* argues, in its very sub-title and throughout, the continued efficacy of the term avant-garde, but notes, "For Bürger, the failure of the historical avant-garde is to blame for what he claims is the now purely gestural, ineffectual nature of cultural revolution. For scholars, practitioners, and enthusiasts, the persistence of his theory itself proves a formidable obstacle."[5]

The obstacle has been that avant-garde practice seemed to render "art more vulnerable to the re-cuperative forces of the

---

may be at www.robertsheppard.blogspot.com. The book also contains the chapter "Keeping the Doors Open: The Poetry of Lee Harwood in the 1960s and 1970s." See also *The Salt Companion to Lee Harwood*, ed. Robert Sheppard (Salt, forthcoming).

[4] Harwood, *title illegible*, n.pag.

[5] Libbie Rifkin, *Career Moves: Olson, Creeley, Zukofsky, Berrigan, and the American Avant-Garde* (Madison: University of Wisconsin Press, 2000) 15.

culture industry, to pave the way for the precommodified ironies of pop and other neo-avant-gardes."[6] To read such ironies is almost to admit that the avant-garde is dead as a concept. Read "neo" as "postmodern," and Bürger again becomes a useful tool for those claiming a conservative postmodernist position to slam every post-War avant-garde from New York poetry to language poetry, from the British Poetry Revival to Linguistically Innovative Poetry. (I can still hear a Utopian thrust in Lyotard's famous definition of the postmodern position: "The artist and the writer, then, are working without rules in order to formulate the rules of what *will have been done.*"[7])

But Bürger's own relationship with recent avant-gardes is more complex. In "Everydayness, Allegory and the Avant-garde," Bürger identifies Joseph Beuys as "in the tradition of the avant-garde," which, after looking at Harwood's statements of belatedness, seems less of an oxymoron, and, referring specifically to his earlier book, and its description of the 'failure' of the avant-gardes, Bürger says: "If one compares the project with what became of it, this talk of failure is certainly apposite; indeed, it would appear to be constitutive of the Utopian impulse of the avant-garde."[8] He adds: "It seems questionable whether a Utopian project can ever fail since it is so intimately connected with that hope that can never be disappointed."[9] He re-phrases the case, more interestingly for my purposes: "Failure is the mode in which the avant-garde artist reaffirms the Utopian quality of the project, a project that would always be transformed into something else if it were to be realised." The aim of Beuys can be no longer to destroy "art as an institution separated from the practice of real life," however

[6] Rifkin, *Career Moves*, 14.
[7] Jean-François Lyotard, *The Postmodern Condition* (Manchester: University of Manchester Press, 1984) 81.
[8] Peter Bürger, *Theory of the Avant-Garde* (Minneapolis: University of Minnesota Press, 1984) 153.
[9] Bürger, *Theory of the Avant-Garde*, 153.

much he distrusted it. He wanted to have his cake and eat it. "Dependent upon what it rejects," in Bürger's words, Beuys's practice makes him "a transgressor who simultaneously transposes the borderlines that he constantly violates"; he "is working from an impossible position—one that is located neither inside nor outside of art as an institution but on the borderline that constantly negates at the same time."[10] Khalid Hakim's desire for contemporary British Linguistically Innovative Poetry, or at least his own, "To be poetri & not poetre at th same tiyme, (sic)" reflects something of this aporetic contradictoriness and impossible utopianism, even as its expression balances on the cusp of English and non-English.[11] Indeed, for Bürger, this tricksterism seems to provide a limit case for his own theorising: it 'shows how the practice of the artist already finds itself in advance' (for what else can the military metaphor signify?) "of the legitimate fears of the theoretician."[12]

Rifkin argues that "Once we realise that the theory of the avant-garde universalises one moment in European modernism, and that aesthetic autonomy is just one of the problematics that innovative art addresses, we can see that poetic avant-gardes continue to emerge in the second half of this (sic) century, and that their breakthroughs as well as their failures have complex and continuing effects," particularly the "failure" of the Utopian after-shock.[13] The switch to the popular word "innovative" aside, this formulation leaves room for artists such as Beuys, who have exceeded the theory that trails him. Rifkin continues, with reference to the assimilation of the avant-garde within art: "Recognising the 'perpetual institutionality' of avant-gardist practice need not then amount

10 Bürger, *Theory of the Avant-Garde*, 153-5.
11 Nicholas Johnson (ed.) *Foil: defining poetry 1985*-2000 (Buckfastleigh: Etruscan, 2000) 52.
12 Bürger, *Theory of the Avant-Garde*, 161.
13 Rifkin, *Career Moves*, 16.

to an acceptance of de facto complicity."[14] Bürger's own reading of Beuys may be read as suggesting as much. Some avant-gardes develop conterminously with theoretical developments. "Contemporary avant-garde poets have, as Ron Silliman puts it, 'grown out of the same historical conditions that raised the question of theory itself within the academy'"; Silliman's argument is, of course, concerned with Language poetry and its institutions, and Rifkin extends this to "their postwar forebears."[15] I would extend that to moments in British poetry, both Lee Harwood's 1960s, and after.

Of course, the term avant-garde has fallen into disfavour for other reasons. It is not one I use myself with ease. Jed Rasula thinks the term should be "retired," since certain artistic practices which he no longer wishes to call avant-garde "need to be disencumbered of that label," and he warns, "and of any other (like 'postmodernism')," or—we might remind ourselves—of all those variants on "innovative."[16] "The diagnostic task of the labelling impulse has long served as a pre-emptive strike" against its radicalism, as we have seen in the case of the versions of Bürger. While any label becomes part of the assimilation of the concept, who "can now imagine that avant-garde is anything but a designer label for momentarily fashionable mindware"?[17] Indeed, I go for a walk around my

---

14 Rifkin, *Career Moves*, 17. The phrase in quotation marks comes from Paul Mann's *The Theory Death of the Avant-Garde* (Bloomington and Indianapolis: Indiana University Press, 1991).

15 Rifkin, *Career Moves*, 16. After a couple of very suggestive pages on the theme of the avant-garde, Rifkin's book explores the field of literary production of his chosen posts in a post-Bourdieuean framework, leaving behind the questions raised here.

16 Jed Rasula, *Syncopations: The Stress of Innovation in Contemporary American Poetry* (Tuscaloosa: University of Alabama Press, 2004) 194. I chart the evolution of the term "linguistically innovative" in "Linguistically Innovative Poetry 1978-2000," *The Poetry of Saying: British Poetry and its Discontents 1950-2000* (see note 2). The reader will see that I am not innocent of its propagation. Beside "linguistically innovative" I have heard the terms "formally innovative" (from Charles Bernstein) and "formally investigative" (from Karen MacCormack).

17 Rasula, *Syncopations*, 194.

corner of Liverpool to gather my thoughts for this piece, and I pass this improbable legend on a parked van: "Advanced Attics" (it is the vehicle of some loft conversion company, not a slogan of the Greek avant-garde); and then I pass the—more disarming—hair salon: "Avant-Garde."

3 *The Avant-Garde and Redefinition*

As I've said, some avant-gardes develop conterminously with theoretical developments. And some theories develop in direct relation to avant-garde practice, however distanciating the metalanguage employed. One such book, it seems to me, is Krzysztof Ziarek's *The Force of Art*,[18] and I will spend the rest of this meditation considering its importance for a theory of avant-garde work and for contemporary innovative artists of all kind, particularly poets (including myself, as one who might find it useful for theory and practice, and for my poetics which is neither).

The Force of Art is one of those immersive books, not unlike the conflicting aesthetics of his two heroes, Heidegger of "The Origin of the Work of Art" essay and Adorno of *Aesthetic Theory*. He compares the two in terms of their theories of power with the same alarming boldness he displays throughout. Its thesis builds slowly and leaves any summary or selective quotation inadequate to the whole. This is not to mystify the book, though it may be to acknowledge my own inadequacy, but to acknowledge that its urgency—which speaks to me as a writer—matches its intricacy and dispersion—which exercises my more intermittent faculties as a critic, and that to be possessed of Ziarek's vocabulary is to be inhabited by concepts—in a Deleuzoguattarian sense—not merely to try on the fashionable motley of a jargon.

Ziarek is curiously free of the inhibiting obstacle of Bürger and others who have worried away at the term avant-garde which he refreshingly uses "to refer both to the early-twentieth-

[18] Krzystof Ziarek, *The Force of Art* (Stanford: Stanford University Press, 2004). Page references cited in-text.

century avant-gardes and to the continuing avant-garde radicalism in contemporary art and poetry," and he opposes Raymond Williams's claims that modernism is a spent force (16). Ziarek, in contradistinction, states of his notion of the avant-garde: "We have not yet sufficiently addressed the problematic of freedom and power as it has been *redefined* in avant-garde artworks" (16, my italics). Ziarek does, however, admit to the "disappearance of avant-garde movements and their provocative statements and performances" but also argues that "what is sometimes called the 'death' of the avant-garde nevertheless has a more interesting and complex obverse side" (183). By this Ziarek means that this "death" decentralises both arguments about the importance of the stylistic shock of the new of the avant-gardes, and arguments for the direct social and political radicalism of avant-garde movements.

The business of Ziarek's book is both to define this redefinition within the avant-garde and, "in response to ... pessimism concerning art as a transformative force in the midst of the globalising works of power" (17), to analyse "art's relation to power," and to "rethink art's force beyond the boundaries of aesthetics" (3).

In the next section I shall attempt to summarise this theory.[19]

4a. The Very Rhythm of Relations

Ziarek conceives of the work of art as a force field. It is not an object but an event, and this eventness makes the artwork a forcework, in his central neologism. Inhering in neither form nor content, the forcework is beyond aesthetics; the artwork is beyond traditional aesthetic categories. No longer being an object, the work of art evades both culture and capital, though it is inscribed by both, and is not a commodity.

Forcework is a non-violent power-free thrusting; it re-orients "aesthetic commodity" in "aphesis," defined as "a letting be or

---

[19] I do, however, for the sake of clarity, leave aside Ziarek's consideration of race and gender.

a letting go," a benign process rather than a seizure of power (22).

In the work of art, forces—conceived of in a Deleuzean and Foucauldian way—are no longer tethered by the social, and in a redefinition of the autonomy of the artwork, as that is theorised by Adorno, to address the staticness and sense of separateness implied by his *Aesthetic Theory*—its lofty metacritique—Ziarek insists not only that artworks transform and re-work their forces (as Adorno would have agreed), but that they transform the ordinary relations of social power, and the receivers of the artwork can carry this non-violent, power-free relationality into social praxis.

The event of this transformation is an interruption of the real, a rupture as the artwork *works* (a term Ziarek valorises), by its "modalities of relation," not in terms of its content (28). Artworks' "importance for praxis is not in the thematic critique or even in formal subversiveness," but essentially in the forcework (60). The particular moment of the reception of this event will transform our sense of judgement. The event will involve a qualitative enhancement, a letting be, and enhancement does not imply technical efficiency. Enhancement's Heideggerrean opposite he calls, almost quantitatively, "increase," or sometimes "production" (45).

One example of all these processes is Stein's transformative "release of things from the closure of their naming" in *Tender Buttons*. Such enhanced transformations, Ziarek claims, are beyond power (and beyond aesthetics and commodification) (47).

Force is a "temporality of happening," forces in the plural; they are flows of interpenetrating parts, multiplicities, shifts, reflecting well the positivities of the postmodernist lexicon. "The force of art is the poiētic momentum into which the artwork transforms the force relations it has brought into its field" (34).

Technicity is the term Ziarek uses to determine the pernicious power of our technologically dominated world, to which are opposed the non-violent forces of artworks, as it were. Occasionally Ziarek is aphoristic: "Technicity aims toward power, while art attempts to let be, in aphasis" (34). However, technicity and art share characteristics, in this case Heidegger's pairing of the technē and the poiētic; only context determines on which side of the divide—in which field—a force will play. If it emerges as forcework, it becomes a "nonideological version of art's social significance," an Adornoesque formulation of the critical function of the work of art (42). "What makes art critical … is that its significance cannot be formulated into a set of propositions, a worldview or theory—that it eschews the socially and philosophically acceptable parameters of critique" (42).

Enhancement is, therefore, non-power, defining the forcework of art as free or "de-powered," not as participation in increase and production. "In art … forces are 'empowered' to be "otherwise" than powerful" (51). This implies neither a negation of power or of powerlessness, which would suggest an *absence*, and therefore still participating in the logic and language of power. The "otherwise"—as in Levinas's theory, from whence it derives—is a radical unworking of power, a new modality of relation, which we might define as "turning power's logic … into the power-free momentum of the event"[20] (59).

However, Ziarek does not shy away from "technopower"'s most potent recent developments, the advances in electronic technology and the biopower inherent in the decoding of DNA, and his critique of Eduardo Kac's *Genesis*, which is a mutating art work that exposes the logic of genetic engineering, is useful in determining the presence of forcework (or not) in both these

---

[20] In *The Poetry of Saying* I precisely base my theory of innovation upon Levinas's distinction between the saying and the said, and I also offer an account of Ziarek's previous work, *Inflected Language*, in a long footnote to my "Introduction." See also my poetics essay, *The Anti-Orpheus*, which is available as a free e-book from Shearsman Books at www.shearsman.com/pages/books/ebooks/ebooks_pdfs/Sheppard.pdf.

areas. Ziarek identifies the levels of artistic complicity in recent e-artworks, particularly through the manipulative logic of the internet. This is most evident in so-called "interactive" works which suggest freedom to the "operator" but in fact are as pre-programmed as a Las Vegas slot machine. While the aleatoric in the work of Cage was a genuine avant-garde strategy, such a mode has been long rendered complicit by its assimilation into the day-to-day workings of global capital's world wide web, as in the stream of "random" blogs that pop up as links on my blogzine's dashboard, for example. Forcework is severely compromised under these conditions, even while many artists embrace the technology without reflection. Nevertheless new avant-garde potentialities exist here: "In the context of the Internet revolution, this 'otherwise' to power gives a new meaning to revolt—the possibility of a turn in the increasingly technic organisation of relations in contemporary culture" (198), negotiated through "the avant-garde problematic of art's relation to technicity." (This is found in e-poetry, telematic art, the gestural rhetoric of Orlan and in the work of Bill Viola, the artist Ziarek looks to effect an ethical turn at the heart of technicity) (198).

Ziarek comes closest to Bürger's position when he argues that the growth of artistic autonomy in the eighteenth century was the way aesthetics could turn the event of forcework into an art object and thus a commodity (as art lost its direct social function). This is the source of the distrust of aesthetics (and poetics) I sense throughout the book, to which I shall return. The more critical art tries to be in orthodox terms, the more complicit with the postmodernist consumer society which assumes the art object a production—a product, we might say—and denies forcework as an inscription of othered and transfigured social relations, as non-power.

More positively, and by re-writing Adorno through Marx, Ziarek argues: "In a consumer society art is socially meaningful because its forcework remains irreducible to aesthetic object and aesthetic categories, on the one hand, and to the laws of exchange, commodification, and commodity fetishism, on the other" (112).

Unlike Adorno, though, Ziarek does not valorise high art over low. The presence (or not) of forcework is his only concern, whether in popular culture or in the poetry of Amiri Baraka (or Krzysztof Wodiczko's public art). Surprisingly, but necessarily, he uses Baraka to formulate a definition of forcework in action (almost) *despite* the overt political content of Baraka's work. Ziarek does not diminish the radicalism of content; it has to be abstracted to the operations of the deeper radicalism of the forcework. "Side by side with their militancy, avant-garde artworks gain social and political significance as a result of such transformation of the very rhythm of relations" (139).

4b. Not Another Poem
Often I am permitted to return to a field. And it is full of forces

Something is happening here, saying whatever, but saying all the same. But not. The same there's nothing to exchange. No need to

Forces don't build up in power. Or domination. A thoughtful, forceful relinquishing

Inside this field you are safe but not safe. All that is the world is not. The world. A bullet flies as the idea of a bullet (flies) but its trajectory is turned. To words like "sleet" turning to "snow." To slow. It is a bullet that stands. In relation to every new thing

Everything here is transformed; every thing out there is interrupted. A snowball frozen in mid-air becomes the off-centre of a new constellation from where we see it transfigured our selves. What we think of it is the new thing

There's more of it. And more and more of it in a different way there's nothing. We can do with what we find here. It's not stock, like the priest's stash of smuggled cigarettes in his confessional. This is where. I want to make some thing. Something elsed, but disavowed—disallowed, even—in this

A carafe, a blue guitar. Beyonding art

I don't want to only make relations. I make. The loopy woman in glasses in my making. I make her trip back from her car to number 99 in her strappy party shoes to search out the Christmas present she has forgotten. Then I will make the thoughts she has as she returns

Outside of her there is dominance. House numbers telephone wires. Humming with Power or Poetry. And all the antinomies. Satellite navigation. Data shadow. Inside. They share the world is not escaped, but elsed

Empower me to be so. Unpowered powerful. In my relinquishment critical. By distance not elevation to keep the saying unsaid. To speak against is to speak. Let me do it I need to do it but let me speak something elsed. From somewhere elsed. Of something

I have *made* something. For you. Now you are someone else

5. *Innovative Technique and Re-envisioning the World*
I didn't know I was going to write the last section. Its first draft appeared almost spontaneously as a "text and commentary" on the un-revised text of part 4a.[21] As such it is my response—not poetry, not criticism, not theory, but certainly poetics—to Ziarek's book. Through it, I think, I have arrived at a critique of his ideas, or maybe a particularised sense of disquiet with what

---

[21] See my *Hymns to the God in which My Typewriter Believes* (Exeter: Stride Books, 2006), for nearly an entire volume of "texts and commentaries."

is one of the most serious attempts to re-think—dare I use the word?—aesthetics that I have read in at least a decade. (Another is Derek Attridge's *The Singularity of Literature*.) It recognises the continuing efficacy of the avant-garde, and I feel it is appropriate that I have addressed it in an innovative form, to write poetry and not poetry at the same time.

Ziarek's distrust of production allows him to set up a definition—out of Heidegger—of poiēsis as a turn within technicity away from production, "a power-free poiētic technē that releases forces from the grip of machination, ordering, and maximalisation" (54). Ziarek's central notion of an alternative rhythm of relationality I find an attractive one, but he adds: "In using the term 'poiētic' I indicate that the kind of transformative forcework evident in art remains irreducible to a poetics and therefore does not fall under the rubric of aesthetics" (54).

As a writer, maybe an avant-garde one, poetics is vital to me—and the previous section is proof of this, I hope—as an ongoing speculative discourse about the formal possibilities of my artistic practice. I have theorised the nature of writerly poetics elsewhere, but my point here is that the nature of *making* is not so easily dismissed, particularly as Ziarek valorises the work involved in bringing artworks into being.[22]

While one major strength of this book is its re-articulation of Adorno's account of the critical function of the work of art, his corollary dissolving of the artwork as an object in order to maintain its forcework, means that artistic *making* (and poetics as formulations of that), artistic *materiality* and *medium* (and aesthetics that account for the negotiation of these) are ruled out of court, so that formal innovation as a factor in contemporary avant-garde practice is underplayed.

Perhaps this always happens when theory confronts practice. (This confrontation might be thought of as the provenance of poetics, but poetics can eschew particularities as

22 See particularly my *The Necessity of Poetics* (Liverpool: Ship of Fools, 2002). A slightly earlier version may be read at www.bbk.ac.uk/pores/1/index.htm.

well when it seeks to be speculative, which is why Ziarek's book is so suggestive to me.) While I agree with Ziarek's negotiation of the *content* of artworks—his approving disregard of Baraka's overt radicalism, for example—his disavowal of *formal* considerations does not ring true, particularly when he talks of the poiētic in Stein's *Tender Buttons* as "a transformative event redisposing the forces of language in such a way that they no longer work according the normative criteria of correctness and sense but let things unfold with a poiētic force of intensity so that things are no longer commodities or objects of everyday use" (47). Such redisposing, he is forced to admit, must be the result of technique; his phrase "a run-on syntax of everyday existence" at least suggests that syntax is at least as important an issue as the everyday (47), as are the functions of "naming and defining," which are disrupted quite concretely in Stein within the praxis of the innovative technique of displaced reference (46). Likewise, when he notes of Baraka's work, "for it is in terms of the rhythm, of the timing and scansion of relations, that Baraka proposes to re-envision the world and call into question the operations of power that stratify and polarise it," Ziarek similarly superimposes his concepts, his metaphors, upon the very technical devices that are prominent in the work, and give Baraka's poetry such power (particularly in performance) (129). In my own piece, for example, the refiguring of the world I attempt to *describe* in the force-field of art is also articulated precisely by the syntactic play provided by redefining sentence barriers. In Ziarek's terms I have re-ordered the syntax of the world to demonstrate a new relationality, but I have effected it by technical means (if I have been in any way successful, of course).

In fact, these three examples demonstrate clearly what Ziarek contends about the critical function—the revitalised relationality—of the work of art, more particularly about the world's transfigured (or re-envisoned) appearance in avant-garde works which, remember, are the ones Ziarek says *redefine* questions of freedom and power in the most radical ways. It is a shame that (at times) he seems to take artistic *creation* to be akin to commodifiable *production*, which brings him oddly close to the proponents of the death of the avant-garde.

6. *Affirmed by the Struggle*

The reader will not be surprised to realise that I regard the avant-garde as a viable contemporary phenomenon. Although I avoid the term—perhaps think it should be retired—I have written of the British Poetry Revival and of Linguistically Innovative Poetry in Britain with exactly the same attitude as writers such as Rifkin and Ziarek, critics who have little anxiety over the term and the various practices they denote. I also feel, as a member (or past member) of one of these avant-garde groupings, that theory—including the theory of the avant-garde, whether that is Bürger's canonical history or Ziarek's conceptual weave—has developed conterminously with avant-garde work. Most linguistically innovative poets I know are conversant in differing degrees with the works of the theorists (and perhaps Ziarek will be added to their number). Formulations of avant-gardism feed directly into avant-garde practice, in a way that is unprecedented, and which I have sought to demonstrate in this piece. Theory feeds directly into poetics.

Ziarek's book will be read in many ways but few will doubt his belief in, and commitment to, the transformative powers of contemporary avant-garde radicalism, even if the idea of avant-garde groupings and movements has had its day.[23] Perhaps the

---

[23] The reason I ponder my possible "past" membership of an avant-garde is not my fear that I've not kept up my subscription, or that a modern-day Breton has expelled me for having a bourgeois face or something, but that I feel geographically remote from the centres of avant-garde practice, and that I've reached an age when perhaps one's poetics—which is hopefully still avant-garde in some sense—is developed for the individual and less for the group, though I hope it is of use to others. I'm frankly not looking over my shoulder to see whether I adhere to the manifesto. The wolfish packing mentalities of avant-gardes are their least attractive aspects, despite the historical necessity of exclusivity and a decent supply of the drug of choice.

very technicity which Ziarek ambivalently discusses, in its development of global communities of exchange and risk, via the internet, will replace that isolation, and develop the "otherwise" ever more strongly.

Ziarek says little about the Utopian impulse of the avant-garde, balancing as it does on the cusp between art and its abandonment, but his sense of a relational transformation of the world, through the non-violent exercise of the dynamising forcework, his sense of enhancement over increase—which is also a valorisation of art over commodity, local play over global capitalism—is a Utopianism of sorts, predicated on its ultimate success but guaranteed only by its inevitable failure. Meanwhile the avant-garde compensation has to be, as Harwood learnt from Tzara in *his* moment, affirmed by the struggle.

Trey Strecker

Narrative Ecology and Encyclopaedic Narrative

It is interesting to contemplate an entangled bank, clothed with many plants of many kinds, with birds singing on the bushes, with various insects flitting about, and with worms crawling through the damp earth, and reflect that these elaborately constructed forms, so different from each other, and dependent on each other in so complex a manner, have all been produced by laws acting around us … There is grandeur in this view of life, with its several powers, having been originally breathed into a few forms or into one; and that, whilst this planet has gone cycling on according to the fixed law of gravity, from so simple a beginning endless forms most beautiful and most wonderful have been, and are being, evolved.

—Charles Darwin, *The Origin of Species*

A relation, which we all are.

—Joseph McElroy, *Women and Men*

"It's a mutual, joint-stock world," Herman Melville tells us, foreshadowing our time's awareness of the complex, reciprocal relationships between human beings and the earth that supports global life.[1] In his classic ecocritical study *The Comedy of Survival*, Joseph Meeker asks a pointed question: "From the

---

[1] Herman Melville, *Moby-Dick. Melville: Redburn, White-Jacket, Moby-Dick*, vol. 2, ed. G. Thomas Tanselle (New York: Library of America, 1983) 859.

unforgiving perspective of evolution and natural selection, does literature contribute more to our survival than it does to our extinction?"[2] The informed, innovative, and demanding novels of a new generation of American encyclopaedic authors do; among the best and most important contemporary American fiction, these books develop a living systemic network, tracing multiple trajectories between the individual, society, politics, history, science, and nature. These new encyclopaedic narratives traverse the limits of the global and the local, ecology and economy, and science and literature toward the ecological wisdom that our species' survival depends upon our adaptability to, not our dominance over, our environment.

In 1866, Ernst Haeckel coined the term "ecology" to describe the nascent science that would study "the household of nature" and "the interaction of organisms and their environment."[3] Encyclopaedic novels like William T. Vollmann's *You Bright and Risen Angels* (1987), Richard Powers's *The Gold Bug Variations* (1991), Bob Shacochis's *Swimming in the Volcano* (1993), Evan Dara's *The Lost Scrapbook* (1995), David Foster Wallace's *Infinite Jest* (1996), Colson Whitehead's *John Henry Days* (2001), and Jeffrey Eugenides's *Middlesex* (2002), among others, are profoundly ecological fictions about relationships between the individual and the big picture, the emergence of the macroscopic from the microscopic, and the interdependence of information and narrative. Recently, Richard Powers has described his own novels as "dialogues between little and big," exhibiting our need to understand "how parts of the whole can see the whole, come to know it, suffer the consequences of it."[4] Unlike many of their contemporaries, these talented novelists recognise the

---

[2] Joseph Meeker, *The Comedy of Survival: Literary Ecology and a Play Ethic* (Tucson: University of Arizona Press, 1997) 4.

[3] Ernst Mayr, *The Growth of Biological Thought: Diversity, Evolution, and Inheritance* (Cambridge, Mass.: Belknap, 1982) 121.

[4] Laura Miller, "The Salon Interview: Richard Powers," *Salon* (23 July 1998): http://www.salon.com/books/int/1998/07/cov_si_23inta.html

prolific complexity of life's "planetary pageant,"[5] and they strive to create fiction that engages the breadth and width of the world across all scales. Here, the concept of narrative ecology provides a valuable model which attends to the symbiotic interconnections and ecological processes active between different systemic levels and demonstrates how various cultural, social, and biological networks join us to our complex environment.

The genre of encyclopaedic narrative prefigures the emergence of narrative ecologies. In 1976, Edward Mendelson wrote two groundbreaking articles, "Encyclopaedic Narrative: From Dante to Pynchon," and "Gravity's Encyclopaedia," distinguishing encyclopaedic narrative's epistemic function to synecdochicly render a scientific, technological, or artistic field through a diverse range of literary styles and narrative forms. For some reason, however, Mendelson separates this informational structure of encyclopaedic knowledge from the narrative act that allows us to move across this space.[6] While his delineation of the intrinsic formal framework for a genre of encyclopaedic narrative can effectively describe Melville's cetology, Pynchon's thermodynamics, and even Powers's genetics, it cannot account for the densely complex unfolding of

---

[5] Richard Powers, *The Gold Bug Variations* (New York: Morrow, 1991) 178.

[6] An equally significant flaw in Mendelson's formulation of encyclopedic narrative is his insistence that these books must assume the status of "a single monumental work that can serve as a cultural focus" before their inclusion ("Encyclopedic" 1268). Thus, a text can only assume its place within this genre after the fact, based upon "extrinsic matters of reception and expectation" (1267): "Only after an encyclopedic narrative has taken its place as a literary monument, surrounded by curators and guides, can it be recognised as a member of its small and exclusive genre" (1268). Mendelson narrowly defines the genre based upon seven examples—the *Commedia, Gargantua and Pantagruel, Don Quixote, Faust, Moby-Dick, Ulysses,* and *Gravity's Rainbow*—neglecting William Gaddis's *The Recognitions* and *JR,* John Barth's *Giles Goat-Boy,* Don DeLillo's *Ratner's Star,* and Joseph McElroy's *Lookout Cartridge,* among others.

multiple interactions within "an indefinite field of relations."[7] Fiction, as Powers argues, should co-evolve as "a two-way product, one that involves both data and its narrative collaborator."[8] My criticism of Mendelson's approach is that it overemphasises the static spatio-informational dimension of the encyclopaedia and neglects the importance of diachronic narrative. Narrative transforms closed encyclopaedic spaces of entropic dissolution into complex narrative ecologies of emergent organisation.

Although narrative ecologies generally display many of the intrinsic formal criteria of Mendelson's encyclopaedic narratives, the novels' complicated informational structures are supplemented by their authors' awareness of biological and ecological processes. Process-orientated connections between diverse systems, subsystems, and components evolve out of the temporal movement represented by narrative processes. Moreover, because narrative resists large systemic abstractions with its own insistent particularities, it negotiates the balance between the individual and the big picture. In an interview with Laura Miller, Powers explains how this tension manifests itself:

> There's this sense of wanting to get the big picture. Wanting to really see, get the aerial view. And see the implication and the grandeur and the movements. The huge arcs that we don't see in our own lives. That's a monumental thing that fiction can do and that's the kind of fiction that I often seek out. But I think what we really want to do is link our own lives to those emotions and see how they intersect and see how they conflict and negate each other. We want the sense of our own story — the beginning, middle and end — to somehow make sense inside this bigger story.[9]

[7] Michel Foucault, *Power / Knowledge: Selected Interviews and Other Writings, 1972-1977* (New York: Pantheon, 1980) 192.

[8] Jim Neilson, "An Interview with Richard Powers," *The Review of Contemporary Fiction* 28.3 (Fall 1998): 16.

[9] Miller, "The Salon Interview: Richard Powers," n.pag.

Narrative allows us to travel across systemic hierarchies and to see how localised individual events in a nonlinear environment both compose and intersect with the big picture. "The world isn't simply taking place at eye-level view," Powers explains. "There's lots going on above us and below us."

In the 1980s and 1990s, many scientifically cognisant young authors turned away from physics-based tropes of entropy and chaos and chose biological concepts of order, complexity, and self-organisation as their dominant metaphors. Their encyclopaedic fiction models a new narrative ecology emerging from the metaphors of complex systems science. Complexity scientists claim that the nonlinear processes of self-organisation and the emergence of complexity "at the edge of order and chaos" provide the mechanism through which the biosphere has evolved its wondrous abundance of life. Complexity theory describes a new strategy for thinking about the emergent, collaborative, integrated behaviour of a large number of interacting elements, connected in multidimensional networks "that are endowed with the potential to evolve in time."[10] The emergence of complex narrative ecologies from the nonlinear interaction of local narrative events creates the complexity of these novels, a new naturalism that follows historian of science Fritjof Capra's observation that late twentieth-century science's recognition that living systems are at the centre of the ecological paradigm signals "a shift from physics to the life sciences."[11]

"Our new, scientifically and aesthetically sophisticated naturalists,"[12] these authors' understanding of complex systems teaches them to see this complex order, not as a by-product of chaos, but as a natural occurrence within living systems. Their novels serve as informational narrative ecologies, mimetic

---

[10] Peter Coveney and Roger Highfield, *Frontiers of Complexity: The Search for Order in A Chaotic World* (New York: Fawcett, 1995) 7.

[11] Fritjof Capra, The Web of Life: A New Scientific Understanding of Living Systems (New York: Anchor, 1996) 12-3.

[12] Tom LeClair, *The Art of Excess: Mastery in Contemporary American Fiction* (Urbana: University of Illinois Press, 1989) 17.

analogues of living systems in a natural environment, and revise the old naturalistic conception of individuals battered by a mechanistic universe to show humans intertwined in coevolving technological, scientific, political, and ecological networks. For this reason, the density and reflexivity of their encyclopaedic novels should not be dismissed as postmodernist play, but regarded as serious, "primarily reconstructive" efforts to reconcile narrative ecology and the natural ecosystem.[13]

"Major literary works," Meeker notes, "resemble ecosystems in that they present a large and complex panorama of experience in which the relationships of humans to one another are frequently represented in the context of human relationships to nature and its intricate parts."[14] From this structural homology between natural ecosystems and narrative ecologies, these texts strive to reproduce the richness and complexity of life on this planet and to address the effects of humankind's impact upon it on a global scale, because the global scale is the scale of nature. Both natural and narrative ecologies are complex webs woven together of systems and subsystems operating on the basis of multiform relations, where the system's constituent parts compete against each other in such a way that the system survives, adapts, and evolves. Connections in an ecosystem evolve based upon the needs of specific species and the necessities of the local environment "bound together by a web of complex relations."[15] Because the constant evolution of these interconnections can threaten the survival of the system as a whole, the most successful systems in the long-term of evolutionary biology and ecological processes balance the adaptability and the stability of complex systems.

Narrative ecologies replicate nature's evolutionary emergent processes and self-reflexive systems, urging us to rediscover

---

[13] LeClair, *The Art of Excess*, 21.
[14] Meeker, *The Comedy of Survival*, 7.
[15] Charles Darwin, *The Origin of Species* (New York: New American Library, 1958 [1859]) 82.

our connections with the living world and with each other. In recent years, the science of complex adaptive systems has drawn attention to the co-evolutionary reflexivity between humans and the natural world inherent in biological processes. Complexity theory describes the large-scale interaction of many diverse local components operating together in a nonlinear environment as an integrated system. The following list provides a synopsis of the general features of complex systems:

1. Complex systems are open systems that emerge from the dynamic interplay of a large number of elements and subsystems. Because complex systems contain too many elements and exchanges to be understood individually, our attention shifts from the individual parts to the behaviour of the whole system.

2. Local activity contributes to global systemic behaviour. Complexity emerges at the systemic level from the relationships between the diverse individual elements that constitute the system.

3. Nonlinear interactions mean that small, local causes can have disproportionately large, global effects.

4. The systems that display the most adaptable behaviour are poised "on the edge of order and chaos"; that is, these systems exhibit a moderate degree of connectivity. Systems that are too loosely connected cannot adapt and remain frozen in order. In systems that are too closely connected, every minor perturbation propagates endlessly throughout the system, which is driven into a state of anarchic chaos. With moderate connectivity, complex systems balance stability and flexibility.

5. Complex systems have a history. Evolutionary biology recognises change as well as continuity. Complex systems (brains, individuals, economies, ecosystems) are not *tabula rasa*. Past behaviour feeds back into the system.

As Paul Cilliers explains in *Complexity and Postmodernism:*

Understanding Complex Systems, "a complex system is not constituted merely by the sum of its components, but also by the intricate *relationships* between these components."[16] In a complex economy, Cilliers points out, individual agents and aggregates of agents "interact by lending, borrowing, investing, and exchanging money for goods," as well as making countless localised decisions which may influence other agents to varying degrees. Complex behaviour emerges in the pattern of relationships among local elements of interconnected systems. Thus we can discuss higher-order complex economic phenomena like the gross national product or stock market indexes as evidence of the dynamic interactions among the various components of the system.[17]

To delve deeper into crucial concepts from complexity theory like self-organised criticality and distributed causality, we must first examine the fundamental differences between closed linear systems and open nonlinear systems.[18] In the algebraic logic of linear systems, all of "the pieces add up" in a one-way chain of cause and effect.[19] Observing such a system, a scientist can isolate the discrete elements of a process and exhaustively document the linkage between a single cause and a single effect. This causal, deterministic worldview achieved its fullest expression in Pierre Simon Laplace's dream that the universe itself was ultimately explainable. If scientists could observe and record a complete explanation of each individual part, then they could ultimately understand the combined whole as "a perfectly manageable system of simple, linear, rational order,"[20] where "nothing would be uncertain."[21]

[16] Paul Cilliers, *Complexity and Postmodernism: Understanding Complex Systems* (New York: Routledge, 1998) 2.

[17] Cilliers, *Complexity and Postmodernism,* 5-7.

[18] The following discussion does not preclude the very real existence of discrete linear behavior within open, living systems; however, for simplicity's sake, I have chosen to focus on these alternatives.

[19] James Gleick, *Chaos: Making a New Science* (New York: Penguin, 1987) 23.

[20] Donald Worster, *Nature's Economy: A History of Ecological Ideas* (New York: Cambridge University Press, 1994) 406.

But because living systems are always open systems, "our knowledge of them is always partial, approximate, at best."[22] An extremely large closed system may be quite complicated, but only open systems have the potential to be complex, since only open systems maintain a reciprocal feedback relationship with their environment. As Anthony Wilden explains: "All systems involving or simulating life or mind are open systems, because they are necessarily in communication with another 'system' or 'environment.'"[23] This extra-systemic relationship is "indispensable to its survival,"[24] because the constant influx of energy or information allows living systems to defy the Second Law of Thermodynamics, at least locally, and to increase in complexity.

"You will want cause and effect," predicts the narrator of *Gravity's Rainbow*,[25] an encyclopaedic forerunner of narrative ecology. Throughout Pynchon's novel, the epistemology of linear causation imposes closed systems thinking onto open systems and turns reciprocal feedback loops into unidirectional power relations, reducing complexity. Since nature is not a mechanistic system where specific causes produce specific, exact effects, the scientist Lazlo Jamf lectures Franz Pökler's class to "move beyond life, toward the inorganic" (580) in order to tame the complex biological processes of "lovable but scatterbrained Mother Nature" (324). Science tries to transcend the natural world in the same way that the cartels attempt to dominate the planet and its natural resources. In a well-known scene, Pynchon contrasts Kekulé's dream of the benzene ring as a singular, closed System, "the Great Serpent holding its own tail in its mouth," with the view of the earth as an open, living

21 Laplace, quoted in Capra, *The Web of Life*, 184.
22 John Horgan, "From Complexity to Perplexity," *Scientific American* (June 1995): 107.
23 Anthony Wilden, *System and Structure: Essays in Communication and Exchange* (London: Tavistock, 1972) 36.
24 Wilden, *System and Structure*, 203.
25 Thomas Pynchon, *Gravity's Rainbow* (New York: Penguin, 1973) 663; subsequent page references are in-text.

ecology[26]:

> The Serpent that announces, "The World is a closed thing, cyclical, resonant, eternally-returning," is to be delivered into a system whose only aim is to *violate* the Cycle. Taking and not giving back, demanding that "productivity" and "earnings" keep on increasing with time, the System is removing from the rest of the World these vast quantities of energy to keep its own tiny desperate fraction showing a profit: and not only most of humanity—most of the World, animal, vegetable and mineral, is laid waste in the process. The System may or may not understand that it's only buying time. And that time is an artificial resource to begin with, of no value to anyone or anything but the System, which sooner or later must crash to its death, when its addiction to energy has become more than the rest of the World can supply, dragging with it innocent souls all along the chain of life. (412)

These "closed symbolics, predicated on absolutes," trap individuals in totalising systems of domination that contravene life's natural processes.[27] Within Pynchon's novel, proponents of the System "find it convenient to preach an island of life surrounded by a void" (697). "Our compulsion to construct and maintain closed, isolated systems," Robert Nadeau explains, "induces a sense of dislocation and fragmentation in relation to the whole."[28]

Like "a maniac bent on suicide" (412), we are "driving the life crystal back to inertness."[29] Mechanist scientific knowledge's reference to technological control and scientific rationality dredges up the residue of domination and codifies our perception of an absolute, indifferent, manageable nature. In *Steps to an Ecology of Mind*, Gregory Bateson perceives seven destructive ideas at the root of our current ecological crisis:

[26] LeClair, *The Art of Excess*, 41.

[27] Robert Nadeau, *Readings from the New Book on Nature: Physics and Metaphysics in The Modern Novel* (Amherst: University of Massachusetts Press, 1981) 139-40.

[28] Nadeau, *Readings from the New Book on Nature*, 140-1.

[29] Powers, *The Gold Bug Variations*, 332.

1. It's us *against* the environment.
2. It's us *against* other men.
3. It's the individual (or the individual company, or the individual nation) that matters.
4. We *can* have unilateral control over the environment and must strive for that control.
5. We live within an infinitely expanding "frontier."
6. Economic determinism is common sense.
7. Technology will do it for us.[30]

Bateson reveals the essential flaw of this antagonistic logic: "*The creature that wins against its environment destroys itself*"[31] While closed systems can be observed and known from the outside, a view that is incoherent with nature, open systems cannot be separated from the environments in which they are embedded. Our alienation from, and disregard for, "the living, interlocked world" have drawn us to the verge of ecological crisis.[32] "There is no escaping the ecological matrix," warns environmental historian Donald Worster, because no transcendental position outside the system exists.[33]

The Earth is not a closed system, rather it is "the largest observable whole of which man is a part; its processes are the processes of its constituent parts; its reciprocal information and governance systems are replicated in all life."[34] Open systems allow us to develop a reflexive conception of multiple relations across all scales, an interdependent view in which elements, subsystems, and systems are connected in reciprocal feedback loops where the emergent behaviour of a system might be different from its component parts. Such systems are more like dynamic mosaics of living and nonliving things than the accumulated activity of their individual elements.

---

[30] Gregory Bateson, *Steps to an Ecology of Mind* (New York: Ballantine, 1972) 492.

[31] Bateson, *Steps to an Ecology of Mind*, 493. Wilden reiterates this point when he writes, "THE SYSTEM WHICH DISPOSES OF ITS ENVIRONMENT DISPOSES OF ITSELF" (207).

[32] Powers, *The Gold Bug Variations*, 411.

[33] Worster, *Nature's Economy*, 333.

[34] LeClair, *The Art of Excess*, 47.

No transcendent position exists outside our natural environment. Significantly, Pynchon's novel opens with an evacuation scene that depicts "not a disentanglement from, but a progressive *knotting into*" the "coral-like and mysteriously vital growth" of increasing complexity (3). Although individuals may step free of History's linear arc, they remain forever connected in multiple, shifting "webs of complication."[35] As individuals and collections of individuals entangled within our evolving, self-organising universe, these novelists demonstrate how it is in our self-interest to act wisely and ecologically.

Within this new literary naturalism, the study of complex systems surrenders mechanist illusions of control and manipulation as authors, characters, and readers dispense with the assumption that humans are separate from other species and the natural world. Instead, as Powers's bioscientist tells his student, science "is about cultivating a perpetual condition of wonder in the face of something that forever grows one step richer and subtler than our latest theory about it."[36]

The theory of self-organised criticality explains how large complex systems evolve to a critical regime between order and chaos where complex behaviour can emerge. Scientist Per Bak of Brookhaven National Laboratory has conducted a famous sandpile experiment to demonstrate how global complexity emerges from the dynamics of individual, local interactions. In Bak's experiment, sand is piled onto a flat platform one grain at a time until it begins to form a sloping pile. Small, localised avalanches occur as the sandpile becomes steeper, but these small events only have small effects. The sandpile remains linear and noncritical. The sandpile achieves criticality when the slop cannot increase and the amount of sand added to the pile is balanced by the amount falling off the edges of the table. As the sandpile moves from a regime of linear cause and effect

[35] Susan Strehle, *Fiction in the Quantum Universe* (Chapel Hill: University of North Carolina Press, 1992) 59.
[36] Powers, *The Gold Bug Variations*, 411.

to a nonlinear state, a single grain of sand can trigger cascading global avalanches.

Simple rules generate unpredictable, richly complex behaviour; in Bak's sandpile, "The simple behaviour of the individual elements following their own simple local rules [conspires] to create a unique, delicately balanced, poised, global situation in which the motion of any given element might affect any other element in the system."[37] In the critical state, complexity emerges as the co-evolutionary product of the system, as rules adapt to one another and their constantly changing environment. A global structure emerges from local interactions, and positive, negentropic feedback from the larger system restructures the local sites.[38] This interdependence between other systems and parts of systems creates recursive feedback loops that link individual systems into larger ecological networks, increasing the stability and adaptability of the global environment. Bak explains that the complex dynamics of self-organised criticality allow systems to react to local disturbances by a co-evolutionary process that keeps the global system poised in the critical region between order and chaos where complexity emerges. As the co-ordinated behaviour of the system moves toward the critical regime, the system adapts. Traces of past iterations feed back into the system, allowing it to "learn" from experience.

Whether a system reaches criticality largely depends upon how the individual elements of the network are connected. The density of connections within a network and between connected networks determines the system's adaptability. In loosely connected networks, the system settles into stagnant patterns, while in densely connected networks, each element cycles among the countless conflicting messages it receives from its neighbours, which sends the system spinning into

---

[37] Per Bak, *How Nature Works: The Science of Self-Organised Criticality* (New York: Copernicus, 1996) 48.

[38] Roger Lewin, *Complexity: Life at the Edge of Chaos* (New York: Collier, 1992) 12-3.

chaotic behaviour.[39] Maximum adaptivity occurs in the critical regime, where systems with a moderate degree of connectivity are "orderly enough to ensure stability, yet full of flexibility and surprise."[40] Global communication across the network enables small, local events to have disproportionately large-scale effects.

Reciprocal relationships create dense, nonlinear assemblages, where systems are connected with their environment and each other. Systems participate in the environments in which they are embedded. After years of believing that our planet is merely "a big dumb rock," Pynchon's Lyle Bland recognises that the "Earth is a living critter" with interdependent atmospheric, climatic, chemical, physical, and biological systems (590). Biological systems, from molecular levels through the nervous system, through the individual, through species, and through ecosystems, are organised hierarchically.[41] Diverse, complex behaviour emerges from robust interaction at the local levels and from intricately linked loops that cross systemic levels. In *Gravity's Rainbow*, Franz Pökler, "the cause and effect man," argues with his wife Leni about how to explain how "changes out there produce changes here" (159). Leni rebuts her husband's simplistic view,

---

[39] In *Gravity's Rainbow,* the polarities of order and chaos might be represented by the one and the zero, the rigid authority of the System and the mindless anarchy of the Counterforce, or the novel's "rigid, imposed, serial connections" and its "chaotic disconnectedness"(Strehle 30). Father Rapier sermonises, "Once the technological means of control have reached a certain size, a certain degree of being connected to one another, the chances for freedom are over for good" (539). Strehle notes that when Slothrop trades paranoid order for anti-paranoid chaos, "He [Slothrop] brings Newtonian assumptions to his reading of reality until his experience forces him to abandon them; then, unable to imagine other alternatives, he simply turns Newton's cosmos on its head and envisions its binary opposite" (38). In similar fashion, postmodernism has shied away from the search for complex order, often finding it easier to claim that there is no real order and that nothing makes sense.

[40] Stuart Kauffman, *At Home in the Universe: The Search for the Laws of Self-Organisation and Complexity* (New York: Oxford University Press, 1995) 87.

[41] Frederick Turner, *The Culture of Hope: A New Birth of the Classical Spirit* (New York: Free Press, 1995) 219.

which depends upon the System's totalisation of the mechanistic logic of causality. "Not produce … not cause," Leni insists. "It all goes along together. Parallel, not series. Metaphor. Signs and symptoms. Mapping on to different coordinate systems, I don't know" (159). In *The Gold Bug Variations*, Powers describes the interlocked systems of "those plastic anatomical overlays in biology books": "Each transparent sheet contains its own, separate hierarchies—circulatory, skeletal, nervous. But each overlay, flipped on the stack, adds its system, compacts its parts into a surprising, indivisible composite."[42] These intermeshed systems and subsystems connect in vast parallel processing networks.[43]

Distributed control challenges the mechanistic view of linear causality with a complex network of multi-directional causality composed of many competing agents. Reciprocal perturbations can draw systems to the critical regime and generate new complexity, but no one can control or predict this effect due to the complex interaction of an incredibly large number of factors. Complexity emerges not from discrete individual elements within a system, but from the unfolding pattern of relationships between them.

"Engaging with complexity," according to Cilliers, "entails engaging with specific complex systems."[44] Complex narrative ecologies demand large investments of time and energy, but they reward such dutiful attention. In an interview with Tom LeClair, Joseph McElroy explains how he uses the word "attention" in his fiction in a way that is particularly helpful for understanding the kind of attention these difficult books require and reward:

> "Attention" is a rather cold word I use to suggest that the ways in which we embrace the world and embrace other people can

---

42 Powers, *The Gold Bug Variations*, 208.
43 Tom LeClair, "The Prodigious Fiction of Richard Powers, William Vollmann, and David Foster Wallace," *Critique* 38.1 (Fall 1996): 27.
44 Cilliers, *Complexity and Postmodernism*, ix.

be more precise and clear than we sometimes think. We can express allegiance with other people, whether or not this is love, by thinking closely about what they say. Look terribly closely but neutrally. Love is at odds with possessing.[45]

McElroy's attention, which crosses boundaries, circulates and consumes without possessing, and increases complexity, produces narratives that navigate "the great multiple field of impinging informations."[46] In many ways, narrative ecologies ask for the same attention that their authors lavish upon the complexities of the world. The reader, Wallace explains, must "put in her share of the linguistic work," "connecting [interpolated systems, subsystems, and diverse elements] to each other and to the narrative."[47]

Yet unlike the authors of massive modernist encyclopaedias who bombard us with the certainty of their knowledge, these authors actively enter the texts and the systems under study as interpreters of our world. According to Susan Strehle, "making the author visible, personal, and active inside the text removes the artist's mystified authority *over* it; single and limited, even openly biased, the author exposes the text's multiple and relative sources, rather than withdrawing to the unassailable— invisible, detached—absence that confers absolute authority on traditional authors."[48] These authors interface and collaborate in a reciprocal relationship with the reader. As living, evolving systems, their immense and challenging books address the complexities of an immense and challenging world, and they invite and depend upon the participation of the reader. According to Thomas Jackson Rice, "the individual reader's response alters the behaviour of the 'system,' the book, with

[45] Tom LeClair, "An Interview with Joseph McElroy," *Anything Can Happen: Interviews with Contemporary American Novelists*, ed. Tom LeClair and Larry McCaffery (Urbana: University of Illinois Press, 1983) 248.

[46] Joseph McElroy, *Lookout Cartridge* (New York: Knopf, 1974) 465.

[47] Larry McCaffery, "An Interview with David Foster Wallace," *The Review of Contemporary Fiction* 13.2 (Summer 1993): 137-8.

[48] Strehle, *Fiction in the Quantum Universe*, 221-2.

each 'iteration,' or reading."[49] Furthermore, these iterations feedback increasing complexity into the evolving narrative system.

If the primary feature of literary studies is, as William Paulson argues on *The Noise of Culture: Literary Texts in a World of Information*, its intrinsic interdisciplinarity as a global system where knowledge thrives through relations of ecological interdependence,[50] then narrative ecologies which mine this knowledge and examine the cultural and biological networks that entwine us with our complex environment offer an extremely powerful demonstration of the efficacy of literature in contemporary life. In this context, narrative movement across an interdisciplinary ecology provides an apt model for the complex cognitive processes of consciousness, adaptation, and learning. Complexity emerges through narrative *passages*, as readers circulate between diverse systems and subsystems, continually organising and reorganising the dynamic informational ecology of the narrative metasystem.

At the end of *Gravity's Rainbow*, with the threatening rocket poised over the crowded theatre, Pynchon (the author) turns to the audience and invites them to collaborate in reformulating the world: "Now everybody—" (760). This reminder that we are collectively responsible for the natural, social, and political environments within which we live points outside the novel. In our time, we need ecological fictions that do not underestimate the complexity of our environment or our complicity with it and that take the risk of making an honest attempt to represent the individual's place in our "living, interlocked world."[51] Narrative ecologies succeed because they chart the connections

---

[49] Thomas Jackson Rice, *Joyce, Chaos, and Complexity* (Urbana: University if Illinois Press, 1997) 103. Rice continues: "The same and many different additional readers perform subsequent iterations/readings; in all cases the products of the experience will differ, often subtly, but sometimes with unpredictably vast shifts in the results (e.g. the most recent 'new critical insight')" (103).

[50] William Paulson, *The Noise of Culture: Literary Texts in a World of Information* (Ithaca: Cornell University Press, 1988) 114.

[51] Powers, *The Gold Bug Variations*, 411.

between the little and the big, the part and the whole, and enable us to better understand our interdependent relations with the natural world and with each other. The ecological survival value of these powerful texts rests upon "the exploration of where we are,"[52] which can illuminate "the possibilities of being alive and human."[53]

---

[52] Neilson, "An Interview with Richard Powers," 23.
[53] McCaffery, "An Interview with David Foster Wallace," 131.

Michael S. Begnal

The Ancients Have Returned Among Us: Polaroids of 21st C. Irish Poetry

Careless and ancient, like a myth,
you step into view, spitting shadows from your mouth.
—Alan Jude Moore, "Galway Road (into Dublin)"

It would probably not be too much of a risk to make the observation that, very generally speaking, Irish poetry has been dominated by a conservative tendency which often seems to have the upper hand in the contemporary scene. Given that Ireland's literary tradition stretches back approximately a millennium and a half, this can really be no surprise. Of the poets of the Gaelic Order, for example, Joep Leerssen has written,

Their social position was one of great importance and can perhaps best be described as a combination between a censor in the Roman republic, a member of the Académie française, a minister of culture, and a representative of the modern media. His professional qualifications included (apart from his descent from a family of established bardic renown) a command over the highly complex rules of Gaelic prosody and a vast store of historical, genealogical and mythological knowledge. All this knowledge was transmitted orally and part of it can be traced back into the pre-Christian era; the poet is originally a *seer* who, until the arrival of Christianity, had been vested with pontifical powers ... The poet did not aim at providing entertainment, but rather at applying his lore and his craftsmanship with language to a celebration of the events of his day, thereby establishing a link between past and present. The poet was the cultural guardian of the Gaelic heritage, whose task it was to guarantee historical continuity, to legitimise the present in terms of past history.[1]

This is a great and interesting thing and shows perhaps that Ireland has a traditional respect for poetry not often found elsewhere, and which survived the rupture of language from Irish into English (the Famine having almost delivered a *coup de grâce*). It also implies a long-standing cultural insularity attaching to Irish poetry, which once again became pronounced in the early 20th century after Southern independence from Britain.

Nobel Prize winner Seamus Heaney perhaps best exemplifies the role of the modern-day bardic poet. Certainly he is a great poet—of this there could hardly be any dispute—and his influence is of course very wide. But, as David Butler wrote of him in the literary magazine *The Burning Bush*,[2] "In far too many workshops one gets the impression that the laureate is being invoked by one or another participant like a benign Buddha in whose honour he/she has penned a biographical *mot juste* poem cow-heavy with metaphor. How different things would be if, say, the protean Ciaran Carson were instead to be made Chief Household Deity."[3] At the turn of the century, when *The Burning Bush* came into existence, there was a sense that a certain style of writing, and a certain gravity it projected, received almost the imprimatur of officialdom. That there was

---

[1] Joep Leerssen, *Mere Irish and Fíor-Ghael: Studies in the Idea of Irish Nationality, its Development and Literary Expression prior to the Nineteenth Century* (Cork: Cork University Press, 1996), 153.

[2] *The Burning Bush*, which ran from 1999-2004, was edited by myself for all eleven of its issues (co-edited with the poet/critic Kevin Higgins for the first four).

[3] David Butler, "Remembrance of Things Pastoral," *The Burning Bush* 9 (Spring 2003): 14.

an identifiable "mainstream." I realise this may be unfair to Mr. Heaney, who has done absolutely nothing wrong, but call it a Heaneyan, or rather a sub-Heaneyan, style. Aside from the aforementioned seriousness, it is marked by a strong rural focus, lyric form, a concern with the meaning of Irishness (though admittedly this concern can apply to anyone), and, perhaps, membership of Aosdána.[4] Despite the fact that over the last few decades Irish society has undergone a radical transformation from an agrarian economy to one now heavily based on information technology (with an accompanying shift in the population toward urban centres), poetry for some was just not poetry if it wasn't pastoral.

In a review of Moya Cannon's republished collection *Oar*, in 2001, Alan Jude Moore delineated the state of play quite succinctly:

> The landscape is that of familiar rural Ireland, of stereotypically put-upon ancestors, and, crucially, decay. Things that are long since decayed form the bog, which is the spiritual dwelling of this collection. No criticism can be levelled at a poet just because they choose to examine this well-trodden ground (it's as boringly subjective when an "urban" writer insists that a "rural" writer has no solid claim to poetry as it is vice versa) ... The poetry, though, can be too comfortable. There is decay but no new decay. This is poetry as social history, not as living commentary. Not as a reminder of how things are and could be, but how things were ... It is no fault of the poet, but the reissue of such a collection sends a clear message as to where poetry as part of Irish culture lies. History did not begin and end with the bog; the bog is not the landscape of importance in Ireland at the moment. It is not where great sea-changes are taking place, where cultures are being reinvented.[5]

---

[4] Aosdána is the Irish government-funded academy of artists, an "establishment," one might say—although this is not to suggest there is complete homogeneity among its members in regard to ethos or style.

[5] Alan Jude Moore, "Review of Moya Cannon's *Oar* (The Gallery Press)," *The Burning Bush* 5 (Spring 2001): 63-64.

Against this, Moore does situate his own poetry in an urban environment, where the decay is the decay of bird feathers in a drain at Connolly Station, and "pigeons drinking / from a pool of steam and oil."[6] Not unlike the stance of Apollinaire almost a hundred years ago, Moore consciously incorporates the disjointed images and media of the modern city, both the Irish and the European (a Dubliner, he currently lives in Moscow). The thing is not to parrot the historical avant-garde, of which Apollinaire was one progenitor, and to be therefore as retrograde as Moya Cannon is in her own way, but to mediate a constantly evolving present in the absence of old poetic certainties. Moore's writing is composed of images, like Polaroids, tawdry and profound at once, unexpectedly tacked next to each other on an apartment wall. Thus history for Moore is not about any reconnection with perceived folkways, but rather the disconnection of "[t]he sun bleeding like a bullet hole / through the windows and the bars, / over graveyards and processions."[7]

To say it again, Ireland is a society which has been undergoing a radical social and economic transition, and therefore it becomes necessary for Irish poets to seek new forms, as others have done for their own times and places. It strikes me as almost bizarre that in the country which produced James Joyce, Thomas MacGreevy and Samuel Beckett, Alan Moore's collection *Black State Cars* should be greeted with near-bewilderment in the newspaper of record, *The Irish Times*. Delivering something of a backhanded compliment, James J. McAuley's review there stated that Moore "is a thirty-something tyro whose talent burns as brightly as that of Rimbaud or Hart Crane. Moore might be flattered by such comparison, but for all but a few poems the strange hallucinatory juxtaposing of images and phrases is too fragmentary or inconclusive to effect little more than

[6] Moore, "Connolly," *Black State Cars* (Cliffs of Moher: Salmon Poetry, 2004), 29.
[7] "The Prisoner Speaks of a Woman," *Black State Cars*, 19.

astonishment."[8] While McAuley recognises that Moore "could be a truly original poet," he has trouble with his "irritating dissociations and distortions" and "cavalier ways of abusing (or not using) the courtesies of punctuation and other helpful directions"[9]—it is almost as if literary modernism never happened. While McAuley is undoubtedly better equipped as a reader than he lets on here, there seems to be a certain laziness among readers of Irish poetry generally if they are still unable to process these basic modernist innovations. And so to step outside the familiar line of Irish poetic nationalism—which stretches from Yeats through Kavanagh to Heaney (though I realise this is a simplification)—can still be dangerous for an Irish writer.

Conversely, in a review of *Black State Cars* in the Dublin journal *The Stinging Fly*, Michael Wynne raves about Moore's writing—his "building up [of] a complex interchange of intimate moods with an inventory of expressionistic detail"—but gets it totally wrong when he says that Moore "wryly and ruefully imagines the innocence of a previous age" and "point[s] up the paucity of our current condition of 'progress,' with all the efficient, denatured blandness that typifies it, a condition underneath which the presences of tradition and nature insistently and indignantly pulsate...."[10] This seems to me a complete misreading of how Moore deals with history, and his ambivalent (at best) attitude to tradition and the past. While Moore stands opposed to the consumerist machine that is contemporary Ireland, he is most definitely facing forward instead of backward. The poem "Heading into Darkness outside Athlone" could be said to function in verse as his review of Moya Cannon does in prose:

... battlefields, externalised historical centres.

8 James J. McAuley, "Found in translation," *The Irish Times*, 12 February 2005.
9 McAuley, "Found in translation."
10 Michael Wynne, "Review of *Black State Cars* by Alan Jude Moore," *The Stinging Fly*, Volume 2, Issue 1 (Summer 2005): 89.

Tiny pities of the aristocracy still roll down hills
to mingle with the smell
of bogwood and treacherous bog.
In rooms where no-one laughs
(or has even come close to a tear for some time),
sentiment is wrapped in a paper bag ...[11]

The Irish-language poet Gearóid Mac Lochlainn, while retaining an overt political nationalism (or more specifically, Irish republicanism), subverts tradition in his own way. Where much contemporary Gaelic poetry understandably dwells along the stark, rocky, Western seacoasts (notable exceptions come to mind, such as the work of Louis de Paor), Mac Lochlainn is an Irish-speaker from Belfast—Ireland's second-largest city, located in the industrial northeast, a region of the country still occupied by the British army. Partly in reaction to the ongoing British domination of the North, Belfast has developed a strong present-day Irish-language movement among segments of the population, one that has become self-sustaining. Raised in a bilingual environment during the Troubles, it is unavoidable that Mac Lochlainn would be confronted head on with questions of cultural and linguistic identity:

– Keep yer fucking 'ands on the wall, Paddy.

Chuala mé mo *details*
ag dul thar an raidió
chuig strainséir eile ag an *base*,
m'ainm do-aitheanta
smiota ag cnagarnach *static* Bhéarla.[12]

– *Keep yer fucking 'ands on the wall, Paddy!*

I heard my details passed over the radio

[11] Moore, *Black State Cars*, 12.
[12] Gearóid Mac Lochlainn, "Teacht i Méadaíocht/Rite of Passage," *Sruth Teangacha/Stream of Tongues* (Indreabhán: Cló Iar-Chonnachta, 2002) 42-43.

to another stranger at base,
my Irish name now unrecognisable,
carved up by the crackling blades of English and static.

Yet neither would it simply be enough to choose gritty, urban subject matter, nor even to write about the Irish war from a radical republican point of view. It is in the interplay between the different versions of Mac Lochlainn, the original Irish poems and their English translations, that he becomes especially interesting. As he writes in the notes to his bilingual collection *Sruth Teangacha/Stream of Tongues* (2002), "In the original poems sound shaped syntax to a large extent and for this reason I believe it is impossible to really 'translate' Irish poetry."[13] Languages are not merely hoards of words with direct correlation to each other, as anyone who speaks more than one language can tell you. Instead, each individuates a world-view inherent in its grammar and idiom; each defines a unique mode of consciousness. Mac Lochlainn (with his numerous co-translators) often departs from his own original versions, sometimes significantly—"a playful jibe thrown out at the monoglot who seeks truth in translation."[14] Thus *Sruth Teangacha* becomes a type of meta-work, composed not just of Irish poems and English translations, but of the interaction between the two.

The result of this, though, is that neither the originals nor the translations can any longer be considered authoritative in their own right. While each comments on its counterpart, it also undermines any claim that the other might have to being the "real" poem. Certainly this is what Mac Lochlainn intends in regard to the translations; he is cognisant of the danger of allowing the English versions to "gain an autonomy of their own and eclipse the Irish."[15] What is more problematic is the effect on the original poems: the fact that a parallel version

---

[13] Mac Lochlainn, "Author's Notes," *Sruth Teangacha*, 188.
[14] Lochlainn, "Author's Notes," 190.
[15] Lochlainn, "Author's Notes."

exists destabilises the authority of the original just as much as vice versa. There can be no wilful ignorance. However, given that only a small percentage of people will be able to understand the Irish, the troubling contradictions inherent in Mac Lochlainn's project could be lost on most. I suspect that a lot of his readers do not fully grasp the deeper implications being made about language, both as a cultural manifestation and as an entity unto itself, and instead take him as an energetic, Beat-influenced Irish rebel. If so, they are only getting part the story.

Mac Lochlainn and Moore are but two of the more disparate voices that began to come to prominence as the 21st century dawned. Both of these poets consciously work in opposition to aspects of the established tradition, albeit in much different ways from each other. Both have reacted to the pastoral trend in Irish poetry which, while not at all irrelevant in itself, has in some respects become a static convention as society continues to evolve in other directions. As a corollary to this new social context, both writers have reached for new poetic forms, Mac Lochlainn making the leap into macaronic language and the interplay of versions of text, Moore often subjecting his English to lucid derangements recalling earlier avant-garde models. There are others, though, who might be said to verge even further in the direction of linguistic exploration.

***

in a way humming thru crystals of light—most unexpected—
the ancients sizzle and dazzle
not as we imagined nor can put our machines to nor
make comprehensible by words or songs or metaphors
The ancients have truly returned to us
and have unfurled flags of sudden Cloud Rings
from rivers crossing the most ordinary streets ...
—Philip Lamantia, "The Ancients Have Returned Among Us"

In the first issue of *The Burning Bush* I naïvely asked, "Where is the experimentalism? Is there an Irish underground?"[16] It turned out that there was, but at that point it simply had not been visible (actually the definition of an "underground"). As the turn of the century approached, however, things were beginning to change relatively quickly. As early as 1998 even *Metre*, known primarily as a journal of formalist poetry, went so far as to publish an article by John Goodby entitled "Who's Afraid of Experimental Poetry?" In it, Goodby argued that more attention ought to be paid to Irish poets like Trevor Joyce, Maurice Scully, Randolph Healy, Billy Mills and Catherine Walsh (most of whom have been published by Healy's Wild Honey Press, and form a group of sorts), which, he humbly asserted, would "improve the range of all Irish poetry."[17] Goodby's piece provoked a swift reaction in *Metre*'s next issue, with a panicky Mac Oliver calling for a return to "dutiful" Wordsworthian language.[18] But the genie was out of the bottle—the likes of Joyce, Scully and Healy were soon being written about everywhere, it seemed.

Joyce's collected volume, *with the first dream of fire they hunt the cold* (2001), really put contemporary Irish "experimental" poetry on the map, garnering favourable reviews; but this overnight success was over thirty years in the making. Joyce had been co-founder, with Michael Smith, of New Writers' Press, and co-editor—also with Smith—of the important journal *The Lace Curtain*, which published six issues between 1969 and 1978. (Perhaps in a way similar to the role of *The Burning Bush* decades later, *The Lace Curtain*'s "primary function … was to publish a wide range of poetry and polemicise against the generality of Irish poetry."[19])

16 Michael S. Begnal, "Editorial Note," *The Burning Bush* 1 (Spring 1999): 1.
17 John Goodby, "Who's Afraid of Experimental Poetry?" *Metre* 5 (Autumn/ Winter 1998): 41-48.
18 Mac Oliver, "Violent Stimulants, or Who's *Not* Afraid of Experimental Poetry?" *Metre* 6 (Spring 1999): 110-118.
19 Goodby, *Irish Poetry Since 1950: From Stillness into History* (Manchester: Manchester University Press, 2000), 126.

with the first dream of fire gathered all of Joyce's work previously published with NWP and Wild Honey Press, and for the first time a wide audience had a chance to behold the range of his achievement. Avoiding the fallacy of representational art, which would have us pretend that any artistic medium (in this case language) is neutral, Joyce views poetry as an active process rather than a collection of finished lyrics. Nothing is taken for granted:

> Cul-de-sac words. parables: fraud.
>
> how come to terms?
>   how compromise?
>
> the rooks are garrulous and strong
> the fox is strong as fire.
>   how celebrate? ...[20]

Joyce has also occasionally utilised versions of the cut-up technique (first elaborated by Dada founder Tristan Tzara), and put them to original, more ambitious uses in poems like "Syzygy," which takes phrases from history, folklore, financial news reports and a line from Pablo Neruda, and recombines them via computer spreadsheet software[21]:

> thrones and dominations fell
> attending as joints lost their grip
> throughout the deadlocked centuries
> as new wood broke
> disordered from old stock
> voices were joining

---

[20] Trevor Joyce, "Death Is Conventional," *with the first dream of fire they hunt the cold: A Body of Work 1966/2000* (Dublin: New Writers' Press, and Devon: Shearsman Books, 2001), 66-67.

[21] As previously noted, Ireland's new economy is after all largely based on the IT industry, a factor Goodby specifically links to Joyce's writing (*Irish Poetry Since 1950*, 304).

in a round of bones[22]

This reads almost as a précis of Joyce's poetic method and practice, and can hardly be only a simple accident of device. Rather, new meanings have been brought out through the act of recontextualisation, meanings hitherto unsuspected, which were hidden in the words all along. Joyce himself has said in an interview that "instead of trying to dominate language, to show a mastery of language…what I want to do is learn increasingly to listen to language…."[23] "Syzygy" is but one example of this, where Joyce acts almost as a medium to the latent power of words, rather than trying to force them into a preconceived notion of how a poem should work. The poem here virtually forms itself through Joyce, and not the other way around.

In early 2002, Michael Smith published an opinion piece in *Poetry Ireland News* which was a scathing attack on the complacency of the poetry establishment in Ireland. Echoing some of his own earlier statements in *The Lace Curtain*, Smith wrote:

> Naïve assumptions are made about language, without any serious thought being given to the nature of language, not to speak of language as it may be employed in the writing of poetry. For example, it is commonly assumed by poets in Ireland that it is possible by a few stylistic tricks and repetitive subject matter to express one's personality, to communicate that personality in a distinctive personal voice, a notion that flies in the face of what for a long time we have known about language and its collective communal genesis and nature.[24]

A year or two before, and such assertions would most likely have been completely ignored, or worse, refused publication.

---

[22] Joyce, "Syzygy," *with the first dream of fire*, 141.
[23] Michael S. Begnal, "Interview with Trevor Joyce," *The Burning Bush* 7 (Spring 2002): 48.
[24] Michael Smith, "Poetry as an Art: New Year Reflections on an Old Theme," *Poetry Ireland News* (January/February 2002): 4.

But, again, times were quickly changing, and voices such as these could no longer be easily shunted aside. In fact, Smith was suddenly given the rotating editorship of *Poetry Ireland Review*, Ireland's largest poetry journal. A late-flowering "revolution of the word" was maybe in some small way taking root. Smith's first editorial for *PIR* took up where his *PIN* piece left off, challenging the "poetry of accommodation and consolation" and criticising its lack of awareness of the major developments in 20th century poetics.[25]

Among those appearing in Smith's first issue of *PIR* was Maurice Scully. Scully has been called a "Heraclitean" poet,[26] and this description is not off the mark. The ancient Greek pre-Socratic philosopher Heraclitus is probably best known for his aphorism "All things are in flux," and Scully's world is indeed a constant flux—he has been said by Robert Archambeau to write "out of an aversion to the idea of the poem as closed system."[27] Vast and ambitious, his work is composed of long, ongoing sequences. (When his collection *Livelihood* finally appeared in 2004, what I assumed would finally be a free-standing book collecting the earlier pamphlets and shorter extracts Scully had published over the years—the book totals 330 pages!—turned out to be but volume two of a trilogy.) While his is a huge undertaking, there nonetheless remains the sense in Scully's work of a singular consciousness, the only possible unifying factor available in such a sprawling corpus. From section C of "Adherence":

A fly cleaning itself precisely
by the window in the sunlight
forelegs back (rest) head eyes
shadows wings brittle-quick & quite
like writing really. Out there. That.[28]

25 Michael Smith, "Poetics and Related Matters," *Poetry Ireland Review* 73 (Summer 2002): 3-8.
26 Robert Archambeau, *Another Ireland: An Essay* (Bray: Wild Honey, 1997) 17.
27 Archambeau, *Another Ireland*, 17
28 Maurice Scully, *Livelihood* (Bray: Wild Honey Press, 2004), 256.

These lines do not truly attempt to convey an image of a fly in itself. Instead they observe a mind observing a fly, and it is from such a fundamental shift that much of Scully's poetry proceeds. It is also what differentiates it from most "mainstream" poetry, which Michael Smith has likened to "painting innocent of the invention of the camera."[29]

There is with Scully too an overt critique of the received tradition. For example, a stanza from "Steps":

> PASTORAL
> Valleys, villages, coastline. A map
> of a stain on the wall. Alive & living,
> not a crammed glasshouse of pistillate
> verba. Grass bends back. The book
> is fat, contains code. The world,
> the water planet. The code contained in
> this thing in the world, the book, changes
> the things, the world …[30]

By retaining a rural subject matter this is a pastoral poem, technically—but a poem that explodes the Heaneyan lyric from the inside. It is only in the consciousness of writing ("the code," "the book") that transformation is possible, not in a fossilised way of life or in a represented landscape. In this sense Scully can loosely be called postmodern, the self-reflexivity of the writing being a characteristic of postmodernism. Yet Scully's work remains utterly vigorous, highly autobiographical, and fully situated in the material world. It is work, in fact, which examines the minutiae of the world (and the human comprehension of it) much more deeply than the romanticising action of the traditional lyric poem can allow.

Randolph Healy also appeared in the first Smith-edited *PIR*, and even more so than Scully or Joyce has adopted a scientific approach in his writing, being himself a teacher of maths and science by profession. Poetry for Healy begins as logical

29 Smith "Poetry as an Art," 4.
30 Scully, *Livelihood*, 228.

inquiry, and in an early essay he has written that "the syntax of logic allows for a much higher loading of information. If one wishes to turn to outside data and not depend on one's own inner resources, this can be extremely useful. If one wishes to use poetry as a means of demystifying the complexities of the modern world it becomes indispensable."[31] A Healy poem might open something like this:

> Because their senses register only
> zero to five per cent of the world
> and because the short-term memory
> jettisons most of this and because
> the conscious mind is limited
> to seven or eight ideas at one time
> it is hardly possible for them to be
> anything more than inaccurate.[32]

So Healy starts from a totally empirical standpoint, but he has to allow for a large degree of uncertainty about what can be finally known. The conclusions drawn are not comforting. In another poem he writes,

> Tonight, standing in earth's shadow,
> close your eyes and see
> that this universe is itself a statement
> within which every statement made
> is partial and uncomprehending,
> that every detail suggests a total
> at which one may not arrive …[33]

Finally, and again, the interrogation turns toward the medium, language being subjective and culturally dependent, and

[31] Randolph Healy, "Logic as a Starting Point for Poetry," *the Beau* 3 (1983/4): 11.
[32] Healy, "Change & Response," *Green 532: Selected Poems 1983-2000* (Cambridge: Salt Publishing, 2002), 46.
[33] "The Size of this Universe," ibid., 54.

Healy's observation: "Writing is mind made visible / I think and watch what I say …"[34]

Like the other poets under discussion, Healy's stance is also to some extent formed out of a reaction to the dominant trends in Irish poetry. "Irish poetry was very much centred on its own Irishness at the time, 'a sense of place' being the mantra of the workshop," Healy has said, adding, "The wild and drunken poet was still very much the model too."[35] Peter Riley has gone so far as to assert that "you have to forget that Randolph Healy is Irish. Because he doesn't trade in that substance: nationality, Celtic *duende* … To Healy Irishness is purely where he finds himself and what he is surrounded by."[36] This of course is easier said than done, to erase considerations of nationality altogether, if for no other reason than that it provides one ineluctable context in which to read the writer. In fact Healy deals with Irishness to quite a surprising extent, even as he is concerned with orientating his own work outside the literary Irish nationalist/tribalist ethos. But instead of ignoring this element, he, like the others, subverts it. For example, "Anthem" is a deconstruction of the lyrics to the Irish national anthem, while "(The) Republic of Ireland" is composed of anagrams derived from the phrase "Republic of Ireland" (with or without the "the"). The latter piece can be read as an overt political commentary on the state of modern Ireland, with lines such as "price trouble in fleadh," "her pro-life bit unlaced," "creed liable if up North,"[37] etc. At the same time there are many references to and uses of the Irish language in Healy, and the poem "*Aisling*" is an oblique take on that Gaelic poetic convention which emerged with Aodhagán Ó Rathaille after the Battle of the Boyne.

---

34 "Vertices," ibid., 92.

35 Archambeau, "A Poet in the Information Age: An Interview with Randolph Healy," *ND[re]VIEW* (online version of *Notre Dame Review*) 7 (Winter 1999): http://www.nd.edu/~ndr/issues/ndr7/archambeau/interview.html

36 Peter Riley, "'anxious fuchsia ocean': The Accomplishment of Randolph Healy," *Chicago Review* 49:2 (Summer 2003): 135.

37 Healy, "(The) Republic of Ireland," *Green 532*, 40-41.

Healy, Scully and Joyce have all drawn on elements of Irish literary history, both modern and ancient. Joyce has translated Ó Rathaille, for example, and on a larger scale he has also translated *The Poems of Sweeny, Peregrine* (1976) (published seven years before Heaney's version, *Sweeney Astray*). Not extremely different from what Gearóid Mac Lochlainn does to his own work, Joyce's sequence makes no attempt to faithfully convey the original. Rather it is referred to as "A Reworking of the Corrupt Irish Text," and draws primarily on J.G. O'Keefe's English translation of *Buile Suibhne* published by the Irish Texts Society in 1913 and 1931. As Joyce himself has written, "The relation in which *The Poems of Sweeny, Peregrine* stand to the original Irish of *Buile Suibhne* may perhaps best be described by that phrase which Clarence Mangan used of his own inventive translations: they are 'the antithesis of plagiarism.'"[38] Elsewhere, Joyce's technique of recombining pieces of text has an ancient analogue in a manuscript of the *Seanchus Mór*, pictured in *with the first dream of fire*,[39] the lines of which were meant to be read in a similarly disjointed manner. Even the poem "Syzygy," instead of overtly harking to Dadaism or to William S. Burroughs's later cut-up experiments, is said by Joyce to mimic a palindromic mediaeval musical form known as the cancrizan, in which "one or more parts proceed normally, while the imitating voice or voices give out the melody backwards."[40]

Other tactics considered to be "modernist," "postmodernist" or "avant-garde," sometimes utilised by the above writers, might in a sense be parallel to earlier practices. In his poem "*Arbor Vitae*," which deals in part with the subjectivity of language systems, Healy mentions an "alphabet of twenty sacred trees / and a system of Druidic hand signing."[41] Like the druids, the ancient poets were also versed in ogham signing, as

---

[38] Joyce, *with the first dream of fire*, 236.
[39] Joyce, *with the first dream of fire*, 155.
[40] Joyce, *with the first dream of fire*, 239.
[41] Healy, "*Arbor Vitae*," Green 532, 25.

well as even more obscure forms of communication such as *bérla na filed* ("the Language of the Poets") and *iarnbérla* ("the Iron Language"). According to John Minahane:

> The Iron Language consists partly of unanalysable slangwords … partly of common words which are slightly distorted to give a special sense … partly of key syllables of well-known phrases compressed into slangwords … and partly of the bits, fillings and joinings of everyday Irish.
>
> The Language of the Poets, *bérla na filed*, seems to consist of words stuck together to make meaningless slangwords. Some of the words may lose bits … or one word may be hidden in another's middle …[42]

The charge of obscurantism, often levelled at contemporary "experimental" poets, must surely have been made at some point in the Irish Middle Ages as well. And wordplay of this sort is of course present in those currently under discussion. But Minahane points out that, for one thing, "In order to maintain a continuous second sense while composing in difficult metres one needed this extra linguistic capacity."[43] That is, he sees it as a complement to the composing of more conventional or formalist verse, not as opposed to it—and also largely as a mode in which poets communicated to *each other*— yet at the same time as a mode that conveyed a deeper level of meaning than the conventional poetry. Certainly the Iron Language is rather more arcane in its time than, say, Healy is in his. In any case, as Minahane importantly adds, "there is something beneath the iron surface—something a good deal clearer!—for anyone who feels like digging."[44] The same thing should be said for poets like Healy, Scully and Joyce, who on the surface might also appear obscure or difficult, or might occasionally seem to purposely frustrate a straightforward

---

[42] John Minahane, *The Christian Druids: On the* filid *or philosopher-poets of Ireland* (Dublin: Sanas Press, 1993) 212.

[43] Minahane, *The Christian Druids*, 214.

[44] Minahane, *The Christian Druids*, 214.

reading of their work. One main difference is that they have taken their work into the public sphere and assert that it can be read at least on an equal basis with Seamus Heaney, Moya Cannon, et al.

***

Crazy dada nigger that's what you are. You are given to fantasy and are off in matters of detail. Far out esoteric bullshit is where you're at. Why in those suffering books that I write about my old neighbourhood and how hard it was every gumdrop machine is in place while your work is a blur and a doodle. I'll bet you can't create the difference between a German and a redskin.

What's your beef with me Bo Shmo, what if I write circuses? No one says a novel has to be one thing. It can be anything it wants to be, a vaudeville show, the six o'clock news, the mumblings of wild men saddled by demons.

All art must be for the end of liberating the masses. A landscape is only good when it shows the oppressor hanging from a tree.

Right on! Right on, Bo, the henchmen chorused.
— Ishmael Reed, *Yellow Back Radio Broke-Down*

The admittance, grudging or not, of a putative Irish avant-garde into the canon can be put down to a number of factors. First of all, the once extreme marginalisation of the poets under discussion, hidden as they were in hard to find pamphlets, occasional appearances in small literary magazines, or on the web, meant that a wider audience had never actually had the opportunity to examine their work in a consistent manner alongside the more well-known poets of the day. David Butler, commenting on the Wild Honey-associated group, emphasises the often overlooked medium of the internet and makes the point that in the 21st century "it would seem naïve to expect to find the cutting edge of poetry located uniquely within the bounds of printed matter, still less of mainstream publications. Those who caricature contemporary Irish poetry as monolithic, conservative and playing Irishness to an international audience would do well to remember this."[45] This is true, but it means that such figures remained concealed up to a certain point. When Joyce's and Healy's collected volumes appeared in print, roughly coinciding with the publication of Goodby's important study *Irish Poetry since 1950* (2000), which devoted space to Joyce, Scully, Healy and Catherine Walsh, audiences were forced to rethink their conception of Irish poetry. About the same time, *The Burning Bush* had started to appear, and the younger poet Joseph Woods took over as head of Poetry Ireland, instilling new energy into that organisation and paving the way for Michael Smith to be appointed editor of *Poetry Ireland Review* for three significant issues. All of this helped generate an interest in a sort of writing that had not really been seriously considered in Ireland theretofore. The time was ripe for a new departure; perhaps readers had become bored with the usual fare of stone walls and green fields. Butler, in any case, makes another worthy point: "Nor is the Irish 'establishment' quite so conservative as some commentators might like to maintain. Trevor Joyce has this year [2004] been elected as a member of Aosdána."[46]

The more strident opposition to the notion of an avant-garde came from some who, oddly enough, would identify themselves as being on the political left. Kevin Higgins, former co-editor of *The Burning Bush*, launched an attack on the magazine after splitting from it. Making clear that he was now writing "from a Marxist point of view," Higgins contributed an opinion piece to a British poetry journal in which he claimed, "There are those who believe the role of the poet is to turn his or her back on the grubby world of contemporary political affairs, concentrating instead on the search for great eternal

45 David Butler, "Where to Look for the Wild Honey," *Poetry Ireland Review* 79 (Summer 2004): 58.
46 Butler, "Where to Look for the Wild Honey," 60.

truths, like a secular priest of sorts."[47] He was reacting to an editorial I had written in *The Burning Bush* issue five, which was in part an attempt to put an emphasis back onto poetics where Higgins and others at the time were seemingly more concerned with making political statements.[48] Yet in that same editorial I had written,

> *The Burning Bush* has always published a certain amount of poetry with a political or satirical focus, and does so in this issue. But it would be a mistake for a poet to think that the strength of his or her convictions, however deeply felt, daring or radical, can compensate for the lack of an ability to write interestingly ... Art for art's sake? No, but neither can art be subjugated for the sake of ideology.[49]

Certainly the piece was framed by aesthetic concerns in places; but the fact that it in no way discounted a political element in poetry seemed to be lost on Higgins, and I was personally condemned for attempting to construct a "divide" between politics and art, and to "rubbish an entire literary genre, the political satire."[50]

Another attack came from the Galway poet Maureen Gallagher. A member of a Trotskyite group called Workers Power Ireland, Gallagher targeted not only myself but Michael Smith as well. In a rather convoluted essay in the *Cork Literary Review*, she advanced the faulty claims that with this *Burning Bush* editorial I was "reiterating a commitment to Art for Art's

[47] Kevin Higgins, "Reacting to the Nine O'clock News: In defence of political satire," *The Journal* 6 (Autumn 2002): 29.

[48] For example, anarchist poet Rab Fulton had recently attacked the Beat generation in his own publication, the Galway-based freesheet *muc mhór dhubh*, on the grounds that the Beats "are regarded as something innovative and radical...whereas they were just one part of a long line of colonial empire-building scum" (Rab Fulton, "The continuing adventures of muc mhór dhubh," *muc mhór dhubh* 9 [December 2000]: 2).

[49] Begnal, "Preface," *The Burning Bush* 5 (Spring 2001): 3.

[50] Higgins, "Reacting to the Nine O'clock News," 29.

sake," and that I harboured a "hostility to realism."[51] She criticised Smith's first *Poetry Ireland Review* editorial for "bemoan[ing] the lack of avant-garde modernist writing," and continued on to say, "There is very little postmodernist poetry in Ireland, a good thing indeed, in my opinion."[52] For in postmodernism, she writes, "Language becomes a value in and of itself without regard to relations in the real world: relationships within the text are all that count."[53] In place of this she posits a type of social-realism, mentioning names like Linton Kwesi Johnson, Miroslav Holub and Arthur Miller. Gallagher exhibits little understanding of what she attacks, however, essentially dismissing Smith's essay without engaging with the modalities of it in any way, thus avoiding the deeper implications of ideas which she finds unpalatable or which run counter to her own argument. Ironically, Smith is an old socialist himself, having, for example, written of the war in the North: "That a solution has been found outside of socialism I am not aware."[54] Whether Smith still subscribes to socialism is unclear, but surely it remains an influence on his thinking whether or not it reflects his current beliefs.

In any case, the question of poetry's political and social function is a valid one. It is something, in fact, that Smith grapples with in his *PIR* piece. Dismissing Surrealism and Dadaism as overly preoccupied with an inner, rather than an outer, reality, he looks instead to the experimentation of Beckett as "genuinely exploratory and constructive in its drive," something which "could also be viewed as a valuable exercise in subverting the corrupt language of politics and business."[55] Gallagher studiously avoids this point, but it is something which the poets under consideration are concerned with also.

---

51 Maureen Gallagher, "Art for Art's Sake," *Cork Literary Review* 10 (2003): 187-88.
52 Gallagher, "Art for Art's Sake," 189.
53 Gallagher, "Art for Art's Sake," 189.
54 Smith, "A Personal Statement," *The Lace Curtain* 5 (Spring 1974): 2. In the same piece he called for a "worker's republic."
55 Smith, "Poetics and Related Matters," 5.

As Trevor Joyce said in his *Burning Bush* interview, "I can't, as a person, not be interested in politics now," before continuing,

> And it seems to me…that a new politics has to emerge. And it probably will be a global politics, maybe an anti-globalist global politics. But that because of the way that international business, and the military, are increasingly dominating discourse and the media, it's going to be necessary to fight from the ground up.[56]

David Annwn, writing of Healy, Scully and Billy Mills, notes that in all three there is a strong "awareness of the dire threats posed by global consumerism,"[57] which accords well with Joyce's comments. The way that these writers grapple with such threats is through language, the most important tool they have at their disposal as poets in an age when the media has become supremely powerful and language a vital weapon in the current imperialistic war (e.g., Donald Rumsfeld on the subject of Iraq). While not associated with the Wild Honey group, Alan Jude Moore has nonetheless arrived at a similar position as they:

> Making a claim for language is important, reclaiming it from the ever increasing use of "international" English and business-speak. The bastardisation of the meaning of words. Meaning is taken away from everything in an effort to desensitise us to what actually happens in the world. Literature is not important to most people in the world. Computer-speak and business English are more important. These things though don't strike any human chords; they subjugate us to the machinations of neo-capitalism.[58]

This again finds expression in Moore's poetry:

---

[56] Begnal, "Interview with Trevor Joyce," 46-47.
[57] Davis Annwn, *Arcs Through: The Poetry of Randolph Healy, Billy Mills & Maurice Scully* (Dublin: Coelacanth Press, 2002), 22-23.
[58] Moore, e-mail to the author, 4 December 2005.

Today there is no news on the streets.
They run only with a business, against which
silence is useless:
with a war between sides of whom nothing is spoken.
Within in it we run marathons,
to keep in shape for the next one.[59]

As opposed to Gallagher's rigidity, and her hesitance to engage with the other side, Kevin Higgins's position seems to open up a bit by the time he reviews Trevor Joyce, implying that some of his earlier statements were possibly provisional or sprang from the need to stake out a position separate from that of the literary magazine he had recently left (or that at the very least he is able to consider literature beyond the bounds of a stated ideology). Of Joyce, Higgins later wrote:

> An experimentalist he may be, but Joyce is light years away from those "Avant-gardists" who make poems consisting just of semi-colons or solitary free floating words. And though he is certainly not a social poet (or a moralist) like, say, Peter Reading or Tony Harrison, his poetry does come from, or at least is a reaction to, a recognisable social world.[60]

Higgins is right. Of his own poetics, Joyce has written: "That's my starting point for understanding: not breathing some experimental and wholly artificial atmosphere, high and impersonal; rather a sense that language, the medium it wholly inhabits, is saturated with the pleasures, the suffering, hopes and terrors of individual people ..."[61]

A lot of the thinking in Gallagher's article would appear to be lifted from Trotsky's *Literature and Revolution* (1925), especially Trotsky's exegesis of Symbolism as "the artistic

---

[59] Moore, "The Hook," *Black State Cars*, 15.

[60] Kevin Higgins, "Review of *with the first dream of fire they hunt the cold* by Trevor Joyce," *Poetry Quarterly Review* 20 (Summer 2003): 23.

[61] Trevor Joyce, "Interrogate the Thrush: Another Name for Something Else," *Vectors: New Poetics*, ed. Robert Archambeau (Lincoln, NE: Writer's Club Press, 2001), 139.

bridge to Mysticism" and "the intelligentsia's escape from reality."[62] Certainly the attempt to transmute this into a criticism of contemporary Irish experimental or avant-garde poetry (label it what you will) fails. To take another example, from Joyce's "The Fall":

> I have mouthed names
>   that are names no longer,
> draw no reply now
>   only hard silence and an image
>   of graven stone. [....]
>
> Stone cracked in the jaws of ice,
>   splintered, grinding,
>   mixed with moisture,
> becoming dirt.[63]

This is a clear instance of a materialist view, the image of a graven stone monument stripped of an earlier mythological or religious meaning, being ground to dirt through the passage of time. Healy's logical approach is pertinent here too. What both these poets are really doing is taking poetry out of a possible mystical setting into one more scientific. In any regard, it would be worth remembering that Trotsky himself later made common cause with the avant-garde of his era, co-authoring a "Manifesto for Independent Revolutionary Art" (1938) with Surrealist leader André Breton. The manifesto affirmed the necessity of "individual liberty" for the artist and stated that "the imagination must escape from all constraints and must under no pretext allow itself to be placed under bonds," before concluding:

> The independence of art—for the revolution;
> The revolution—for the complete liberation of art![64]

[62] Leon Trotsky, *Literature and Revolution*, trans. Rose Strunsky (New York: International Publishers, 1925), 234-35.
[63] Joyce, *with the first dream of fire*, 69.

Breton is certainly one of the more abstract poets imaginable, but essentially what this tells us is that Surrealism for Trotsky was not finally an empty form or distanced from reality—or "art for art's sake."

The more recent figure of Amiri Baraka is another prime case of experimentalist literary technique converging with left-wing politics. The former Beat/former Black Nationalist poet announced himself a Marxist-Leninist in the early 1970s, yet according to Baraka editor William J. Harris he "has also created an original body of work that belongs in the forefront of innovative avant-garde writing."[65] It is not simply a case of grafting a "style" onto a political content, however. "Ironically," Harris says, "avant-garde ideas of form cohered perfectly with the new black artist's need to express his or her own oral traditions; the free verse and eccentric typography of the white avant-garde were ideal vehicles for black oral expression and experience."[66] Harris calls Baraka a "process artist," and in this sense a comparison can be drawn to Maurice Scully's embracing of flux as poetic method. Furthermore, Randolph Healy has stated: "This is a starting point for poetry. That one does not have to inhabit a single philosophy or set of convictions ... A dialogue with experience *is* possible ..."[67] And Baraka himself has written:

> My writing reflects my own growth and expansion, and at the same time the society in which I have existed throughout this longish confrontation. Whether it is politics, music, literature, or the origins of language, there is a historical and

---

[64] Trotsky and André Breton, "Manifesto for Independent Revolutionary Art," cited in Dickran Tashjian, *A Boatload of Madmen: Surrealism and the American Avant-Garde* (London: Thames & Hudson, 1995), 165-67.

[65] William J. Harris, "Introduction" to Amiri Baraka, *The LeRoi Jones/Amiri Baraka Reader* (New York: Thunder's Mouth Press, 1991), xvii.

[66] Harris, "Introduction," xxvii.

[67] Healy, "Logic as a Starting Point for Poetry": 11.

time/place/condition reference that will always try to explain exactly why I was saying both how and for what.[68]

The immediate parallel here between Baraka and the likes of Joyce, Healy, Scully, Alan Jude Moore, et al., if not a direct political correlation, is that the latter's techniques nonetheless arise out of a particular context—both society and the individual in transition—and the need to give expression to the "confrontations" this engenders in a newly befitting manner. There is no attempt at consciously affecting "postmodernism."

Ideologies are contingent, but they may certainly at times feed into the wider project: Smith's, Breton's and Baraka's socialism (and Baraka's earlier cultural nationalism), Gearóid Mac Lochlainn's republicanism, Trevor Joyce's contemplation of a new politics altogether, etc. But rather than a question of one ideology versus another, it is a question of open forms of thought versus closed systems. Whether working against the perceived conservatism of an Irish poetic mainstream, or in opposition to the proscriptive elements in certain bodies of political criticism (be they Marxist, nationalist, or what have you), it is clear that progressive Irish poetry's evolution into the 21st century can no longer be restricted by the old templates. Terms like "avant-garde" and "experimentalism" in this case are merely shorthand for the articulation of new material realities. Often an urban reality is implied. But, equally, the process of change cannot help but impact on rural society and the poets it produces, and so in a sense Irish poetry as a whole has been challenged. Whether and how this challenge is taken up further remains to be seen, but for many the pre-millennial status quo is no longer a realistic option. The future, therefore, ought to be interesting.

---

[68] Baraka, "Preface to the Reader," *The LeRoi Jones/Amiri Baraka Reader*, xiv.

Contributors

ROBERT ARCHAMBEAU's books include *Word Play Place* (Swallow/Ohio), *Vectors: New Poetics* (Samizdat), and the poetry collection *Home and Variations* (Salt), and the forthcoming study *Laureates and Heretics*. He edited the international poetry review *Samizdat* from 1998-2004, and has taught at the University of Notre Dame and Lund University, Sweden. He presently lectures in English at Lake Forest University, and co-directs the &NOW Festival of Innovative Art and Writing. www.samizdatblog.blogspot.com.

LOUIS ARMAND is Director of Intercultural Studies in the Philosophy Faculty of Charles University, Prague. His is the author of *Inexorable Weather* (Arc, 2001); *The Garden* (Salt, 2001); *Malice in Underland* (Textbase, 2003); *Strange Attractors* (Salt, 2003); *Menudo* (Antigen, 2006); and *Solicitations: Essays on Criticism and Culture* (Litteraria, 2005). He is also the editor of *Contemporary Poetics* (Northwestern University Press, 2006). www.louis-armand.com

MICHAEL S. BEGNAL was formerly the editor of the Galway-based literary magazine, *The Burning Bush*. His first collection of poetry, *The Lakes of Coma*, appeared in 2003 from Six Gallery Press (US). His latest, *Ancestor Worship*, was published by Salmon (Ireland). He has appeared in the anthologies *Breaking the Skin: New Irish Poetry* (Black Mountain Press) and, in Irish, *Go Nuige Seo* (Coiscéim).

R.M. BERRY is professor of English at Florida State University, and author of the novels *Frank* and *Leonardo's Horse*. He has also published collections of short stories including *Dictionary of Modern Anguish* and *Plane Geometry and Other Affairs of the Heart*. His literary criticism has appeared in *Symploke*, *Philosophy and Literature*, *Soundings*, *American*

Book Review, Narrative, and other periodicals. He is publisher of Fiction Collective Two.

CHRISTIAN BÖK is the author of *Eunoia* (Coach House Books, 2001) and *Crystallography* (Coach House Press, 1994). Bök has created artificial languages for two television shows: Gene Roddenberry's *Earth: Final Conflict* and Peter Benchley's *Amazon,* and has also earned many accolades for his performances of sound poetry. His conceptual artworks (which include books built out of Rubik's Cubes and Lego Bricks) have appeared at the Marianne Boesky Gallery in New York City as part of the exhibit *Poetry Plastique.* Bök currently teaches in the Department of English at the University of Calgary.

MAIRÉAD BYRNE is Assistant Professor of English at Rhode Island School of Design in Providence. She immigrated to America from Ireland in 1994, and earned a PhD in Theory & Cultural Studies from Purdue University in 2001. Her recent publications include a poetry collection, *Nelson & The Huruburu Bird* (Wild Honey Press, 2003); three chapbooks *Vivas* (Wild Honey Press, 2005), *An Educated Heart* (Palm Press, 2005), and *Kalends* (Belladonna, 2005); as well as a talk, *Some Differences Between Poetry & Standup* (UbuWeb, 2005).

JOHANNA DRUCKER is currently the Robertson Professor of Media Studies at the University of Virginia and Professor in the Department of English. She is known for her work as a book artist and experimental writer of visual texts. Her most recent title, *From Now,* was published by Cuneiform Press in 2005, and her most recent academic work is *Sweet Dreams: Contemporary Art and Complicity* (University of Chicago Press, 2005).

RACHEL BLAU DUPLESSIS is the author of *Drafts 1-38, Toll* (Wesleyan, 2001) and *DRAFTS. Drafts 39-57, Pledge with Draft, unnumbered: Précis* (Salt, 2004) and the forthcoming *Torques: Drafts 58-76.* In 2006, University of Alabama Press republished *The Pink Guitar: Writing as Feminist Practice* and published *Blue Studios: Poetry and Its Cultural Work.* Her critical publications include *Genders, Races, and Religious Cultures in Modern American Poetry, 1908-1934* (Cambridge, 2001), *Writing Beyond the Ending: Narrative Strategies of Twentieth-Century Women Writers* (Indiana, 1985), and *H.D. The Career of that Struggle* (Harvester and Indiana, 1986). DuPlessis also edited *The*

Selected Letters of George Oppen (Duke, 1990). She is a professor in the English Department at Temple University. wings.buffalo.edu/epc/authors/duplessis

VADIM ERENT graduated from the University of California at Irvine in Postmodern Studies. He has published articles on contemporary Russian art, and a monograph on the painter Oleg Tselkov.

LISA JARNOT is the author of three collections of poetry including *Some Other Kind of Mission, Ring of Fire,* and *Black Dog Songs*. She recently completed a biography of the San Francisco poet Robert Duncan which will be published by University of California Press in 2007. She currently teaches in the Creative Writing Program at Brooklyn College.

LAURENT MILESI teaches 20th century American literature and critical theory at Cardiff University and is a member of the Joyce ITEM-CNRS Research Group in Paris. He is the editor of *James Joyce and the Difference of Language* (Cambridge, 2003), and his translation, together with Stefan Herbrechter, of Jacques Derrida's *H.C. pour la vie, c'est a dire...* was recently published by Stanford. He is currently completing two monographs, on Jacques Derrida (in French) and on postmodernism (*Post-Effects: Literature, Theory and the Future Perfect*).

ESTHER MILNE lectures in Media and Communications at Swinburne University of Technology, Melbourne. She publishes in new media theory with a focus on the production of intimacy, affect and presence across email and epistolary circuits of communication. She is also a facilitator for *Fibreculture,* the online network for critical Internet research and culture in Australasia: www.fibreculture.org

BONITA RHOADS earned a Ph.D. in Comparative Literature from Yale University in 2006 with a dissertation that considers the impact of nineteenth-century visual culture on the development of literary genre. Since 2004 she taught at Charles University, Prague, and Masaryk University, Brno.

ROBERT SHEPPARD is Senior Lecturer in English and Writing at Edge Hill College (soon to be University) in Ormskirk, England. He lives in Liverpool and Liverpool University Press published his most

327

recent critical volume, The Poetry of Saying: British Poetry and Its Discontents 1950-2000, last year. He has written a monograph on the novelist, poet and documentarist Iain Sinclair for the Writers and Their Works series. The author of many articles on, and reviews of, contemporary poetry, he is also a poet, and his most recent volumes are Tin Pan Arcadia (Salt Publishing 2004) and Hymns to the God in which My Typewriter Believes (Stride Books, 2006).

www.robertsheppard.blogspot.com

TREY STRECKER teaches English and sport studies at Ball State University. His essays on contemporary American literature have appeared in *Critique: Studies in Contemporary Fiction, The Review of Contemporary Fiction,* and *ISLE: Interdisciplinary Studies in Literature and Environment.* He is the editor of *Dead Balls and Double Curves: An Anthology of Early Baseball Fiction* (Southern Illinois University Press, 2004).

KESTON SUTHERLAND lectures in English at the University of Sussex. He is the author of several books of poetry, including *Antifreeze, The Rictus Flag, Neutrality* and *Neocosis.* He is also the editor of *Quid,* a journal of poetry, politics and aesthetic theory, and co-editor (with Andrea Brady) of Barque Press (www.barquepress.com). He is currently working on an edition of the collected critical prose of J.H. Prynne.

ANN VICKERY is a Research Fellow at Monash University, Australia. She is currently working on two large projects, the first focusing on the career paths and reputations of contemporary Australian women poets and the second investigating the affiliations and influences between women writers and artists of the New York School. She is the author of *Leaving Lines of Gender: A Feminist Genealogy of Language Writing* (Wesleyan, 2000) and was editor-in-chief of *HOW2,* an international journal of innovative women's writing and scholarship, between 2000 and 2002.